PASSION FOR PIZZA

A Journey Through Thick and Thin to Find the **Pizza Elite**

PASSION FOR PIZZA

A Journey Through Thick and Thin to Find the **Pizza Elite**

CRAIG WHITSON • TORE GJESTELAND
MATS WIDÉN • KENNETH HANSEN

SURREY
BOOKS

AN AGATE IMPRINT

CHICAGO

Printed in China

Originally published in Norway by Kagge Forlag AS, 2014

All photographs by Mats Widén

Library of Congress Cataloging-in-Publication Data

Whitson, Craig, author.
Passion for pizza : a journey through thick and thin to find the pizza elite / Craig Whitson, Tore Gjesteland, Mats Widén, Kenneth Hansen.
    pages cm
 Summary: "A collection of 50 recipes for pizza featuring the history of and tributes to the people and places that make pizza a worldwide favorite"--Provided by publisher.
ISBN 978-1-57284-160-4 (hardback) -- ISBN 1-57284-160-5 (hard cover) -- ISBN 978-1-57284-746-0 (ebook)
1. Pizza--Italy. 2. Pizza--United States. I. Title.
TX770.P58W48 2014
641.82'48--dc23
                    2014040236

Surrey Books is an imprint of Agate Publishing. Agate books are available in bulk at discount prices.
For more information visit agatepublishing.com.

Tore and Craig took the initiative to write this book, which the entire team of authors has developed further. Kenneth contributed to concept development and art direction, while Mats took fantastic pictures and contributed his unique experience with food and cookbooks. Tore and Craig picked out who we were going to visit and where to go, in addition to overseeing the interviews, recipes, and the book's contents. The text is penned by Craig, while Tore organized the baking for photos accompanying the recipes. This is how the book came into being. Help with proofreading, correcting and valuable help with translation by Thomas Muravez for Semantix.

Semantix

To the angels, demons, saints, and fools

CONTENTS

FOREWORD ix

INTRODUCTION xii

Section 1:   Italy...1
Chapter 1:   Naples 3
Chapter 2:   Other Pizzas in Italy 21

Section 2:   USA...**51**
Chapter 3:   New York 53
Chapter 4:   Chicago...79
              Phoenix 97
Chapter 5:   California 99

Section 3:   Ingredients and Equipment.....137
Chapter 6:   Ingredients 139
Chapter 7:   Equipment..171

Section 4:   Recipes..**181**
Chapter 8:   Let's Make a Pizza 183
Chapter 9:   Dough Recipes 187
Chapter 10: Sauce Recipes 197
Chapter 11: Pizza Recipes................................... 203

RESOURCES 284

ACKNOWLEDGMENTS 286

ABOUT THE AUTHORS 286

DOES THE WORLD REALLY NEED ANOTHER BOOK ABOUT PIZZA?

Countless pizza cookbooks have been published. The history of pizza's origins is also richly presented in book form. The Internet is teeming with recipes, advice, tips, and opinions on numerous websites and blogs. All of which begs the question: Does the world really need another book about pizza?

Tore Gjesteland and Craig Whitson think it does. Confirmed pizza aficionados, Tore and Craig have known each other for years. Together with Chef Trond Moi, they participated in the unofficial world championship of pizza baking in Las Vegas in 1998. The trio won the contest for their dessert pizza, which was a variation of a pecan pie. The following year they released the book *JazzPizza,* which contained recipes they had developed for the competition, as well as other favorite recipes.

In 2011, Craig and Tore were invited to a summer party by a mutual friend. The host made a variety of pizzas in his wood-fired oven, and the conversation naturally turned to pizza. As it happened, Craig had started a book about pizza, and Tore was in the early stages of his own book project on the same topic. They joined forces and created the book together along with a third friend, Kenneth Hansen.

After much talk about recipes and what is right and wrong in the pizza world, they decided to find out the following: What stories have not yet been told about pizza? The authors determined that there was a need for a book of stories from behind the scenes in the pizza world. The book would show pizza lovers the amount of work that goes into the making of their favorite dish.

Fast-forward to spring 2012. In monthly meetings that followed, the trio explored the pizza world. The Swedish photographer Mats Widén, who had worked previously with Kenneth, then came on board—and the trio became a team of four. Together, they started planning trips to Italy and the United States. Great pizza and pizza connoisseurs can of course be found elsewhere in the world, but there was no question that the book would focus on the two most important countries for pizza: the United States and Italy.

No one knows for sure where pizza comes from, and it would be great if this book could tell the world who started it all, or if there were a prehistoric drawing of the first pizza baker, perhaps dressed in animal skins, with a club in one hand and the very first pizza gripped proudly in the other. But in truth, there is no such thing as the one original pizza on which all others are based. The idea probably sprang to mind spontaneously in many places across the world, because it's a short jump from harvesting grain to using fire to make some bread and then topping or filling it with something good—that is the very definition of a pizza.

It can certainly be argued that Naples is the center of the pizza universe, but the Neapolitan *pizzaioli* are not the only ones who are passionate about pizza. Some of the best pizzas come from the strangest places, such as Phoenix, Arizona, where brothers Chris and Marco Bianco and their team make one of America's most sought-after pizzas. And in Caiazzo, Italy, Franco Pepe has dedicated his whole life to pizza. Every morning he makes dough based on the weather, and after lunch he puts on his finishing touches before the customers arrive.

Pizza bakers pride themselves on making the perfect dough, experimenting with different toppings, and baking their inventions to perfection, but the producers of cheese, tomatoes, flour, and other ingredients also play an important role in the final result. Let's also not forget the producers of wood, gas, coal, and electric ovens, who build their products according to exactly defined standards and in line with the traditions and innovations

There is no such thing as the one original pizza on which all others are based.

made by many generations of oven designers. The world of pizza includes a variety of occupations such as restaurant owners, farmers, people delivering pizza, historians, journalists, and people repairing pizza equipment. All these and many more are included in this book.

In their travels, the authors have seen how important traditions and family affiliations are. In the pages of this book, you will get to meet several of the most highly respected pizza families around the world, including the Sorbillo, Bari, Starita, Malnati, and Barlotti families, as well as many more. These pizza professionals, alongside competitive bakers and other individuals, have dedicated their lives to producing the perfect dough, a specific type of cheese, or simply the world's best pizza, day in and day out. This is their book.

In addition to behind-the-scenes insights, this unique book also offers information about ingredients, equipment, and techniques, as well as recipes for the very best pizzas. The world's best pizza bakers have provided this information, and their recipes and tips will help you create pizza you've only dreamed about making, in your own oven at home with a few simple tools and techniques.

As devout pizza lovers, we have created this book with reverence. Along the way, we have constantly gotten to experience what true craftsmanship is (*artigianale* in Italian). Behind every pizza, there are skilled people who produce the ingredients, manufacture the equipment, and bake the pizzas that we all know and love. We had high expectations when we started the book—and all of them were fulfilled. We are immensely pleased to share our experiences with you.

Sit back and join us on an unforgettable culinary adventure!

Tore, Kenneth, Mats, and Craig

OUR FIRST ENCOUNTERS WITH PIZZA

Blood, Sweat, and Tears In the early 1960s, I was playing with my new friend Misha at a playground in Stockholm. We were both seven years old and were to start school together in the fall. I remember that there was a scent of cherry and lilac in the air. It's peculiar when I think about it today, especially because I can remember that particular scent, but I can't recall which of us started the altercation. Suddenly we started to fight—over what, I couldn't tell you. With neither aim nor forethought, I hurled a tin soldier at Misha with all my might. It lodged itself into his cascade of black hair, which soon became quite red in color—and a shocked, screaming Misha disappeared down the hill toward Hälsingegatan.

When I got home, my mom ordered me to get myself cleaned up, put on a new shirt, and come with her to Misha's house to apologize. The sign on the door had a foreign name, which turned out to be Italian. Misha's dad opened the door, and boy, was I relieved when I saw that he was not angry. Misha came out, proud as a peacock, with a large white bandage and three stitches in his head. He too was neither angry nor upset. All I had to do was shake his hand and apologize.

To my astonishment, I was invited to a party at Misha's house the following Saturday. When I returned to his home, I discovered a table covered with several platters of a thin kind of bread with red sauce on top. Nowhere did my searching eyes spy the cake or cinnamon rolls that I was expecting. Just as clearly as I remember the scent of cherry and lilac that fateful day a week before, I remember the wonderful aroma and flavor of *pizza!* It smelled delicious and tart with tomato and spices and something I could not identify, but which I now assume was basil or perhaps sardines and garlic. There was no cheese. The bread was both crunchy and slightly chewy. I had never tasted anything like it. The pizza had the same effect on me as M&M's: once I started eating, I couldn't stop.

It was eight or nine years later that I had my next pizza experience; I was graduating from ninth grade. My friends and I ordered pizza from a new pizza restaurant in the neighborhood. The food that we received came in greasy boxes that smelled of wet cardboard and was made with canned mushrooms, canned ham, and a metallic-tasting tomato sauce the taste of which revealed it had to be canned. The crust reminded me of the box it came in more than anything else. The tough and stringy cheese got stuck in my throat. After that experience, my attitude toward pizza changed and I considered it nothing more than junk food.

Many years later, Kenneth Hansen asked if I could help create a book about pizza. At first, I politely declined, because I thought everything worth writing about pizza could be scribbled down, amounting to nothing more than a page. But I was so wrong!

On our first day in New York, we joined a multiday outing organized by Scott's Pizza Tours. I was immensely skeptical, but then something happened on the third day: We visited Motorino and had a pizza with a fantastic crust topped with Brussels sprouts, pancetta, and pecorino. All my taste buds stood up to applaud, whistle, and shout, "Hurray!" And so it continued, with new taste sensations one after the other. When we came to pizza's home country, Italy, it was like I had just fallen in love and had an open mind and a silly smile.

A few months later, I came home with 20 pounds of stone-milled Italian flour in my hand luggage. And I've been infected with an almost maniacal obsession to take a peek into almost every pizzeria I come across. I am no longer in love—I am, to some extent, in the grips of madness. **Mats** ◮

It's Not the End of the World, But I Can See It from Here This is just one recollection of the many encounters I've had with pizza—and it is one of the strangest.

With all the trips made, all the interviews conducted, all the images and text combined into this book, there is one particular experience that still sticks in my mind. To me, this encounter said something about what happens when everything is in a state of change.

When we visited this particular pizzeria, regular customers were not present because new people with a very different background and culture had moved into the neighborhood, and pizza was definitely not on the top of their "to do" list. The owner—the force behind the place—was proud and had not adapted to the arbitrary changes surrounding him. During the hour we were there, only one other patron came in, and she was old enough that she wasn't exactly scarfing down pizza, cola, or anything else.

The pizzeria occupies a large space that is close to the street and is clearly marked with neon lights that glow in the windows between plastic flowers and translucent curtains.

The booth seating felt typically American; the walls were full of ancient history, revealing days of glory past, and the host mostly rummaged about behind the bar.

We chose this place because it was typical of Brooklyn, with huge New York pizzas that were classic in content, presentation, and taste. They were tasty and quite good, actually. Louis Migliaccio of Sam's Restaurant (see page 65), which was established more than 80 years ago, had a sign in the window, "Pizza & Lunch," advertising what he offered. It was probably a recent, last-ditch attempt to draw guests in, but the emptiness of the place suggested the sign's effectiveness was dubious at best. In addition to the solitary guest, the owner, and us, there must have been someone who worked in the kitchen, but we never saw him. It is easy for me to imagine him, though: appropriately overweight from eating up all the leftover dough and pizza sauce lying around, perhaps with cheese and a can of anchovies now and then; dressed in a low, white chef's hat with a sweat brim, white apron, plaid pants, clogs, and with a few days' or a week's worth of stubble. He probably has to do everything in the kitchen, including washing the dishes, although there are not many of those anymore, so it's of little consequence. He stands his ground but only looks forward to getting out of the door after closing time to show the owner, who does little more than poke around at the bar, that the chef takes his job seriously.

It is a kind of living theater of change, where the last man is left to turn off the light. The sell-by date has come and gone. A little sad, but it's thought-provoking for others who follow the times and change along with them. If Sam's is still open, I recommend you pay a visit. If Louis isn't in the bar, then he is probably in the apartment above, where he lived when we were there. That is, of course, if he hasn't sold it to the neighborhood's newcomers. **Kenneth** 🍕

It Started with Potatoes Some might find it strange that I would eventually apply to study culinary arts at a vocational secondary school. Eighth grade for me often involved traumatic weeks of going to class and doing homework, after which I was then put to work peeling potatoes in a hotel basement in Sandnes, Norway. But even the darkest cellars and most blistered fingers failed to kill my dream of becoming a chef. (I thought, as it so happens, that the chef's workweek was about eating tasty, expensive food.) A couple of years later, in 1974, I started culinary studies at the Bergeland secondary school in Stavanger.

Just up the street from the school, No. 28 Pizza Pub had just opened its doors. It was the first pizza restaurant in the district and had become very popular among the region's youth.

I had barely heard of pizza at the time and had certainly never tasted it. The kitchen fan blew the previously unknown pizza smell right out onto the street and down to the school yard. I'll never forget it! It was the best aroma I had ever known. And then I tasted my first slice—wow! It was absolutely the best thing I had ever tasted. The crispy crust, the tomato sauce, industrially made Scottish mozzarella, and seasoned salt. And last but not least, the irresistible aroma: dried oregano sprinkled on red-hot, brown-spotted mozzarella—straight from a Bakers Pride stone oven!

A few days after my first encounter with pizza, I got a part-time job at that very same pizza pub. In the evenings, there was a long queue outside the dark premises, which were located in the basement of a residential building at Bergelandsgata 28. The job quickly made me popular among my friends. The "We know Tore!" factor vastly shortened one's waiting time. Likewise, a boxed-up No. 28 Special always did the trick at get-togethers before going out on the town or upon coming home afterward.

The pizza pub was incredibly popular for a long time in Stavanger, but it was eventually replaced by pizza chains and others who predicted that pizza was not just a flash in the pan. Today, it's strange to think of the first pizza makers who stubbornly refused to remove garlic, or rather garlic powder, from the popular dish, even though the management of the city's businesses resented the fact that their employees came back from lunch with garlic breath!

Take-out pizza was also a big thing, but there were no pizza boxes to take it home in. Large, white paper bags were puffed up by a special technique and sealed off with a stapler. At Burt's Place in Chicago (see page 91), we saw the same bags—40 years later!—a delightful flashback.

No. 28 Pizza Pub was my first encounter with pizza, and it was the start of a lifelong relationship. Pizza has in many ways become my life. Sometimes I wonder how it could have happened, but then I close my eyes and think back. The first aroma. The taste. The surprise. An experience I am lucky to have been able to help to convey to others. And I have yet to meet anyone who does not like pizza! **Tore** 🔺

Shakey's Rattle & Roll Needless to say, Oklahoma was never any Mecca for pizza—at least not like Naples and New York—and unfortunately for us Okies it was Phoenix (or was it San Francisco?) that took the prize for America's best pizza. Who on Earth would have believed it possible?

I clearly remember the popular, local pizza places in Oklahoma City, in addition to all the Pizza Hut locations and the several pizza stands. We also had a famous pizza chain, Hideaway, which still supplies hungry Oklahomans with good pizza.

Let's first take a look at American pizza in the 1960s and 1970s. The pizza itself was the superstar, but the tabletop extras were just as important: grated Parmesan cheese and red chili flakes, preferably served from a shaker with a metal top. You never see these shakers on tables at Italian pizzerias, although the Italians occasionally use Parmesan—and even more seldom, chili flakes of one kind or another—on their pizzas.

As a child, I was delighted to dine at a pizzeria, and when I got into my teens, eating pizza had evolved into a science. I still remember the trips to My π (My "Pie"—get it?) and other good pizza restaurants in Oklahoma City.

It was key to eat the right kind of pizza, but more important it was all about eating pizza at the appropriate establishments. This is where Shakey's comes into the picture. I was utterly obsessed with Shakey's pizza when I was in junior high school—even more so after I started high school. I was more than a Shakey's regular. *Stalker* is probably a more accurate description. My favorite meal was Bunch of Lunch, which was Shakey's lunch buffet with fried chicken, Mojo potatoes, and a multitude of different pizzas. It may well be that salad was part of the offer, but I have in any case suppressed this detail. The important thing was the chicken, potatoes, and pizza.

Shakey's restaurant chain is no longer in Oklahoma, but they still have locations in California, Washington, and Alabama and have opened restaurants in Mexico. Bunch of Lunch is the company's trademark, and the buffet is as popular as ever.

We visited Los Angeles on our pizza tour of the United States, and I felt obligated to give Shakey's another chance after a space of almost 40 years. When we rolled into the parking lot and saw the sign that read "Bunch of Lunch," the memories came flowing back. I had eaten lunch here every second or third week in my youth, and now I was delighted to taste the food that my old favorite place was making in the new millennium. And then judgment was passed: The pizza tasted just like another commercial pizza— the type of pizza I've avoided for years. I can't say whether the pizza at Shakey's is similar to what I ate in my youth. The big surprise was that both the Mojo potatoes and the chicken were just as I remembered them. I'll bet you a year's salary that I would have been able to pick out these two dishes in a blind test.

I am glad that my taste buds have developed and that my stalking days are over, and I am sure that this was my last visit to Shakey's. I've probably become a pizza snob, although I'm not a fan of fancy gourmet pizza either (whatever that is). For me it's all about the perfect balance—and of course the pizza crust. The crust is the most important factor when determining the quality of the pizza. Incidentally, I have never tasted a phenomenal crust that isn't topped with the best cheeses, sauce, and other toppings—just as a good pizza should be. **Craig** 🍕

ITALY

Even the most jaded non-Italian pizza maker will surely admit that without Italy, there would be no pizza.

All four of us have spent time in Italy—quite a lot, to be honest. Tore and Craig have taken various pizza tours throughout the country, and Mats and Kenneth have spent longer periods working on cookbooks in Italy. What none of us realized, however, was just how much we did not know about pizza. Being able to recite the story of Queen Margherita visiting Naples in 1889 does not a pizza aficionado make. This famous pizza with tomatoes, mozzarella, and basil was, as we learned on our journey, probably born several years before the queen's visit. Some experts believe that this historical event was, in fact, quite different from the modern version of the story.

But there is no doubt about Italy's key role in the pizza universe. Naples is the capital of this universe, but exciting pizzas are found throughout Italy. Italians are extremely proud of their traditions, and when it comes to food and wine, they are staunchly patriotic. There is a strong focus on local produce, local history, and local traditions. A resident of Naples will most likely proclaim that the only true pizza anywhere is the Pizza Napoletana. In Rome they often scoff at this idea: Those Neapolitans with their soft, puffy pizza—no thanks!

Pizza in Italy today has been escalated to an entirely different position from its earlier status as "food for the people." Pizza today has entered the world of sophisticated and professional gastronomy, and the humble pizzaiolo has become a superstar. There are lots of "new" pizzas in Italy, and there is an entire movement in the North, with the arrival of the much-discussed Pizza Italiana. This has made many of the Neapolitan pizzaioli even more protective of their pizza's history, and for those of us who love pizza, this world of Italian pizza has never been more exciting.

Today we can taste the Italian pizza from generations past as well as some of the most innovative pizza anywhere. Meeting the Italians featured in this book was a joy. The interviews with them were sometimes like riding a roller coaster—we moved quickly from one topic to another, speaking with animation and mutual excitement. A question, for example, about salt could quickly lead us to something that happened on a Tuesday in the 1980s or even a story about how Mama would have made the dough. Experiences like these cannot be made up. We hope you enjoy reading the interviews as much as we enjoyed conducting them.

CHAPTER 1

NAPLES

PIZZERIA DI MATTEO **The Classic Pizza** p. 5

PIZZARIA LA NOTIZIA **Artigiani** p. 6

PIZZERIA GINO SORBILLO **The Largest Pizzaiolo Family in the World** p. 8

L'ANTICA PIZZERIA DA MICHELE **Pizza Originale** p. 11

MARIA CACIALLI **The President's Daughter** p. 12

PIZZERIA STARITA A MATERDEI **The Pizzaiuolis' Pizzaiuoli** p. 14

MONICA PISCITELLI **Neapolitan Pizza in the Blood** p. 16

TRUE NEAPOLITAN PIZZA ASSOCIATION **We Have Our Methods in Naples!** p. 18

THE CLASSIC PIZZA

Pizzeria Di Matteo, located in the heart of the historic city center of Naples, was started by Salvatore Di Matteo in 1936. As you approach the pizzeria, you usually meet a long line of people waiting to buy deep-fried snacks or pizza slices. A trip upstairs is well worth it for pizza lovers. Visiting Pizzeria Di Matteo is one of those things you should put on your bucket list.

Lovers of classic Pizza Napoletana—soft and chewy pizza with a lightly charred crust, San Marzano tomatoes, and creamy white mozzarella—will get all this and more at Pizzeria Di Matteo, which is also known for making one of our other favorite dishes: *pizza fritta*—fried pizza. The iconic pizzeria also makes what has

to be Italy's most American-style pizza, with pieces of hot dog and—we love it—fries. Don't be thrown off by this variation, as most of the pizzas at Di Matteo's are classics.

One of Pizzeria Di Matteo's claims to fame is President Clinton's 1994 visit during the G7 summit in Naples. We met Nunzio Cacialli, who had been a pizzaiolo at Pizzeria Di Matteo for years (he has since opened Pizzeria di Nunzio Cacialli). His brother, Ernesto, also worked there for years but has since passed away. The brothers contributed greatly to the pizzeria's popularity, and when President Clinton visited them, it was Nunzio and Ernesto who received him.

Nunzio Cacialli

> My only passion is to make pizza. I start early in the morning and finish very late. I fell in love with pizza at a young age. My life is all about fulfilling this passion. The most important thing for me is tradition.
>
> **NUNZIO CACIALLI**

ARTIGIANI

"Naples is the city that can tell the truth about pizza. It all started here in Naples and spread to the rest of the world. As early as the 1800s, there were 200 pizzerias in Naples, according to the state archives. By that time, there was a document that recognized pizzaiolo as a profession. They were not called pizzaioli at the time, but *artigiani*."

So began our visit with Enzo Coccia, who comes from a pizza family. His grandmother had a pizzeria in downtown Naples, and everyone in the family is a pizzaiolo. According to Enzo, Naples is the most important city for pizza, and his family is very keen to introduce Pizza Napoli as a separate "brand" to distinguish it from Pizza Italiana and Pizza Americana. "There is a lifetime of work behind our product, which we are immensely proud of," says Enzo.

"During the last ten years," he says, "the pizza profession has changed, especially in relation to the economic crisis in the world. No matter how bad things are, people can still go out and eat pizza. Pizza is available to everyone, whether they live in Japan, Italy, or Norway, and the pizzaiolo has come out as some kind of star. They have actually done something good for people, even in difficult times."

Enzo says an authentic Neapolitan pizza must have a soft crust and high-quality products. "Those who make the best pizza find the best ingredients," he says. "Sea salt from Sicily is of very good quality. I use oil from either the Sorrento Peninsula or the outskirts of Salerno." La Notizia is proof that tradition and quality count, as people come from all over the world to taste their Pizza Napoletana. "People stand two hours in the rain under an umbrella to get a table. They simply want to eat pizza with good ingredients." He has written to the European Commission for certification of Pizza Napoletana.

Enzo also advocates for gourmet pizza, as well as pairing certain pizzas with champagne.

"I have two pizzerias [both named La Notizia] that are slightly in contrast to each other: One is very traditional, while the other is a bit more modern and innovative," he says. "And why not drink good wine with pizza made with premium ingredients?"

> *I have many favorite pizzas, but if I had to choose my favorite, I would choose a pizza that is soft and made with the best ingredients, and I would drink Jacques Selosse champagne with it.*
> **ENZO COCCIA**

▸ **An evening with Enzo Coccia (pictured top right)**

THE LARGEST PIZZAIOLO FAMILY IN THE WORLD

We arrived at Pizzeria Gino Sorbillo during lunch service; a good idea only if you have a reservation or if you truly don't mind waiting for an available table. The food *is* worth the wait.

We got a table on the extremely busy first floor. The boss appeared in his chef's whites shortly after we were seated and let us know immediately that he had only a half hour for the interview. The reason: a film team, seated a few tables away, was also waiting for him. The allotted half hour turned into a couple more wonderful half hours with the heated Gino, who spoke about pizza and passion at a coffee shop down the street—and followed that up by leading us on a full tour of his amazing pizza studio. After the interview, we were shuffled off to the equally busy second floor, where we sampled a succession of classic and less classic Neapolitan pizzas.

The pizzeria was opened by Gino's grandmother, mother to 21 children, most of them pizzaioli. The Sorbillo family is, in fact, the largest family of pizzaioli in the world; Gino is a fourth-generation pizzaiolo. There are three Sorbillo-manned pizzerias close to each other, but Pizzeria Gino Sorbillo is the most famous.

What makes this pizzeria so special? For one thing, there is always a Sorbillo family member or two present. Gino explains that he is pretty much always at work. He points toward a man wearing what is traditionally called a "do-rag" in the United States: "You see the man in there right now?" he asks. "That is my father, Salvatore (who, by the way, is number 19 of the 21)."

Gino considers it his job to provide food for everyday people—a group with which he identifies, having been born in a poor neighborhood in Naples. He spends a lot of time away from his family, so it is a pleasure for him to meet the people visiting his establishment. The Sorbillos' goal is to have their guests relax and enjoy themselves. The fact that they enjoy themselves is the reason they come back again and again.

"Each and every person should be able to eat Neapolitan pizza! It is a human right," he says. "We must see the Pizza Napoletana for the slice of tradition that it is. The pizzas of Naples vary and are colorful and very direct, just like the people. The tradition of Pizza Napoletana is strong and will remain so."

The pizzas at Gino Sorbillo are huge. There are the standard pizzas: Marinara, Margherita, Capricciosa, and 4 Stagioni, but also a large selection of other pizzas such as Osvaldo (fresh tomato, provola cheese, and basil) and Gennaro

It is a human right to eat Neapolitan pizza!
GINO SORBILLO

(mozzarella, cream, cooked ham, corn, and basil). You will also find the Amnesty Bianco and Amnesty Rosso (with €1 per pizza going to Amnesty International).

Gino has worked with chefs from all over Italy and the world, and he knows that Neapolitan pizza is something special. "Before, there were pizzerias that were also restaurants. Many of these dropped the pizzeria because of its low status. Today, it is just the opposite," he explains. Sorbillo gets calls from people who own restaurants, asking him to help introduce pizza into their business concept.

PIZZA ORIGINALE

Many consider Michele Condurro's pizzeria to be the best in Italy, or even the world. The pizzeria is called L'Antica Pizzeria da Michele, although pizza aficionados know it best as "da Michele." Condurro opened his first pizzeria in 1906, bringing with him all the knowledge and experience from a family of pizzaioli who had been making pizza since 1870. In 1930, he moved his pizzeria to Via Cesare Sersale, and today, if you are lucky, Michele's son Luigi (one of four brothers) will be making your pizza.

It is a surreal experience visiting da Michele for the first time. The pizzeria's facade is as undistinguished as any we have seen, making it hard to believe that some of the best pizza on the planet is made inside. The entryway to this famous pizzeria is not the only thing that is disconcerting. L'Antica Pizzeria da Michele only offers two types of pizza on their menu. Michele Condurro's message is simple: "There are only two types of Neapolitan pizza: the 'Marinara' and the 'Margherita.' No junk should be used in preparing the pizza, because it would only alter its world-famous authenticity and taste."

Paying further homage to minimalism, da Michele completes its menu with a choice of water, beer, cola, and Fanta. These are all sold, by the way, at the same price. With only two types of pizza to choose from, available in just two sizes, it is a shame to not order both. After all, Margherita and Marinara pizza are, for many pizza lovers, the best litmus test to the true quality of a pizzeria.

You might be wondering how hard it can be to make only two pizzas. But cracking the

◄ Behind the scenes at Pizzeria da Michele

da Michele code is as baffling as cracking da Vinci's. Of course they use the best ingredients available. Of course they have a great oven. And of course they have experienced personnel. The kitchen is visible to diners, and there surely have been scores of pizza bakers, pizzeria owners, home pizza cooks, and others who have sat in the brightly lit pizzeria with its green-and-white-tiled walls. They sit observing, concentrating, but never quite figuring out just what da Michele does that nobody else has managed to do.

MARIA CACIALLI

THE PRESIDENT'S DAUGHTER

A female pizzaiola is a rare sight in Italy. Maria Cacialli's father, Ernesto, was the pizzaiolo who served pizza to then President Clinton in Naples in 1994. Maria Cacialli is also a trained chef. We spoke with her about pizza and about her life as a pizzaiola.

"I was born into the world of pizza," says Maria. "My father started working when he was 5 or 6 years old. He had 16 brothers, and everyone in the family had to contribute so that they could have food. My youngest is 12 and does 'freestyle pizza'—also known as acrobatic pizza—while my oldest is 20 and has already been given a pizza world champion title in the categories of stuffed pizza and innovative pizza."

Maria Cacialli has two brothers and is deeply moved when she talks about her father, who she describes as a parent, a teacher, a friend—everything. They were very close, and he unfortunately died far too early, before she could open her own pizzeria.

Maria's pizzeria is a tribute to her father. President Clinton was in Naples in connection with the G7 summit in 1994. "The staff at the Pizzeria Di Matteo, where my father worked, heard that the president was coming across the street and then saw my father run out with a large pizza in his hands so that Clinton had no choice but to have a bite. My father managed to persuade him to come into the pizzeria, where he ate more. Afterwards, President Clinton appointed my father as his personal pizzaiolo. That is where the name 'Pizzaiolo del Presidente' came from. I wanted to dedicate my pizzeria to his memory, so I called it, 'La Figlia del

Presidente' [The President's Daughter]."

Maria is a woman in a male-dominated profession. Usually she is the only woman when traveling to an event or competition.

"I am called 'the female demon,'" she says. "When I enter competitions, all the pizzaioli come in white. They are all exactly alike with white coats and a red hat. I have a custom-made coat, and I wear a little extra makeup, earrings, and high heels, and everyone claps when I enter. The other competitors might be a little jealous, but that is partly the goal."

Another pizzaiolo has actually threatened Maria, she says. "Some think that I have no business being here. But it is a calling. I shall carry on my father's tradition, and that, to me, is what matters. I do not care about the bullying, but it is not easy for other women to be part of this world. I would absolutely like to see more women working with pizza!"

La Figlia del Presidente is located in an old bomb shelter. To Maria, this makes all the sense in the world.

"Neapolitans are a bit special. They believe in the spiritual, and they believe in life after death. I drove around for a while looking for the right place, and one evening I found this place. It was completely dark; I walked around and it felt right. This was where we were supposed to be."

THE PIZZAIUOLIS' PIZZAIUOLI

A pizzeria having survived for more than 100 years is reason enough for us to want to visit it. Pizzeria Starita is more than a century old, but it's also the pizzeria where Sophia Loren worked in the most famous pizza film in history, *L'oro di Napoli*. In addition, Antonio Starita has made pizza for the pope. This place is one of the most popular and important pizzerias in Naples, and, for that matter, Italy. It was high on our list of pizzerias to visit and learn about.

You work here with your wife, son, and daughter. How did you come to run your own pizzeria?
I have lived all my life in Naples, and I am the fourth generation. Initially, this was a cafeteria where they served wine and food. In 1947, it was made into a trattoria, and that is when we started making pizza.

I have four sisters and was very young when my father died. Everyone expected me to become a lawyer or doctor, but I took over the pizza restaurant. It was a bit random, and there was not really a "calling" for me.

How did *L'oro di Napoli* come to be filmed at your family's pizzeria in 1954?
Originally, they wanted to make the film in the city quarter called Marte Dei. They wanted to use a pizzeria that was at street level, so that they could also serve pizza out on the street. But in the end they chose us. The whole place was at

their disposal, the entire premises, for one week. And my father had to teach Sophia Loren how to make pizza.

It was very important to the film crew that we made pizza fritta, and ours was one of the few places just starting to make it in the quarter. The pizza's original name was pizza Otto Adotto, and this pizza has an interesting story. The way it worked was that one would eat pizza Otto without paying for it. Eight days later and after eating a second pizza, one would then pay for the first pizza they had eaten eight days earlier. One could eat the pizza on credit. This was the start of the credit controls, or financial authorities.

> *All serious pizzerias have an important pizzaiolo in the family, and everyone has a secret.*
>
> **ANTONIO STARITA**

This was also reflected in the film. This area was full of small factories at that time. Conditions were cramped and not as open as they are today. Factory workers made shoes and gloves, and those who worked in the factories ate at the pizzeria for lunch. As soon as you got a customer who ordered pizza and was going to pay eight days later, you had a regular customer. The customer could not suddenly disappear because he had to come back and buy a new pizza as payment for what he had just eaten. This was also explained in the film.

How did you get to make pizza for the pope?
During an anniversary celebration, a pizzaioli organization decided that the pizzaioli from Sicily and other parts of Italy were to offer the pope pizza. They held a contest, and I was one of three finalists. In the end, I had the honor of serving the pope pizza. It's called Pizza del Papa and is topped with cream of butternut squash, squash blossoms, grilled peppers, and smoked mozzarella.

Is there a house specialty?
Montanara Starita. All serious pizzerias have an important pizzaiolo in the family, and everyone has a secret. Our secret is my mother's recipe for Montanara Starita, a pizza fritta with ragu, or meat sauce, on top. Inside it is filled with the smoked provolone di bufala.

What do you think will be the future of Neapolitan pizza?
I am not afraid for the future of Pizza Napoletana. If you have learned to make Pizza Napoletana in the traditional way, you can take the ingredients and make it in New York or in Japan, or anywhere else.

What do you think about the development of gourmet pizza in Naples?
I am against this development. Pizza must be simple, authentic, and accessible for everyone. Gourmet pizza is something completely different than what tradition dictates. It costs more because the ingredients are so much more expensive, which means the younger generation cannot afford it. Another challenge for us was to take up the fight against McDonald's, hot dogs, and fast food in general. It is challenging to get young people to come to a pizzeria instead of going to McDonald's. If we lose young people, we have a big problem. If we can keep the tradition, the simplicity, and the youthfulness of pizza, then there is no threat. We must teach a new generation of pizzaioli that pizza must be available to all.

MONICA PISCITELLI

NEAPOLITAN PIZZA IN THE BLOOD

Monica Piscitelli has Neapolitan pizza in her blood and a passionate relationship with pizza that you can read about on her blog, Campania Che Vai, or in her book, *Guida alle Migliori Pizzerie di Napoli e della Campania*. We interviewed Monica at Pizzeria Di Matteo in Naples.

Can you tell us a little about your background?
I grew up in a suburb of Naples but moved to the city with my sister when I began studying economics at college. On top of my studies, I worked in a law firm. During that time, I would come to this particular pizzeria almost every day. When I finished my studies I was very interested in agriculture and the use of natural resources: I was fascinated with the study of why southern Italy was not as well developed as the rest of Europe. Italy's strength has come from its food, so I decided to become acquainted with the landscape and natural resources of my region.

Pizza itself is very well known in the world, but the people who make pizza and their history is not as well known. I started visiting pizzerias and concluded that there were many famous pizzaioli who were not comfortable with being pizzaioli in today's world.

What is happening to pizza in Naples today?
In Naples, pizza is taken seriously, and pizza has changed a lot, especially in the last few years. Two or three years ago, a few journalists began showing an interest in pizza, which was rather unusual for experts in food and wine magazines. Most of my colleagues were more concerned about Italian cuisine in general, great chefs,

and culinary tradition. Pizza was not deemed important, and it was believed that people who worked with pizza were not educated.

People across the country are working to improve the quality of pizza and bring attention to this [change]. Simone Padoan (see page 41) and Giancarlo Casa are two people who are working on this in Naples. To begin with, they are changing the outside appearances of pizzerias. Before, pizzaioli would work in a small corner of the room, but now they are being positioned out in front where customers can watch. Customers are more concerned now with what kind of flour is used, the size of the pizza, how flat it is, how the tomatoes taste, and the quality of the mozzarella. Twenty to thirty pizzaioli across the country are now working this way.

How important is Naples for Italian pizza?
Naples stands for tradition and 300 years of history. Here, you are born into the pizza world, and you often have no choice but to work in a pizzeria with your parents.

It is said that Italians are very critical of pizza made elsewhere in the world because it is not Italian.

What one does not know, one criticizes. And since pizza was born in Naples and is Italian, Ital-

> When you have your first girlfriend and a little money, you can at least afford to go to a pizzeria!
> **MONICA PISCITELLI**

ians seem to think that they are the best at making it. An American pizza is not the same as an authentic Italian pizza, just like Neapolitan pizza cannot be compared with pizza from Rome. But it is silly to say that one is better than the other. They are just different.

Who eats pizza in Italy?

Everyone. In Italy we do not say: "Let's go and eat pizza." We say: "Let's make pizza." *Andiamo a farci una pizza*. In Naples, we go out to eat pizza just as you would walk into a café to have a cup of coffee.

So no one makes pizza at home?

Yes, we make pizza at home, but it is much easier and cheaper to go out. A good pizza Margherita in Naples costs €3.50, so it is much easier to go out and buy it or to order it over the phone. When you have your first girlfriend and a little money, you can at least afford to go to a pizzeria. If you have a Saturday free, you meet friends out for a pizza.

WE HAVE OUR METHODS IN NAPLES!

Massimo Di Porzio's grandfather and grandmother, Umberto and Merlinda, founded Ristorante Umberto in 1916. Today, Di Porzio and his two sisters run the restaurant. One part of Ristorante Umberto is a restaurant where pizza is among other dishes on the menu, and the other part is simply a pizzeria. Here's Massimo on pizza's importance to Neapolitans.

What was your first memory of eating pizza?
We start to eat Pizza Napoletana as children. I have a lot of memories from when I was young and spent a lot of time in the restaurant with my parents. At Christmas and Easter, they always served the customers first, and then, at the end of the day, we would have family meals together.

Neapolitans like traditional food, so we serve Neapolitan brunch on Sundays—something that people like to eat with their families. Competition is strong, so it's important to focus on the strengths of your traditions. We started with pizza in 1936, 20 years after my grandfather opened his restaurant.

Things are not as they once were. Today, there are cooking schools and the True Neapolitan Pizza Association (AVPN), which helps with better training for pizza makers. I started as a pizzaiolo when I was young, but now I prefer to be with the customers. I am also vice chairman of the AVPN.

Tell us about the True Neapolitan Pizza Association (AVPN).
AVPN is a nonprofit organization with about 450 members worldwide. It is run on pure passion. We share thoughts and ideas with members and teach about pizza. In 1984, Antonio Pace, the chairman, began a pizza recipe discussion with 25 other pizza makers. At the time, the makers had their own recipes—and secrets—about pizza. After one year, they came up with one "master" recipe.

DOUGH: The dough should not be stored inside a refrigerator. The great contrast in the

Massimo Di Porzio

humidity between the refrigerator and the oven is bad for the pizza, so you have to keep the dough at room temperature. It makes black spots on the crust otherwise. With fermentation, you don't know what is going to happen when the dough rises in five or six hours. But, in my opinion, this is part of the magic of pizza. If you have tender dough, you can bake the pizza at a lower temperature.

Pizza is the first thing babies eat after they have started with milk. It is inside our soul.
MASSIMO DI PORZIO

PRODUCTS: We always say that products from Naples should be used, but that is not possible everywhere, even though it is getting easier and easier. Let's take mozzarella as an example. In Japan, they use a variation of mozzarella that's more like ricotta or butter. It is not as elastic as what we use in Naples. And look at San Marzano tomatoes—their production is very small. We can say that our pizza *must* use only San Marzano tomatoes, but of course, if you have another good tomato, you can use those.

Has the organization been criticized for being too rigid?
The AVPN is strict when it comes to authenticity and membership. The organization is growing rapidly, and we must not lose control. But we must also be practical. Thirty years ago, things were completely different. It was almost unimaginable that someone in the United States, for example, could make Pizza Napoletana. Today, we have volunteers who go around the world to certify our members. We approve 2 or 3 applications out of 15, especially if they come from countries outside Italy. The organization is strengthened as a result of the growth, though, and there are more people involved than ever before. Recently, for example, the chairman and director went on a tour through Brazil and Argentina with the University of Gastronomy to organize workshops and pizza-making demonstrations.

Other Naples Favorites

It would have been impossible to write about all the great pizzerias in Naples, but here are some more of our favorites:

- Ristorante Mattozzi Europeo
- Pizzeria Trianon da Ciro
- Il Pizzaiolo del Presidente
- L'Antica Pizzeria Port'Alba
- Pizzeria Brandi
- Ristorante Ettore di Napoli

CHAPTER 2

OTHER PIZZAS IN ITALY

ANTICO FORNO ROSCIOLI **Pizza Roman Style** p. 23

FORNO CAMPO DE' FIORI **Pizza from the Baker** p. 24

SFORNO **200-Year-Old Sourdough** p. 27

PIZZARIUM **Street Food** p. 29

PANIFICIO GRAZIANO SALVATORE **Sicilian Pizza** p. 31

ANTICA FOCACCERIA SAN FRANCESCO **Pizza Topped with Bread Crumbs** p. 32

PEPE IN GRANI **Remember This Name: Franco Pepe** p. 37

PIZZERIA I TIGLI **With Truffles and Caviar** p. 41

PANIFICIO PASTICCERIA TOSSINI **Focaccia di Recco** p. 43

SQUADRA NAZIONALE ACROBATI PIZZAIOLI **Viva L'Italia** p. 48

PIZZA ROMAN STYLE

If you ask Craig where his favorite pizza slice comes from, the answer is unequivocal: Roman-Style Pizza Bianca with potato from Antico Forno Roscioli at Campo de' Fiori in Rome. The crust is to die for—crispy, yet soft—unbeatable! Roman-style pizza is a long, rectangular pizza, sliced and sold by weight.

The Roscioli restaurant empire consists of a bakery and a restaurant/wine store/deli. The restaurant has an innovative menu featuring classical dishes made from the finest Italian ingredients. Roscioli's, however, is not deterred from using imported ingredients when the chefs feel they will enhance the flavor of the dish. The Tortellini in Brodo we enjoyed featured handmade, meat-filled tortellini, fresh Parmigiano-Reggiano, and broth made from the very French Poulet de Bresse (Bresse chicken). The same menu featured La Burrata di Pisignano topped with Norwegian herring caviar. Who would have thought a Norwegian product would find its way all the way to Rome?

The Roscioli bakery is much more than a pizza stop. The shop offers an ample supply of homemade breads and sweets, which makes the patron's choice extremely difficult. On our visit to the bakery, the manager was made aware that we were there to try the pizza, and he immediately ordered his favorite for us: pizza crust stuffed with thinly sliced mortadella. The exquisite taste was enough to make us want to research housing prices in the city where all roads led to Roscioli's bakery.

PIZZA FROM THE BAKER

Pizza Bianca is the house specialty at Forno Campo de' Fiori, says owner Fabrizio Roscioli. "In earlier times, the oven door used to be quite narrow so it was difficult to use the space well," he explains. "Pizza Bianca was created from people simply throwing some dough into the oven with a little oil and salt. There is no machine that makes the pizza; everything is done by hand. You put whatever you want on it—Nutella, pork, whatever—there are no limits to what can be used."

Pizza Bianca is the best-selling item on the menu. "This is the pizza that kids bring to school," Fabrizio says. "We always use extra virgin olive oil on it, but we are quite focused on product development and researching new types of flour. We are never finished, but we feel we have a very good product just as it is now."

Most bakeries in Rome make this kind of pizza, but it varies considerably depending on where you go. And of course, the dough is key. "You cannot use the same dough as with other types of pizza. Everyone has his or her own secrets, and that is where passion comes into play," Fabrizio says.

Another distinguishing feature of this Pizza Bianca is that bakeries, not pizzerias, tend to make them. "There is a high-heating capacity in a bread oven, so the capacity is completely different than that of a pizza oven. It is like comparing a train moving at 30 mph to a car driving 30 mph. The two have completely different horsepowers. If you fill this [bread] oven with pizza, the temperature will decrease by 40°F, but if you fill a pizza oven to the brink, the temperature will decrease by 105°F. We use an oven temperature of approximately 520°F. The temperature remains fairly constant, with 30 to 40°F variation."

Pizza Bianca was created from people simply throwing some dough into the oven with a little oil and salt. There is no machine that makes the pizza; everything is done by hand.

FABRIZIO ROSCIOLI

200-YEAR-OLD SOURDOUGH

Stefano Callegari owns three pizzerias in Rome—two that make Neapolitan-style pizza, Sforno and Tonda, and one that is more Roman in style, called 00100. Stefano's pizza is innovative—he likes his crust to be crispy, and he uses a sourdough with wild yeast. He is constantly looking for new flavors and new combinations.

Which of your locations opened first, and what is the difference between the three places?
I opened Sforno in Rome first, about ten years ago; it was previously a Chinese restaurant that we converted into this pizzeria with five wood-fired brick ovens from a place near Florence. The second place is called Tonda, also in Rome. The third place, 00100, I opened in the Testaccio area of Rome, and it is more of a carryout place than a restaurant. At 00100, you eat standing or take it to go. We also opened a test kitchen there where we create and test food.

What makes your pizzas unique?
At 00100, we make square pizzas. As you know, in Rome it is extremely popular to fill a simple pizza and make a sort of sandwich. Pizza sandwiches are traditionally filled with "dry" ingredients and then heated up and eaten. I wanted fillings from the ancient Roman cuisine—oxtail, tripe, meatballs with sauce—but it becomes a bit tricky when you press out the dough so all the filling becomes dislodged from the inside. I found a way to solve it: I cut off the corner crust and opened the pizza, so that it becomes like a triangular sandwich.

As for ingredients, I use both wild yeast and normal yeast, both of which come from nature, and which allow more air into the mixture, and create sourdough. It's very characteristic—very crunchy and light.

Also, I cook the Roman pizzas in a way similar to Pizza Napoletana. Roman pizzas generally are cooked at about 570°F. They need more time and are left in the oven longer so they get really crispy. At my restaurant, we bake the pizza more like they do in Naples, at approximately 840°F.

Do you have a signature taste?
My pizzas are very light with a strong taste of being charred—I love the taste of almost burnt bread and don't care if it's burnt black in some places. I also like to play around with toppings. An example of a fun variation is a pizza I call Greenwich, which has classic English Stilton cheese and port wine. I take Stilton cheese and set aside the parts with the most blue mold, putting the whiter parts on the pizza before it is fully baked. When the pizza is done, I put the best part—all the blue—on top. Finally, I take the port wine, make syrup from it, and drizzle it on top of the pizza.

PIZZARIUM

STREET FOOD

Gabriele Bonci is a big guy, but his work is quite delicate. His large hands gently knead pizza dough to achieve an airy, delicious crust. We met Gabriele at his famous Pizzarium in Rome, where he told us about his pizza philosophy: "It's all about street food but in a sophisticated way. If one takes into account the street and all things related to the street . . . then I'm a street artist."

How would you describe your pizzeria?
This place is for everyone. It's a social thing, because anyone can come here, buy a slice of pizza, and eat it while strolling on. Anyone can come here and get top quality—better than Michelin Star quality. You do not have to sit here and eat a gourmet dinner; rather, you can take it with you. It changes the value of what we eat.

Do you swear by the same philosophy as they do in Naples: "Pizza for the people?"
We focus on quality in the dough, the ingredients, the vegetables, the meat, the prosciutto—everything. One can almost go crazy after finding the absolute best bufala mozzarella in Campagna and in southern Italy.

Would you describe your pizza as "gourmet"?
I hate that term and the entire history of gourmet pizza. It should all be about good food that tastes good, but everyone should be able to eat it. You should not have to go to a fine restaurant to sit down and eat well.

How do you describe pizza from Rome?
Pizza Napoletana has a story, a very strong story. But Pizza Romana, or crispy pizza, does

> *It would be ridiculous to say that all ingredients must be produced in the immediate vicinity. In Rome, we are all living in the middle of a big city, so it is clear we cannot use only locally produced food. We must go further out in the country to find our produce. I use products from all over Italy.*
>
> GABRIELE BONCI

not. People from Rome prefer their own pizza instead of the Neapolitan. They want a crispy crust, which they think is better than the soft crust from Naples. The consistency of the crust is a personal taste.

You make a lot of focaccia. What is the main difference between pizza and focaccia?
The flattening of the dough, how long you take to roll out the dough, as well as the cooking time. Focaccia sits and rises before being baked. It is only put in the oven when the dough finishes rising. Pizza is placed in the oven immediately.

PANIFICIO GRAZIANO SALVATORE

SICILIAN PIZZA

Panificio Graziano Salvatore is both a bakery and a pizzeria. The establishment opened in 1955 and serves a wide range of bakery products in addition to both thin- and thick-crust pizza.

We visited Panificio Graziano in mid-afternoon. Rumor has it that Italians take a little siesta after lunch, but this must be greatly exaggerated because the pizzeria was very busy. In fact, it was so busy we had to wait awhile before we could talk to the master baker, Francesco. Luckily, we had some food in the meantime and entertainment as well: An older couple was unable to find parking as all of the spaces were already full of

cars and mopeds, so they parked in the middle of the street! The man went to order pizza while his wife waited in the car. It wasn't long before a line of angry motorists formed, honking their horns. The funniest thing was that the couple sat down and ate the pizza in the car, deaf to all the activity around them.

The first pizza we ate at Panificio Graziano was topped with tomatoes, onions, and anchovies. We also tried the Pizza Rustica with tomatoes, caciocavallo cheese, and salami. Some of the pizzas are the classic large, square Sicilian pizzas with soft, thick crusts. They also serve round pizzas with thin crusts, as well as their specialty: pizzettes, which are small, round mini-pizzas.

We noticed that they were using various tomato varieties on their pizza. They adjust the tomato mixture every day and use seasonal tomatoes as much as possible. Out of season, they use canned tomatoes as well, but fortunately they have good, fresh tomatoes almost all year. We visited the restaurant in November, and the tomatoes were fresh and of excellent quality.

We spoke with Francesco, who is the pizzaiolo and co-owner with his mother, who works at the checkout. His sister runs the café next door. In total, there are 21 lively, friendly employees. We asked Francesco what he thought about Neapolitan pizza versus Sicilian pizza. "I do not like the soft, watery dough that Neapolitans use," he said. "I prefer a more crispy pizza crust."

PIZZA TOPPED WITH BREAD CRUMBS

Court Chef Antonio Alaimo established Focacceria San Francesco in 1834, right in the center of Palermo. The restaurant still serves some of the original dishes Chef Alaimo served nearly 200 years ago. In 1902, Salvatore Alaimo changed the name to Antica Focacceria San Francesco. Today, it is Salvatore Alaimo's relatives, the Conticello brothers, who run the place.

Antica Focacceria San Francesco is a member of the Slow Food movement and the first restaurant to sell DOP-protected focaccia. (DOP is a guarantee of origin.) The pizza at Antica Focacceria San Francesco is classic Sicilian *sfincione*, which is a pizza crust topped with tomato sauce, anchovies, caciocavallo cheese, and bread crumbs. Another specialty is a small focaccia with caciocavallo cheese or ricotta, and spleen and lung (of lamb or calf) boiled in large pots in the middle of the restaurant. This focaccia Maridada resembles the small hamburgers called *sliders* that are so popular with late-night diners in the United States. The restaurant also has a large selection of antipasti, pasta, fish, and meat. The restaurant is frequented by many regulars from the local area as well as by tourists from around the world.

Caciocavallo Cheese: The Cheese from the 1300s

In Sicily, it's very common to find caciocavallo cheese on pizza. The name *caciocavallo* means "cheese on horseback," which stems from the fact that fresh portions of this cheese are tied together in pairs with a rope and then hung over a wooden board or stick to dry and age. There is even an Italian expression that means "to end up like a caciocavallo," meaning to be hanged to death.

There are several types of caciocavallo cheese in Italy, but all are made of cow's or sheep's milk. Its shape is reminiscent of a long-necked gourd, and the flavor is evocative of butter and nuts, and the cheese is also available smoked. The cheese usually weighs in at about three pounds. The cheese was first produced in southern Italy in the fourteenth century and is considered a descendant of some of the first cheeses made in ancient Roman times. Caciocavallo cheese is also produced throughout the Balkans and, since the early 1900s, in the United States.

Sicilian Sea Salt from Trapani

Twenty years ago, most of us were satisfied with the salt we used. Then sea salt became the salt of choice, even if it didn't matter from which ocean it came. After a while, home chefs became familiar with the slightly exotic salts: *fleur de sel*, Maldon salt, and Himalayan salt, to name a few. Today, there is an abundance of different kinds of salts in stores—so many that it is not easy to choose the "right one."

Many think the best salt for Italian pizza comes from Trapani, on the island of Sicily. This salt is very special. We visited Trapani and the salt museum there and were introduced to Alberto Culcasi. Culcasi's grandfather, also named Alberto, started working with salt when he was just 6 years old, and in 1977, he bought the approximately 5 hectares that are run by the family today. We asked Alberto to tell us a bit more about his family's history.

My grandfather, who died a few years ago, began the family business as a bit of an adventure. An earthquake destroyed the whole area in 1964, and he bought land so that he could rebuild the area's salt-production business, create a salt museum, and continue his family's production of high-quality salt. It took many years to build it all up, but today the operation is in full production.

There are several things that make Sicilian sea salt special, and climate is especially important. It is very hot here, with a lot of wind and little rain. In the old days, you could use the salt right after it was brought in to production. It was a very clean product with lots of minerals. The mineral content of the salt today is somewhat lower because it is more processed than before. However, it is still one of the best there is—it can withstand higher temperatures than other types of salt, which is ideal for pizzas cooked at a high temperature. In addition, salt is easily soluble in water, so food actually becomes easier to digest.

My grandfather was not obsessed with making money the way others were—this business was in his soul. For us, the family tradition is what we want to carry forward. I am responsible for the museum, Carmelo is involved in the production, and Salvatore runs the restaurant.

To judge the quality of the salt, I simply taste. If it has a very strong, salty taste, the quality is good. People come here and ask why the salt does not taste like salt, but this is [because of] the process we use. Our salt is hard, and that means the quality is good.

ALBERTO CULCASI

My grandfather got windmills from the area working again and incorporated them into the production process. The windmill where the museum is located comes from Holland and is 600 years old. American windmills also came into use gradually; they are more modern and made of metal. But salt eats metal, so they did not last more than 30 years. We therefore swear by the Dutch windmills, which are made of wood.

REMEMBER THIS NAME: FRANCO PEPE

Naples is known as the pizza capital of Italy. Many people also know that Rome has its own pizza. What most people do not know, however, is that one of the world's most exciting pizza personalities is located in a small town called Caiazzo. The man is Franco Pepe, and his restaurant is called Pepe in Grani. We had heard rumors of Pepe's new restaurant in both Naples and in the USA.

We met Franco Pepe on a Sunday afternoon in November, just weeks after he opened his new restaurant. We walked down a long, narrow alley to reach the restaurant, which is located in a seventeenth-century building that Franco had restored. In addition to the restaurant on two floors, he has a workshop and a few rooms for visiting pizzaioli and others with whom he works. The weather was still good enough to allow us to eat outside on the beautiful veranda overlooking Caiazzo and the surrounding area.

Franco began his career in his grandfather's pizzeria, and eventually he, along with his father and his brothers, ran Antica Osteria Pizzeria Stefano Pepe. Today, Franco is 49 years old and has spent all of his years at a pizzeria. Now, however, he feels a calling to do something more with the business.

Franco has tremendous faith in his product and its quality and some negative feelings about other pizza businesses. He is angered about the number of pizza chains that exist, he is not particularly interested in what is happening with the pizza in Naples or elsewhere, and he does not want to be labeled as Neapolitan. He makes "la pizza di Franco Pepe," he says. While he has been criticized for his attitude and encouraged to be like "others" so that he can earn more money

> *Everything is done by hand. My grandfather taught me how to understand the flame in the furnace, or rather the heat in the oven on the basis of color. Temperature is essential, but I have learned to look at the color of the oven and not at a thermometer.*
>
> **FRANCO PEPE**

and gain success faster, Franco wants a place that gives him energy, motivation, and inspiration—a place where people have to look to find him, off the tourist track and away from the center of a city. People should come to his pizzeria because he is here and because he makes his pizza here.

"I do not want to be compared with any others whatsoever. I almost get angry when someone says I am better than someone else. That's not the goal. I have done all this myself. I have not been helped by anyone else, and I have built myself up very slowly."

After spending some time in northern Italy with another pizzaiolo, he had the opportunity to experiment with his pizza and other pizzas. "That is what makes pizzas move forward; we are developing new types of pizzas. That is what I want to do. Those who are genuinely interested and understand my way of thinking can come here and study pizza with me."

But not just anyone can go to the conservatory to work with Franco. "Certainly not! For me it is very important that the chemistry is good and that I work with pizzaioli who are interested and who do what I do."

Franco says he's not as quick at his craft as others because each pizza is very, very special to him. Every time he makes dough, which is based on techniques he learned from his grand-father, he gets emotional. Many have tried to copy it, without success. Franco's dough is possibly the lightest dough we tasted; it was an amazing experience.

Franco likes to experiment and has a work-shop on the second floor of the restaurant where he simply studies dough. Every morning when he gets up, he looks at the weather, temperature, and climate, and then he mixes the flour(s) he will use that day. Later in the day, he makes his final adjustments to the dough before it is used that night. He finds it impossible to use one type of flour all the time, as both climate and temperature change.

We asked Franco if he makes any adjustments to the grinding of the flour, or whether it is fairly uniform in the various products he makes.

"Generally speaking, I am against the very white and heavy flours. For the most part, the Tipo 00 (the finest-ground) with Tipo 0 (the slightly coarser-ground) flours."

We were treated to several pizzas, each of which was an exciting creation made by a real master. One of our favorites was based on one of the oldest pizzas in Italy's history, interpreted by Franco himself: a Pizza Bianca with pepper and basil, lardo, a rare type of pecorino, and topped with fresh white figs from Caserta as it is taken out of the oven.

WITH TRUFFLES AND CAVIAR

In 2012, food and wine magazine *Gambero Rosso* printed its list of the best pizza restaurants in Italy. Not a single one was in Naples, which caused an uproar. Francesco Borrelli, a Neapolitan politician, called it "culinary racism," and people demonstrated to show exactly how upset they were. One of the pizzerias noted in the article was Franco Pepe's (see page 37), located not far from Naples, but which, according to Borrelli, does not make Neapolitan pizza. The pizzeria that ended up at the top of *Gambero Rosso*'s list was i Tigli in Verona.

"It was great recognition," says owner Simone Padoan, "which is wonderful, of course. But my motivation has never been for my restaurant and me to stand at the forefront of pizza in Italy. We want to ensure that we are ambassadors of good ingredients and of the products that are served on our tables."

Simone is best known for his creative pizzas, but he does not like the term "gourmet pizza." He prefers *pizza degustazione*, which means something along the lines of "pizza for tasting." He serves pizza cut into small pieces, almost like a multicourse restaurant dinner.

In 1994, Simone opened i Tigli; its name refers to the trees that grow in the park just outside the restaurant. For the first few years, Simone made classic pizza, but in 1999, he changed his strategy and began making pizzas that were completely different. Simone uses classic pizza ingredients but is also interested in other toppings, such as truffles or caviar.

There are some who claim that Simone does not make pizza. "I've only moved forward," he says. "I've found my own way with pizza."

Simone is deeply connected to traditional food, which is evident in his use of raw materials from the area where he grew up. The type of pizza he enjoys making the most is actually one with mozzarella and tomatoes.

"I Tigli is perhaps the most criticized pizzeria in Italy, and that is okay because criticism always leads to a lot of positivity and creativity. I have learned to tolerate criticism, but the worst thing for me is a lack of respect for my staff. They work for hours, and it is painful to me when I feel that people do not respect what they do."

Simone explains that there are differences between the North and South, and he is fully ingrained with the innovators of the North. "There are two different cultures and ways of living," he explains. "In the South, they are trying to get back the quality of pizza from earlier times. They have lost a lot along the way, so it is good that they are searching for answers in their roots. In the North, we have a very different type of society. We tend to be more innovative and trendy—we have the world's most innovative car designers, fashion designers, and artists in our midst. The North and South are moving in two distinct directions. There must be room for both."

◄ Simone Padoan works his extraordinary dough (upper left and lower right).

Maurizio Tossini

PANIFICIO PASTICCERIA TOSSINI

FOCACCIA DI RECCO

The seaside town of Recco has a population of 10,000 and is a twenty-minute drive east from Genoa. Recco's claim to fame is its Focaccia di Recco, basically a pizza crust filled with local cheese. We visited Panificio Pasticceria Tossini in Recco and spoke with owner Maurizio Tossini. He explained that the focaccia produced in Recco is not only an icon of Recco but also of the Liguria region.

There are two types of regional focaccia here: the original type with stracchino cheese and another type using the same dough but with tomato sauce and olives in addition to the cheese. All the focaccia is made with very thin dough, which is placed on a tray, topped with small pieces of stracchino (also known as crescenza or formaggio di Recco). The dough is then folded over the filling.

The focaccia at Panificio Pasticceria Tossini is typical of focaccia from Recco. You can eat it as antipasto before lunch or dinner, or as a snack or an entrée, depending on the focaccia's size. Maurizio's company has been making this product since 1966, and he tries to create a better product each year.

"We deliver to supermarkets, cafés, and restaurants, which gives us very different kinds of customers. We have a partner that produces a type of sandwich with our focaccia, because it is a quick and easy lunch. Since many people can no longer afford one- or two-hour lunch breaks, they need quick and easy meals. It is very easy to digest our product because of the simple ingredients."

There are stories passed down about when people in Recco started to make this, but those are just local stories. We don't have an exact date or year. We like to say that this product was born when the people had cows and could then produce cheese. It is a very popular, traditional recipe.

MAURIZIO TOSSINI

Beniamino: Pizza Consultant

We had the pleasure of meeting Beniamino Bilali in Turin. He grew up in Rimini in Romagna, where he still lives, but he is often on the road. In Turin, he was hired as a consultant for a pizzeria that was opening soon. Beniamino is young, eager, and knowledgeable. He is fascinated by pizza and, in particular, by the dough. This quickly becomes obvious when you speak with him. We have become good friends, and it was Beniamino we called when we needed an expert during the photo shoot for this book.

You have helped open several pizzerias. Do you do something different in each new venture?

Every pizzeria I have opened has been a new experience. For example, in Bologna, I worked with a pizzeria that moved the pizzaiolo into the kitchen so that he and the chef could work together. One was good at baking, and he baked the pizzas; the other was good at cooking, so he cooked and prepared the pizza ingredients for the filling. Everything was fresh, and everything was made right before it was used, and this was something new. In Fariza, we did the same thing and used only ingredients that were in season. We worked with a small menu with only eight to ten different types of pizza, which we changed every four months. And the pizzaiolo was always visible.

Tell us how you think about pizza.

Pizza Napoletana is a good product and is DOP protected, but Pizza Napoletana can only use mozzarella products from Naples. Pizza Italiana expands the pizzaiolo's ability to search the globe for new things, showing that pizza is not just one specific type of pizza. That includes quality in the dough and in the ingredients. Anything goes; anyone can make his or her own version.

What is most important about making good pizza?

Each region in Italy has its own pizza, but the most important thing is the dough. The choices with flour, yeast, and water are key. I've experimented with one of the oldest fermentation processes: adding hot water to flour (preferably integrale, or coarse, flour), which creates a type of gel and leads to a natural fermentation process. Yeast is already in the grain, but what happens when you add water is that it always creates something new. People used this technique 2,000 years ago.

What about tomatoes and cheese?

You must use tomatoes and mozzarella to give the pizza a real identity. And it can't be just any cheese; it has to be mozzarella. The tomato sauce must be Italian and contain only the best ingredients. Thus, there are three key ingredients needed to make a good Italian pizza: mozzarella, tomatoes, and good dough. Neapolitan pizza is the exceptional benchmark as they have everything at hand locally. But why should another Italian pizza be bad? We must have the same respect for all Italian pizzas, for the modern Italian pizza.

> You must be intimately familiar with your ingredients. If you have good ingredients, you must feel them, treat them like a child, and be attentive and careful. It is very important in our profession to know the story behind all of the ingredients.

BENIAMINO BILALI

How important is the oven?

Pizza was born to be made in a wood oven—it is best that way. But we must think about the future and find alternative types of energy. Ninety percent of the work is in making the dough—if you have good dough, you can bake it in a good oven heated either by wood, gas, or electricity.

What kind of dough should we use at home?

There are two ways to make dough. You can either mix the yeast with flour and water in one operation and set the dough to rise, or you can first mix a little yeast with a little flour and a little water and make a starter portion of yeast that then stands until it ferments and begins to bubble. The first method is quick and simple, but the dough isn't as tasty; the second method takes a few hours, depending on the temperature, but you will end up with lighter pizza that is more flavorful.

Would you describe yourself as an artist or as part of an industry?

I will always remain an artisan, but to be a good artisan, you must have rules to follow. Art must have an identity to have an impact on the outside world.

VIVA L'ITALIA

In 1987, six or seven pizzaioli in the Ravenna area got together to juggle pizza. They developed pizza dough that was elastic enough to juggle in the air. In 1990, the World Championship in pizza baking was organized, and the same year saw the creation of a national team of pizza jugglers. Italy is the only country with its own national team, and today there are 14 members. The team members are paid, and the national team has its own office where, among other things, they organize their upcoming shows, events, and competitions.

In Modena, we met the group of talented pizza jugglers: Alessandro Coluccino, Christian de Rosa, Alessandro Gullotto, and the leader of the group, Danilo Pagano. They have their own lighting and music for commercial exhibitions and shows, and they always bring the necessary ingredients for the special pizza dough they use.

The pizza acrobats come from all over Italy and have traveled the world. Most have worked as pizzaioli, and several have their own pizzerias around Italy.

The pizza acrobats perform amazing stunts with the special pizza dough, which incorporates a special type of flour that makes it durable, elastic, and strong. Rolling the dough around on the fingertips is nothing compared to throwing it from one hand to another—via shoulder blades. The team members throw the dough from person to person and perform a whole repertoire of tricks. They train hard and often, and the result is impressive—to put it mildly.

USA

Pizza in America

It is impossible to present all the great pizzas made in America—or the world for that matter—in one book. We have made a considered selection, and we are fully aware that residents of New Haven and Philadelphia will be rolling their eyes when they see that some of their local favorites, such as Sally's Apizza, Pepe's, Tacconelli's, Zavino, or any number of other pizzerias, are not included.

The problem becomes exponentially worse when you consider that cities such as Providence, Denver, and Memphis all have local pizzas revered by thousands of pizza lovers. And what about Detroit? The city features pizza, and even pizza pans, unlike anywhere else in the world. All we can do is apologize to all the great pizzaioli and pizzerias we have not yet managed to meet or experience.

Our American pizza journey started in New York, and led us to Chicago, Los Angeles, and San Francisco, with a side trip to Phoenix.

With the exception of Phoenix, all of these cities have numerous outstanding pizzerias. The unique and enticing thing about American pizza is that there is no single pizza that can be called the official "American pizza." A classic New York pizza is significantly different from one found in a San Francisco pizzeria.

Some American pizzas can easily be traced back to their Italian roots, while others are a result of the traditions and creativity found around the country. In Greek communities, you can eat bread-like dough topped with white cheddar and gyro meat. In the South, you might find a pizza crust topped with barbecue sauce and smoky pulled pork. In the Southwest, we tasted pizza with a tortilla crust and toppings from the Mexican kitchen. One thing is certain: no country anywhere offers the variety of great pizzas that can be found in the United States. We recommend all pizza lovers find the time to sample as many of these unique pizzas as they can!

CHAPTER 3

NEW YORK

NEW YORK **Gotham** p. 54

KESTÉ PIZZA & VINO **Pizza's Mick Jagger** p. 57

DI FARA PIZZA **Italian Heroes** p. 58

TOTONNO'S **Pizza & Cookie** p. 61

NEW YORK PIZZA SUPREMA **We All Love NY Pizza** p. 63

SAM'S RESTAURANT **The Old Neighborhood** p. 65

SCOTT'S PIZZA TOURS **On the Road with Scott** p. 69

PIZZA A CASA PIZZA SCHOOL **Hitting the Books** p. 73

BARI RESTAURANT & PIZZA EQUIPMENT **Bari in the Bowery** p. 75

EATALY NYC **In Love with Food** p. 77

GOTHAM

Italian immigrants brought their breads and pizzas with them to New York in the late 1800s; in 1905, Gennaro Lombardi received the first commercial license to sell pizza at his store at 53½ Spring Street.

Other Italians also sold pizza, but Lombardi is credited as being the father of New York pizza. Gennaro was a pizzaiolo from Naples who moved to New York in 1897. He opened a tiny grocery store, and together with his employee, Antonio Totonno Pero, started selling pizzas.

The New York pizza is inspired by the Neapolitan pizza, but New York pizza has always had its own signature: the wood-burning ovens of Naples were replaced by the coal-fired ovens found in New York, and buffalo mozzarella was replaced by *Fior di latte*, a type of mozzarella made with cow's milk.

Wood-fired ovens can cook a pizza in just over a minute, but coal-fired ovens require about five minutes, which produces pizza with a different consistency and look. The coal-fired oven is well on its way to becoming a thing of the past, for environmental reasons, but there are many coal ovens hidden behind walls in New York City. Their persistent existence is due to the fact that they are so hard to dispose of: they take two to three weeks to completely cool, and then the wall encasing the oven, plus the 20 to 30 feet behind the oven, must be removed. Even trying to repair a coal oven is a feat few will attempt. Today, gas and electric ovens are the popular—and environmentally friendlier—way to go.

Ovens aside, American flours are vastly different from those used by Italians, which is an important factor in the resulting crust. Put this American crust into a gas, electric, or coal-fired oven, add some American whole milk, low-fat mozzarella, and pepperoni (not an Italian ingredient, by the way), and presto—you have a New York–style pizza!

Another important, uniquely New York factor is that life in the city is all about location, location, location. A New Yorker's residential proximity to a given pizzeria is a critical factor that often determines his or her favorite pizza. Much of the pizza in New York City is sold in slices, perfect for the fast-paced lifestyle of the "City That Never Sleeps." You will find pizza sold by the slice in Italy, but in New York slices are as essential as the Yankees and the other great slice: New York cheesecake.

> No single pizza is the very definition of a New York pizza, but New York pizza clearly has its own style, or even better: many different styles.

PIZZA'S MICK JAGGER

Roberto Caporuscio was born on a dairy farm in Pontinia, Italy, a small town an hour from Naples. From early in life, Caporuscio's trade was cheesemaking. At the age of 37, however, he decided to study the art of making pizza in Naples.

Roberto moved to the United States in 1999. Today, he serves as the US president of the AVPN (Associazione Pizzaiuoli Napoletani), works as a pizza consultant, and runs a pizza-making school where he teaches aspiring pizzaioli the art of making Neapolitan pizza. He opened his first pizzeria in Pittsburgh, and later, he opened A Mano in Ridgewood, New Jersey, both of which were successes. Roberto now lives in New York and runs Kesté (the name means "this is it" in Italian) Pizza & Vino.

The menu at Kesté boasts more than 40 pizzas as well as appetizers, salads, and paninis. The restaurant was relaunched in 2012, and the new wine list is more than three times as large as the previous list. There are a number of

big-name Italian wine producers as well as an excellent selection of craft beers from Italy.

We visited Roberto at Kesté with one of his biggest fans, Scott Wiener (see page 69). We'd heard Roberto described as "the Mick Jagger of New York pizza," so we looked forward to meeting him and sampling some of his pizza.

In addition to the full-time employees at Kesté, there were students hard at work in the kitchen preparing pizzas. Roberto encouraged them, corrected them, and participated in making pizza while telling us about cheesemaking and the wonderful pizzas of his beloved Naples.

We sampled pizzas from the students and from two of Kesté's pizzaioli. The students' pizzas were good; the Kesté pizzas were extraordinary. Meanwhile, Roberto was preparing to open for the day while supplying us with tips for people and places we simply *had to* visit in Italy. He was busy; we were eating great pizza. What a way to start the day!

ITALIAN HEROES

The young Domenico DeMarco moved to the United States from Caserta, Italy, in 1959. Pizza and bread baking are in his blood, and it is this tradition he brought with him to America. His first pizzeria was located in Bay Ridge, Brooklyn. The location for the pizzeria was not particularly good, and DeMarco ended up closing it. Before that happened, however, there was one significant event. A young woman named Margret had just been dumped by her boyfriend, and she sat alone, brokenhearted, at the pizzeria. The gallant young Domenico came out from behind the counter to talk to her, and the two fell in love. And the rest, as they say, is history.

Domenico DeMarco had already paid the deposit for another location when he and his father, Alexander, found the ideal place on Avenue J. Luckily, Domenico changed course, and he rented that perfect corner spot a few days later. This became Di Fara Pizza, a name that is a combination of DeMarco's name and that of his original partner, Farina. Domenico bought out Farina in 1978.

Shortly after starting the pizzeria, Domenico married Margret, and as the pizzeria grew in popularity, the DeMarco children arrived: Mike, Dominick, John, Margret, Alex, Louise, and Harry. Today, Mike, Dominick, Margret, Alex, and Louise all work at Di Fara.

Early in his career, Domenico believed he would someday return to Italy with his family. His wife, however, a native New Yorker, did not agree. The pizzeria was Domenico's only connection to his homeland. Cooking is an instinct to him—something everybody on the family farm in Italy was accustomed to doing. Making pizza kept him close to his home in the surrounding hills of Naples. This is the heart of the pizza Domenico makes.

Running a pizzeria is an all-consuming job, something we have heard numerous times during our travels. Domenico's son Dominick explains: "My father's goal in making great pizza never had anything to do with making lots of money. He cannot make much with the way he runs the place, as it's only open five days a week from noon to closing at 8:30 p.m., making only one pizza at a time, in one oven, without a break all day."

It's extremely entertaining watching DeMarco & Co. work while waiting for your pizza. His grown-up children take orders, grate cheese, bring him ingredients from the cooler, bus tables, and do pretty much anything except make the pizzas. Papa DeMarco bakes his pizzas himself, often one at a time. He removes them from the oven by hand, the only way to check that the pizzas are perfectly cooked. His legendary use of scissors to cut the fresh basil over the pizza is also something to see.

Dominick DeMarco joined the family business along with his other siblings, Mike, Margret, Alex, and Louise.

New York pizza lovers are a loyal crowd. And there is probably no other New York pizzeria with a more loyal following than Di Fara. Some will complain about the $5 slices, though ordering a whole pizza for $28 or the Di Fara Classic Pie at $32 (with sausage, peppers, mushrooms, and onions) can be considered a steal.

While Di Fara Pizza may be New York's most talked-about pizzeria, DeMarco's son Dominick also sells pizza in Las Vegas: "Vegas is a project that I'm doing. No one else in the family is involved. I have always been interested in the western part of the United States, so I opened Dom DeMarco's Pizzeria & Bar with some good friends."

TOTONNO'S

PIZZA & COOKIE

Antonio "Totonno" Pero started his pizza career working at the original Lombardi's—New York's first pizza place—on Spring Street in the Little Italy area of New York City. In 1924, Totonno left Lombardi's to open his own pizzeria on Coney Island. Totonno's is the oldest continuously operating pizzeria in America; it is still run by the same family, and they still serve the same coal-fire baked pizzas they always have (no slices!). Totonno's is famous for its pizzas but also for its "flexible" hours of operation.

We had a great meal at Totonno's. The owner, Cookie Ciminieri, brought us menus and drinks, and after an acceptably long wait, our

pizzas arrived. The pizzas were wonderful, and the wait gave us a chance to meet some truly unique characters.

Sadly, Totonno's was ravaged by Hurricane Sandy in 2012 and had to close for repairs for several months. After reopening, Antoinette Balzano—Ciminieri's sister and co-owner— told the *New York Daily News*, "I couldn't let my grandfather go down this way. Not from a fire or from storms. I could see if we were too old or something, but the customers need Totonno's."

Today, with new tiles on the floor, new kitchen equipment and electrical wiring, they are back and busier than ever.

Owner Cookie Ciminieri (left) served us delicious pizza; we met some wonderful "regulars," including Paul Randazzo (right), who calls himself "The Calamari King." Randazzo is the oldest grandson of Helen Randazzo, who opened the original Randazzo's Clam Bar, just a stone's throw from Totonno's.

WE ALL LOVE NY PIZZA

If you miss the old-fashioned, romantic pizzaiolo twirling pizza high overhead, there is one NYC pizzeria that serves great pizza with added entertainment.

Pizza blogger Colin Hagendorf (aka "Slice Harvester") has proclaimed the slice at Pizza Suprema ("owned by the same Italian family for over 45 years!") as the best in Manhattan. This is no small feat in the city that never sleeps, or stops eating pizza. Scott Wiener of Scott's Pizza Tours (see page 69) says that Suprema has one of the best pizza slices: "Powerful, robust, earthy, bold. It makes me salivate just thinking about it."

At Pizza Suprema, the tomatoes and mozzarella are Californian. They use imported pecorino Romano cheese on some of the pizzas, and all of the pizzas are baked in the Bakers Pride oven, which Wiener describes as "the definition of New York pizza."

Scott joined us at Pizza Suprema to eat. "Most New York pizzerias use the same ingredients, but each pizza is different. In a place like Pizza Suprema, or even in a place like Kesté, they are all different. It is just such a visceral experience," he says.

We sampled a number of pizzas at Pizza Suprema, and the big favorite is their Upside Down Pizza, which the pizzeria describes as "a first cousin to the 'New York Style' Sicilian." Its crust is thick but light, deep dish, square, and covered with mozzarella and an oniony tomato sauce, and then topped with pecorino Romano cheese and extra virgin olive oil.

SAM'S RESTAURANT

THE OLD NEIGHBORHOOD

The image of the "ultimate" classic New York pizzeria has red-and-white-checkered tablecloths, red vinyl booths, maybe some neon signs outside, a paper sign proclaiming "No Slices," and a slightly grumpy middle-aged waiter inside. Throw in a good pepperoni pie, and the picture is complete. Welcome to Sam's Restaurant on Court Street in Brooklyn. The rustic-looking restaurant could have come from a scene in *The Sopranos*—and, in fact, it was featured in an episode, though Louis Migliaccio's lips are sealed as to what plans might have been made by the New Jersey mafia while they were there.

Louis Migliaccio is waiter, bartender, busboy, and storyteller at Sam's. His father, Mario, owned the restaurant initially, and Louie pretty much grew up there before he became owner. If you believe everything that has been written about Sam's on the Internet, you might wonder if you will even be allowed to eat at the establishment. Upon our arrival, however, we were welcomed with open arms.

Louis told us the story of the 80-year-old restaurant and the joys and challenges his family has faced over the years. We learned that the restaurant's heyday is a thing of the past and that the "old neighborhood" has gone through a lot of changes. Today, the mostly Jewish neighborhood is not as pizza-crazed as the residents were 30 years ago.

Luckily, Migliaccio owns the building, but it is easy to see that he is uneasy about the restaurant's future. This is a common theme among all restaurants we visited on our travels: What will the future bring? Is there a next generation that will take over? Migliaccio told us that banks have offered several times to buy him out because of

the valuable land the restaurant occupies, but for the moment the restaurant will remain.

Sam's Restaurant is the quintessential mom-and-pop place where the red sauce flows and there's an extensive menu with antipasti, soups, sandwiches, and salads. This is New York Italian cuisine of the days of yore, which is a combination of kitchens both in Italy and New York—a restaurant relic of the '40s and '50s trying to survive more than half a century later.

Sam's pizzas are cooked at a piping hot 750°F, giving them a nice char, and the ingredients are carefully chosen. At any time, Louis will have at least five types of tomatoes on hand, and his sauce is made by a combination of these. He also uses the delicious Polly-O high-grade mozzarella.

We ordered two large pizzas—one of them a meatball and mozzarella pie, the other with ricotta, mozzarella, and anchovies. The rich, creamy whole-milk mozzarella and the tomato sauce bursting with flavor make you want to come back for more. Let's just hope places like Sam's are still around for future generations to enjoy.

Other New York Favorites

No single book could possibly cover all the great pizzerias in the Big Apple, which simply leaves room for the debate to continue—and future trips (in the name of culinary research) to be made. In addition to the New York pizzerias we have described in some detail already, we visited some others that simply must be mentioned:

Motorino There are five Motorino locations—three in New York, one in Manila, and one in Hong Kong. Our photographer, Mats, became a lifelong fan of Motorino after sampling their famous Brussels Sprouts Pizza topped with fior di latte, garlic, pecorino, smoked pancetta, olive oil, and, of course, brussels sprouts. Mats has

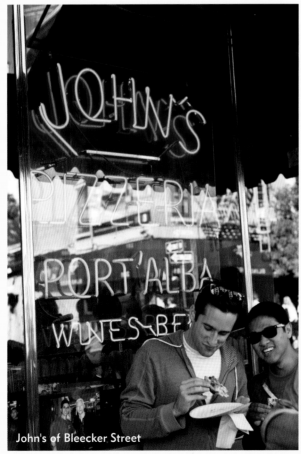
John's of Bleecker Street

created his own version of this pizza; the recipe can be found on page 266. It is also worth mentioning that Motorino's weekend brunch features Pizz' al Uovo, a pizza topped with fior di latte, smoked pancetta, basil, pecorino, chili oil, and fried eggs.

(Famous) Joe's Pizza Joe Pozzuoli emigrated from Naples in the 1950s, and in 1975 he opened Joe's Pizza, which he still operates to-day. Joe's Pizza serves Fresh Mozzarella Pie as well as the Sicilian Square Pie. This is your classic New York pizzeria. The pizzas are delicious, and, in case you were wondering, they have "fresh salads sometimes available for large orders (five pies or more)." A second Joe's Pizza is now located at 150 East Fourteenth Street.

Forcella A visit to Forcella should start with classic Italian antipasti such as arancini, crocchette, or burrata e prosciutto. As far as pizza goes, Forcella has a couple of specialty pizzas well worth trying. The first is the Montanara—a lightly fried crust topped with tomato sauce, homemade mozzarella, Parmesan, and basil. Forcello also offers a fried calzone (calzone fritto) with smoked mozzarella, salami, ricotta, tomato, and Parmesan; both are excellent. Forcella also has other specialty pizzas featuring ingredients such as burrata, truffle oil, kale, and artichokes.

John's of Bleecker Street John's of Bleecker Street was founded in 1929 by John Sasso and is famous for coal-fired oven pizzas. John's doesn't serve slices, but its throngs of loyal customers will tell you no one could ever eat just a slice or two of pizza this good. Try the thin-crust pizza with your choice of toppings or the scrumptious calzones.

Don Antonio by Starita Roberto Caporuscio of Kesté Pizza & Vino (see page 57) and the famous Neapolitan pizza baker Antonio Starita (see page 14) own and operate this pizzeria. Traditional Neapolitan pizzas, as well as other creative pies including Starita's delicious Montanara Starita (a pizza fritte), delight pizza connoisseurs.

Lucali We had the pleasure of watching Mark Iacono, proprietor of the Brooklyn pizzeria Lucali, roll out a ball of dough with a wine bottle. After applying sauce to the pizza, Mark shaved fresh portobello mushrooms onto the pizza with a mandoline before baking it in his custom-built oven that can be fired up with both wood and gas. You'll find soft drinks on the menu but will have to bring your own wine.

The restaurant (pictured on page 52) is modern but has a timeless quality that is thoroughly inviting. Iacono opened Lucali in 2006 to bring more traffic to an area of Brooklyn where a favorite childhood hangout sits: Louie's Candy Shop. Iacono has opened a new Lucali pizzeria in Miami Beach, and it has received top honors from guests and the media alike. Lucali's pizzas are unique, and its calzone is the stuff of legends. Just ask regular customers Jay-Z and Beyoncé.

Motorino

ON THE ROAD WITH SCOTT

There is surely no more avid patriot for New York pizza than Scott Wiener. He is the man behind Scott's Pizza Tours, as well as an extraordinarily gifted pizza connoisseur. Our meeting with him was enriching—not only did we learn more than we had ever imagined about the history of pizza in New York (which means the history of pizza in the United States in general), but Scott also introduced us to many of the most interesting pizza personalities to be found anywhere.

Scott grew up in New Jersey and was well acquainted with great pizza from an early age. He worked as a musician while in college and while touring the country with his bands, he discovered the differences in pizza around the country. He found himself analyzing the different ingredients in pizzas he ate and, in the process, realized that his love of pizza had become a serious obsession.

Once back home he used his free time to visit pizzerias in the New York area, and on his 26th birthday he rented a bus and took thirty of his friends on a trip to some of his favorite spots.

Scott is still interested in music, but work now is all about feeding his pizza passion. In addition to running the pizza tours, Scott writes a column for *Pizza Today* magazine (the country's premier pizza-industry trade magazine), contributes to the website *Serious Eats*, and writes the Scott's Pizza Journal on his website. He knows all the ins and outs of the pizza industry in the New York area, and he is the only person we met who uses—or, rather, needs—an app to control his slice intake. As Scott puts it, "I use the program to limit my slice intake by giving myself a shocking visual of how much pizza I consume. I established a guideline of 15 slices per week; the Daytum app helps me stay within that limit."

Why is 15 slices your limit?
Well, 16 slices would be two whole pies, but 15 is less than two whole pizzas. It just makes me feel like less of an animal. From the information I've collected, it looks like I visited 144 different pizzerias last year. The pizzerias I frequented most often were Lombardi's (see page 54), John's of Bleecker Street (see page 67), and Kesté (see page 57), which makes sense because I cover those three quite a bit on my tours. Other random information: I have visited pizzerias beginning with every single letter of the alphabet except for Q and X; and my total number of slices for the year was *at least* 714 pizza slices, which comes to about two slices per day. That is well within my 15-slice weekly limit! The popular statistic for pizza consumption in the United States is around 50 slices per person annually. Wimps.

What do most people *not* know about the history of New York pizza?
New York–style pizza did not become popular until after the Second World War. Ovens and how cheese works in them played a huge role in the evolution of this pizza. In lower tempera-

ture ovens it takes so long to bake that the crust does not bake first, and the cheese dries out, browns, and then burns. In this scenario, using fresh mozzarella doesn't work, so it was replaced with low-moisture mozzarella. The whole milk, low-moisture cheese that is the shredded cheese you have at Joe's and John's is more expensive. Therefore, pizzerias began using a cheese blend, which became synonymous with New York pizza. It's a combination of 50 percent skim milk and 50 percent whole milk mozzarella. Now they are marketing that all around the United States. You can buy New York–style cheese, an East Coast blend cheese, which is just part skim and part whole milk mozzarella. It all comes down to saving money. Everything boils down to pure economics.

Would you say that true Neapolitan pizza has replaced the classic New York pizza?
It all started when Federal Express started shipping internationally in 1986. That was when we began seeing authentic imported ingredients. ABC—a buffalo-milk dairy from Casserta, Italy—was the first to export legally to the United States. So you see, when this started to happen, people in the United States became accustomed to a different version of the pizza. New Yorkers have always thought of their pizza as fast food, but now, the locals are beginning to realize that pizza has become something else.

What about New York Sicilian pizza?
At the end of the 1800s, immigrants from Sicily brought their sfincione pizza—reminiscent of focaccia—from Palermo. Pizza Siciliana is basically a focaccia that has married a New York pizza. The sfincione and the New York pizzas

Pizza Suprema's Sicilian Pizza: This sauce kills me! It is powerful, robust, earthy, bold, and it makes me salivate just thinking about it.
SCOTT WIENER

use basically the same dough, but the Sicilian pizza dough rises more. The New York variant is also rectangular instead of round.

We joined Scott at one of his favorite Sicilian pizzerias, New York Pizza Suprema on Eighth Avenue (see page 63). "This place and Joe's (see page 66) are my favorites. Here, they have the Upside Down Pizza, a first cousin of the New York–style Sicilian pizza, where the mozzarella covers the crust and is topped by an onion-based sauce, extra virgin olive oil, and Romano cheese."

Joe's Dairy: Vincent and Anthony

Some of us are lucky enough to still be able to visit the neighborhood pizzeria we grew up with, but in the real world, pizzerias and producers of the great ingredients for making our favorite pizzas come and go. Such is the case with Joe's Dairy on Sullivan Street in New York City.

We visited Joe's Dairy in 2012 and were lucky enough to meet the Campanelli brothers. Unfortunately, the store is now closed, though the brothers still produce mozzarella for restaurants at their facility in New Jersey. Vincent Campanelli spoke to us about the history of Joe's Dairy.

How did you and your brother come to own Joe's?
I am 60 years old, and there has been a cheese shop here since I was a baby. My brother, Anthony, took over the business when he was 18 years old. He worked with the gentleman who owned the store, named Joe, who taught my brother the tricks of the trade. That year, Joe decided he wanted to sell the store, and my brother came up with the crazy idea to buy it . . . as a kid! Three days before his 18th birthday, Anthony put the key in the lock.

What's your favorite kind of pizza?
I'm old school. I don't like a lot of stuff on it. Cheese pizza—New York–style—is my favorite; pepperoni, sometimes peppers, and onions. That's all I want and it has to be well done. The guy who created the Hawaiian pizza should be shot. There shouldn't be pineapple—or ham for that matter—on pizza. I like arugula and I like spinach, but not on a pizza!

I've had a few slices in my life and you can tell almost immediately when you open a pizza box. You'll either say, "Oh yeah!" or, "Oh no!" I cannot go for specialty pizzas. Give me a little burn, a little crunch, a good bottle of something, and some garlic powder, and I'm a happy soul.

HITTING THE BOOKS

Mark Bello runs the Pizza a Casa ("pizza at home") Pizza School and store in New York's Lower East Side. Pizza a Casa, Mark's "Pizza Self-Sufficiency Center," was established in 2005 as a catering and educational company. He opened the school in 2010 after spending several years in various venues teaching people how to make pizza at home. The school's participants come from across the United States and around the world.

The walls at Pizza a Casa are covered with pizza-themed memorabilia including articles, awards, photos, cooking equipment, signs, license plates, and more. The room is rather small but cozy, with a two-sided station in the middle for people coming to learn more about pizza making. One wall features a display of equipment and ingredients the participants can purchase for use at home.

Mark has received a lot of attention in the food press, with praise from the *Village Voice*, James Beard House, *Food & Wine*, and *Time Out New York*, among others. He accomplished all this without a commercial oven, a thirty-year-old sourdough starter, or years behind the counter at a crowded pizzeria. His love of great pizza and his dedication to his craft have been the driving forces in Mark's life.

Pizza a Casa offers different types of cooking" classes and workshops for the public, as well as team-building and corporate events. Some of the participants have had very little experience in the kitchen while others are aspiring pizzaioli looking for inspiration.

Mark loves his work and is proud of his pizzas: "I do not just teach how to make pizzas at home. I teach how to make pizzas that are better than 99.9 percent of the pizzas you will ever have at a pizzeria or delivered to your home." This is a lofty promise, but the feedback he has received confirms just how good a job he is doing.

One last thing: Pizza a Casa is right next door to Doughnut Plant, one of America's premier doughnut shops. It is hard to beat a great pizza you make yourself followed by a Meyer lemon, tres leches, or coconut cream doughnut and a cup of coffee. And if you're not in New York, Mark has created an app called DIY Pizza Pie, which is chockfull of tips on how to make pizza, including step-by-step guides and videos.

> *I do not just teach how to make pizzas at home. I teach how to make pizzas that are better than 99.9% of the pizzas you will ever have at a pizzeria or delivered to your home.*
>
> MARK BELLO

You Can Call Me Ray's!

If anyone should ever tell you that the pizza business is not amusing, then they are wrong. Ray's is a perfect example of the humor (and intrigue) the pizza industry offers. Imagine you are going to open a pizzeria, but there is already a pizzeria in the neighborhood that everyone loves. Let's pretend this pizzeria is called Ray's. You are searching for a name for your new pizzeria, and out of the blue, you are hit by the following idea: What if I also called my pizzeria Ray's? Everyone in the area already knows that Ray's makes great pizza. And after all, the other Ray's is four blocks from here, so who will care?

In New York City, there have been, and still are, several pizzerias called Ray's. The issues with Ray's have been so bewildering that there are also pizzerias named Original Ray's (none of which, by the way, were the original Ray's), Famous Ray's (now Famous Roio's), and Famous Original Ray's. And that's not all; don't forget Real Ray's or Ray's on Ice. Or Roy's Pizza. Or our favorite of all: Not Ray's. You just have to love those New Yorkers!

BARI IN THE BOWERY

Good, old-fashioned craftspeople who know their business inside and out can be hard to find. But if you were to visit the Bowery district of New York City, you would find a whole family of them. Bari is a restaurant and pizza equipment company that is almost 80 years old, owned and operated by none other than the Bari family.

Oven wizard Pasquale (Patsy) Cutrone.

Bari builds, repairs, and sells pizza ovens, and their ovens can be found in countless pizzerias in the New York City area. When a pizza oven needs to be modified, repaired, or replaced, just call Bari.

We visited the Bari business and met with Frank Bari to hear the fascinating story of his family and learn more about the company's products. Frank explained to us how coal ovens work, contrasting them with gas ovens. (Bari does not manufacture electric ovens.) "Gas gives you a better distribution of heat, so gas, in my view, is much better," he explains. "Coal ovens give you hot spots. My own customers who have coal and wood ovens tell me that the electric ovens do not cook pies properly; the pies were getting burnt. This was solved by adding a gas flame underneath."

Frank told us that his father invented many tools now common among pizza chefs, including the electronic cheese grater (the machine that shreds up the mozzarella for the pizza), the screens on which pizzas are baked, the plastic dough drawers, individual pizza-dough pans, and a pizza cutter with a finger protector so you don't cut your fingers off. He also built ovens from scratch.

After our conversation, we visited the building where the ovens are built. In the workshop, we met Pasquale (Patsy) Cutrone (now in his 70s), a native of Italy who has lived in the United States his entire adult life. Patsy is the oven guy—he knows every nook and cranny on every oven he has ever made. Throughout the Bari business, you'll find old-fashioned craftsmanship, alive and well, in the Bowery.

EATALY NYC

IN LOVE WITH FOOD

The New York location of Eataly, on Twenty-Third Street between Fifth and Sixth Avenues, includes a total of seven restaurants, 40,000 square feet of space, and more than 10,000 products, all showcasing the food and wines of Italy.

The Eataly concept was founded by Oscar Farinetti in 2007, when he opened a 30,000-square-foot store in Turin, Italy. Today, he runs Eataly with a team of five partners. There are 27 Eataly locations worldwide, including ten in Italy, one in Chicago, and the one we visited in New York City.

Eataly is big, but what is most impressive is the fact that even in Italy it is rare to find such a wide selection of great Italian food. Need some fresh Italian sausage, a bottle of Ligurian olive oil for your pesto, or some cantuccini for your sweet tooth? Eataly has it all, and then some. We were lucky enough to find the last two boxes of fennel pollen in the store and some cookbooks that we just *had* to have. Of course we also sampled dishes from three of the seven restaurants. Sadly, we arrived too early to order the porchetta sandwich at the rosticceria—better luck next time.

During our visit, we met Americo (Ricky) Imperatore. Ricky's family comes from Naples and Sicily, but today he lives in the Bronx. He makes fresh mozzarella from cow's milk (fior di latte), scamorza, and burrata for restaurants in

the Eataly complex; the cheese is rarely more than two hours old when sold. Eataly offers private events, wine tastings, and a wide range of cooking classes, under the expertise of chef and co-owner Lidia Bastianich. The possibilities at Eataly are endless—a half-day visit should give you a good start, but it is really not enough.

Ricky Imperatore making mozzarella cheese at Eataly.

CHAPTER 4

CHICAGO

CHICAGO **Digging Deep** p. 80

CHICAGO PIZZA TOURS **Pizza Paparazzi** p. 82

LOU MALNATI'S PIZZERIA **Classic Chicago Pizza** p. 85

SPACCA NAPOLI PIZZERIA **Every Facet Is Significant** p. 86

COALFIRE PIZZA **Coal in Chicago** p. 88

BURT'S PLACE **Unforgettable Chicago Pizza . . . Just Outside of Chicago** p. 91

JEFF RUBY **Anonymous** p. 94

DIGGING DEEP

Whether the topic is baseball, politics, the weather, or food, Chicagoans have very strong opinions about which team and which pizza is best. One thing is certain: Chicago has some of the most diverse pizza offerings, and without a doubt the pizzas responsible for the hottest of heated debates. They are completely unlike the Neapolitan-influenced pizzas so prevalent in New York or the ultra-fresh pizzas that dominate the California pizza scene.

Chicago has the most unique pizzas in America.

Chicago will forever be known as home to the deep-dish or deep-pan pizza. Surprisingly, though, most Chicagoans prefer their version of the thin-crust pizza, whereas the much heartier pizza is reserved for deep-pan aficionados and out-of-towners.

Texan Ike Sewell of Pizzeria Uno fame invented the thick-crusted pizza as a way of attracting the Italian-American public. Today, there is a wide range of pizza styles found in Chicago, including variations of the classic deep-pan pie, Neapolitan-style pizzas, and—more recently—some gourmet-inspired pies with almost any topping imaginable. Some of the most creative pizzas in America can be found in Chicago, such as those we enjoyed at the now-closed Great Lake pizzeria (see page 93), where Nick Lessins impressed his clientele with an array of unusual toppings and cheeses. Chicago is one of the greatest culinary cities in the world, and pizza is one of its celebrated strengths.

PIZZA PAPARAZZI

New York City isn't the only major US city offering comprehensive pizza tours. Jon Porter of Chicago Pizza Tours took us on an exciting expedition and introduced us to the often-misunderstood Chicago deep-dish pizza. Join us on the unforgettable Chicago pizza tour we took with Jon.

"My name is Jon Porter, and I'll be your tour guide for the day. I assume you all signed up because you like pizza, and just by signing up you told me something about yourselves. You see, people who *like* pizza are the people that call up a place and have it delivered. But those who *love* pizza go to restaurants and order different types of pizzas, as we are going to do now. They whip out their cell phones and start taking pictures of them and post the pictures on

Instagram and Facebook. We call these people 'pizza paparazzi.'"

Jon starts his tours at Pizano's Pizza & Pasta, owned by Rudy Malnati Jr. The Malnati name is extremely important in the world of Chicago pizza. In the '40s, Ike Sewell and Ric Riccardo came to Chicago and began working together. They decided to open a Mexican restaurant, but Ric ultimately thwarted those plans, Jon said. "'Listen here,' Ric told Ike, 'I spent all this time over in Italy fighting the war, and they've got this stuff called pizza over there. It's going to be dynamite here in Chicago, so let's open a pizzeria instead.'" Neither Ike nor Ric had any idea how to make pizza, so they looked to Rudy Malnati Sr. Rudy invented a "deep-dish" pizza, and the three men opened Pizzeria Riccardo. Rudy eventually passed away, and Ike and Ric bought out Rudy's family and renamed the restaurant Pizzeria Uno (or simply "Uno's"), which is still a thriving Chicago pizzeria with multiple locations.

As a side note, Rudy Malnati Sr., was never a legal owner of Pizzeria Riccardo, but he remained loyal to Ike Sewell even after Rudy's son, Lou, left to start Lou Malnati's—a competing pizza giant in Chicago. Ike never spoke to Lou again, but Rudy Sr., continued to work for Ike.

Rudy Sr., was a simple man who was happy with what he had.

The Chicago pizza scene has grown immensely since Ike and Ric's day. And Chicagoans have a pretty specific taste for pizza. "The most popular pizza [topping] in Chicago is sausage, definitely," Jon says. "Across the country, pepperoni is the number one topping by far, but here in Chicago, it is typically all about sausage. A lot of places will create their own signature [taste] by grinding their own blend of seasoning to complement the sausage, while others use such large amounts of sausage that it is not possible to make it themselves."

The pizza tour with Jon Porter was a unique experience. We learned a lot about the history of Chicago, the Chicago Bulls, Chicago architecture, Garrett's Popcorn (another culinary icon in the Windy City), the scandal that plagued former Governor Rod Blagojevich, and much, much more. But the very best part of the tour, of course, was that we ate delicious pizza just about every half hour at some of Chicago's best pizzerias.

LOU MALNATI'S PIZZERIA

CLASSIC CHICAGO PIZZA

Somebody once said, "Avoid chain restaurants!" Actually, that somebody could have been any one of us. The notion of this being a universal truth was crushed after our visit with Marc Malnati at the legendary Lou Malnati's Pizzeria in Chicago—one of the nearly 40 Lou Malnati locations. We met with Marc Malnati, Lou's oldest son, to hear the story of the family-owned and -operated chain of pizzerias.

Marc Malnati's father and grandfather Rudy began making deep-pan pizza in the 1940s, and in the 1950s, they co-managed Pizzeria Uno (see page 82), another legendary pizzeria in Chicago. On March 17, 1971, Lou opened his own pizzeria in the Chicago suburb of Lincolnwood. Lou loved telling the autobiographical story of the Italian who opened a pizzeria in a Jewish neighborhood on an Irish holiday.

Lou Malnati passed away in 1978, at which time his son Marc Malnati joined Marc's mother to run the family business. A few years later, Marc's younger brother, Rick, joined in as well. We spoke to Marc about the pros and cons of operating a large number of restaurants. It was here we learned that the enduring strength of homegrown Chicago-based pizza restaurants has severely limited the ability of mass pizza chains to compete in the Chicagoland market—in stark contrast to their invasion of almost every other city in the United States.

The key to Lou Malnati's success is actually quite simple: Don't change a winning formula. Marc explained that their restaurants make all their pizzas by hand, always using the best ingredients possible. For example, the same dairy has delivered the mozzarella cheese Malnati's uses for more than 40 years.

"Many people use cheese from California," says Marc, "but I like the flavor of cheese from Wisconsin. And it's much better to buy something local, with fewer miles on the road." Because Wisconsin—America's Dairyland—is just about an hour's drive from Lincolnwood, "I can get up to the dairy and see what they are doing and talk to them and have direct contact with them."

The pizzas at Lou Malnati's are classic Chicago pies, in which slices of mozzarella are placed directly onto the dough. Next come the peppers, sausage, or mushrooms, and then the chunky tomato sauce. The "Lou-Mal" pie features a single, pie-wide patty of sausage on top of the cheese instead of chunks of sausage spread over the pie. This is one of the best Chicago pizzas around.

It is important to mention that Lou Malnati's is not just about the pizza: The Malnati family is involved in numerous charitable activities, donating gift cards to local charities and offering a variety of popular "Dough for Dough" fund-raising options to local nonprofit organizations. They also support local youth sports teams and host an annual benefit to raise money for cancer research.

EVERY FACET IS SIGNIFICANT

One of the most interesting Chicago pizza stops we made was Spacca Napoli Pizzeria, one of only about 80 American restaurants certified by the Associazione Verace Pizza Napoletana (AVPN). The pizzeria is run by Jonathan Goldsmith—a native New Yorker—and Chicago artist Ginny Sykes. The couple moved to Florence, Italy, with their daughter, Sarah, in 1988, returning to the United States in 1991. One Italian friend told Jonathan, "You should open a pizzeria. You will make a lot of money. Flour, water, salt, and yeast is all you need!" And that is exactly what Jonathan and Ginny did.

The couple is closely involved in all aspects of the pizzeria. Jonathan is the host and the pizza guy, working his way around the restaurant, talking to guests, managing the activity in the kitchen, and basically doing what needs to be done. Ginny's role is also extremely varied: planning, designing, and just being an irreplaceable business partner. She designed the menus and the restaurant's logo, handles public relations and marketing via social media and other channels, and makes the restaurant a beautiful place.

Jonathan greeted us, and within seconds he was talking about dough.

"Our dough making has evolved over the years. From only one hour of rising before forming the pagnotti (dough balls) to five. We used to mix the dough for a straight 20 minutes. We now mix for 15, let the dough rest for one hour in the mixer, then place it on the table covered with

In Naples, there's a poem that says: "La Ricetta è semper la stessa." Which means "the recipe is always the same" . . . flour, water, salt, and yeast. It's in dialect, and it's what you have in a Margherita. But if you look closely, there is something missing: passion. If there's no passion, there's no feeling. If there's feeling, it can be a capolavoro, a masterpiece whether it's made in Japan, Canada, or America. For me, every facet is significant.

JONATHAN GOLDSMITH

damp linen another four hours. How long we let the pagnotti rise once they are cut depends on when we are going to use them. There are many possibilities; 8 hours, 15 hours, 24 hours, sometimes in the fridge, sometimes not. We mix in the morning, we mix in the evening. Though the basic recipe for the dough is simple (1 liter of water, 1.7 kilos of flour, 50 grams of salt, 2.5 grams of fresh yeast) for an 8-hour rise, there always can be some variation. You learn over time. If it's humid outside, you use less water; if it's dry, you use more. Maybe only half a gram of yeast per liter of water. The amount of yeast used in the mix influences digestibility—less is better. Although we strive for consistency, the dough is alive and can vary day to day. I am always asking, 'How's the dough?'"

The dough is only part of the story, though. "The hardest job is probably the oven. Those responsible for it are one with it—they know exactly how it behaves and the different hot and cold spots."

The products that go into the pizza are high quality—it makes a difference, Jonathan says. "The ingredients speak for themselves. I do not want a single ingredient to take anything away from another. It should be like a marriage, a wedding night. I don't even know how much this oil costs; I just know it's good."

Next up for Spacca Napoli? "I am thinking about bringing the tufa, the volcanic stone, and lining my dough room with it because it is a very controlled environment. The stone has the ability to absorb some of the environment, keeping conditions more constant."

In the meantime, the restaurant makes up to 600 pizzas on the busiest of days. "For me, it's the whole package, and the whole operation together, that is important," Jonathan says. "Everyone here plays a part. Its not one person alone putting that pie on your table."

COAL IN CHICAGO

In Chicago, we came to a little piece of New York: Coalfire Pizza. We spoke at length with Bill Carroll, who co-owns the restaurant with Dave Bonomi. Bill moved to Chicago from Massachusetts and brought his East Coast version of pizza with him.

How did Coalfire get its start?

Chicago is well known for deep-dish pizza. It just wasn't what my business partner [Dave Bonomi] and I were accustomed to, so we saw room for something else. We knew people from New York, New Jersey, and Massachusetts who all asked the same thing: "Where can you get a good thin-crust in this town, or at least the traditional stuff

we are used to?" So we thought if we couldn't find it, we would see if we could make it.

Where does the name Coalfire come from?

We wanted to use the brick oven, whether it was wood or coal; it didn't necessarily matter. We just wanted something a little more unique than a regular gas oven. And then the idea was to do something traditional, something Neapolitan-American. So we have the fresh mozzarella we use for the Margherita pizza, but we also use low-moisture mozzarella on our sausage and regular pizzas. We aimed for a pizza that would be crispier, properly cooked, and lightly charred. So we thought for sure that there wouldn't be anyone else using coal in Chicago—we just felt that it would be a unique product and concept. And sure enough, that is what happened.

Tell us about your ingredients and how you developed your pizzas.

Before we opened, we read a few books about bread baking and dough baking and just did some trial and error with certain dough and sauce recipes. We then tweaked it along as we went. We fed it to our friends and family at different times, and we'd change it a little here and there, until virtually everyone was saying,

"Yeah, this is really good!" Our tomato sauce is generally straight tomatoes, but we add some seasoning and cheese. We wanted to use as many local products as possible—some of our cheese comes out of Wisconsin, and even our fresh mozzarella is domestic. The same goes for our prosciutto. We were never going for fancy Neapolitan-style, just something that we liked and that people we knew liked. Once we found that, that's what we went with.

What's the secret to cooking with your coalfire oven?

There is a science to stoking the fire of the oven, because it's really like a big fireplace. The guys have to stoke the fire constantly to make sure the floor retains the heat. We keep it close to 800°F (the floor itself is usually 700–750°F) and cook the pizzas for 2½ to 3 minutes. That's the key to making sure the bottom gets the char. We look at each pizza to see if it is finished baking, lightly charred and enticing the way we like it.

Will there ever be another location?

We have made it over five years, somehow, and we're hoping to open a second location someday. We just want to make sure that everything is going right before we get ahead of ourselves. If you grow too quickly, especially with this kind of method, you could easily lose the quality control.

UNFORGETTABLE CHICAGO PIZZA . . . JUST OUTSIDE OF CHICAGO

If you are visiting Chicago, plan on driving, grabbing a cab, catching a bus, stealing a horse, or just putting on your running shoes, and heading out to Morton Grove. Morton Grove (23,270 residents) lies just northwest of Chicago and is home to one of America's foremost pizza personalities: Burt Katz.

Burt has been doing pizza for 50 years and has operated several different places in his career. If you Google him, you will see that this guy is a legendary figure in Chicago pizza. He is now in his late 70s with a beard down to his chest, like he was applying for a gig with ZZ Top. In the 1950s, Burt opened The Inferno, and in the 1960s he opened the restaurant Gulliver's (named after Jonathan Swift's novel *Gulliver's Travels)*. Burt sold his business to a restaurant group in the late 1960s, and in 1971, he opened one of his masterpieces, Pequod's (named after the whaling ship in *Moby Dick*). In 1986, Burt decided to sell Pequod's to the current owner, Keith Jackson, and leave the pizza business altogether. Three years after he retired, though, Burt changed his mind again and went back into the pizza business, opening Burt's Place across the street from his original Pequod's location in Morton Grove.

> You make a promise, you keep your promise. I don't play games when it comes to business. I just don't believe in it.
> **BURT KATZ**

We made two major mistakes when visiting Burt's Place. The first was not reading up on the system Burt and his wife, Sharon, have established, which involves ordering, showing up on time, and being flexible. It is expected that you will call to reserve your table, preferably the day before (or even earlier). If you are ordering takeout, the same rule applies. We were there for a little over an hour, and there must have been at least a dozen calls.

Burt and Sharon spend almost an hour cooking the pizza, so advance booking is a brilliant idea. You order your pizza when you book your table, so you won't have to wait an hour for your food once you arrive, unless you're like us and enjoy a chat over a beer or two. Your pizza arrives piping hot right out of the oven. The rest is simple: eat, enjoy, pay your bill, and make room for the next guests.

The second mistake we made on our visit to Burt's was waiting until our last evening in Chicago to head out to Morton Grove, which meant not being able to visit the place one more time before leaving for our next destination. We showed up at Burt's Place in the late afternoon, not having ordered, and probably looking kind of stupid. We explained our situation, apologized for our

ignorance, and shamelessly played the we-came-all-the-way-from-Norway card, hoping it would work. And in an unmatched act of Midwestern kindness, it was decided that we could speak with Burt *and* eat some pizza.

We settled into a corner booth in what must be one of the most unique restaurants any of us had ever visited. There are old radios, musical instruments, and various other paraphernalia and tchotchkes on the walls. Jazz music played from the speakers, and we got the feeling that Burt's Place was just that: Burt and the stuff he likes.

The pizza at Burt's Place is classic Chicago. The crust is caramelized, a phenomenon that is hard to explain. What happens is that some of

the cheese slowly melts into the pan, caramelizing in the butter, while the bread takes on a more rustic appearance (less golden, more burnt mahogany). Don't be surprised if you wake up in the middle of the night craving a small corner of Burt's crust. It's that good.

For those who want to visit, Burt suggests planning ahead. "Yesterday, I was already booked up for tonight," he said when we visited. "I've had people calling for Thanksgiving two months ahead of time. We are small, you know. We don't make promises and [then] keep people waiting at the door. You have to respect the customers. You make a promise, you keep your promise. I don't play games when it comes to business. I just don't believe in it."

We'll Meet Again, Great Lake

Since we began researching and writing this book, one of our favorite restaurants closed: Great Lake in Chicago's Andersonville neighborhood.

The restaurant had a brief existence, opening in 2008 and closing in 2013. It was very popular in the community and was fueled by the dreams of a very determined and tenacious couple, Nick Lessins and Lydia Esparza. In 2009, GQ food critic Alan Richman included Great Lake in his list of America's 25 Best Pizzas. He called their pizzas "creative, original, and somewhat local—representing everything irresistible about the new American style of pizza-making"—not a small feat for a tiny neighborhood pizzeria making pizzas unlike any other in Chicago.

We can safely say that the pizzas of Great Lake were different than any we had ever had before, both in the United States and in Italy. Nick and Lydia have traveled a lot and discovered exciting combinations of flavors, such as the combination of smoked fish, dill, dried local mushrooms, and crème fraiche, which they enjoyed in Finland and incorporated into their pizza menu back home. That said, Great Lake's pizza had serious Italian roots. "We make pizza of Italian origin, but actually it is an American-Italian hybrid style of pizza," Nick said at the time.

Great Lake was known for being uncompromising in its use of local and sustainable ingredients, and they refused to use meat and dairy products from corporate agriculture, as their menu proclaimed: "All meat and dairy products come from animals that are allowed outdoors to graze and are reared on family-owned farms. We do not use meat or dairy products from corporate agriculture or factory farms."

Nick and Lydia cited the challenges of high rent and a landlord's reluctance to invest in much-needed upgrading as two factors leading them to close Great Lake. But they have not yet given up and hope, at some point, to open a new Great Lake. That, of course, will make their former customers—including us—very happy.

ANONYMOUS

Jeff Ruby is senior editor, humor columnist, and chief dining critic for *Chicago* magazine. We met Jeff in downtown Chicago after promising to not take any photographs of his face, since he reviews restaurants anonymously. So we will not reveal the color of his hair or eyes, but the remaining body parts in the photograph accompanying this article are Jeff's own.

What makes Chicago pizza so special?
It reflects Chicago perfectly. Chicago has this reputation of being the City of Big Shoulders and the City that Works. And the legend that grew up around Chicago-style pizza was two guys who weren't content with the small, wimpy Italian pizza. I do not know if that's true, but the legend has fastened its grip on Chicago. There are hundreds of thousands of tourists who come to Chicago every year and say, "I *gotta* get my deep-dish pizza. I *gotta* get it."

In 2005, I wrote a pizza book with co-author Penny Pollack, called *Everybody Loves Pizza*. It featured pizza from all over America, so I ate pizza seemingly nonstop for the better part of a year. I found that, in Chicago, the pizza was inconsistent, even at the best places. There was no place that was doing deep dish consistently well. There were too many variables, like who was making it. I don't know why that was. It was a little disappointing to me.

Pollack and I rated the top 10 pizzas in America, and we did not put a deep-dish pizza on the list. And I got verbally abused by everybody in Chicago. They said, "You know, you are a native *Chicagoan,* and you should have pronounced a deep-dish pizza as the best." Chicagoans are *very* protective of their traditions,

and deep-dish pizza with a thick crust is one of them. I sort of piggybacked off this when I wrote a feature for the magazine, about the 25 best pizzerias in America. I made some off hand comment about how I was qualified to judge these pizzas with a clear eye because I didn't grow up in Chicago. This gave me the freedom to look at Chicago pizzas without any geographical bias. I got reamed for that of course. "Who are you to come into Chicago and tell us which pizza is the best?" they said. "That's the whole point," I replied.

What's your favorite pizza?
I think the ideal is the Neapolitan pizza. I firmly believe that anything that is bread, tomato, and cheese can be pizza. Sometimes you don't even need the cheese, sometimes you don't need the tomato, and it is basically just a meal on bread, where bread serves as a plate for all this other stuff.

What is your approach to reviewing restaurants?
In some ways I take it really, really seriously because people's livelihoods are at stake, money is exchanging hands, and there are a lot of people interested in it. It's not brain surgery, and I am not saving the world, but I am providing a

service of sorts for people and hopefully entertaining them a little bit, too. At the same time, I have always thought there was something inherently funny about food and writing about food, so I don't take it so seriously that I forget there is something absurd about the position I am in. That is not to say that I don't do serious research; I spent a long, long time on the pizza feature that you could probably read in 20 minutes.

Tell us a little more about your fascination with pizza.

There is something about bread, cheese, and tomato that is this elemental, perfect food. When they are used in the right proportions, there is some sort of magic to it. I have been writing about food for 15 years, but I have never gotten sick of pizza. Every pizza is a little bit different, and even ones that look alike don't necessarily taste alike.

Pizzeria Bianco: Sizzling Passion in the Desert

Between Chicago and California is a gem of a pizzeria: Pizzeria Bianco in Phoenix. The guy behind the pizzeria (three locations plus a bakery) is Chris Bianco, who is all about the passion. The winner of the James Beard Award for Best Chef: Southwest in 2003, Chris has long been a leader in the Slow Food movement as well as the trend toward small, independent, artisanal pizzerias across the country.

"I have chosen food as my profession, and there is so much I want to do," he says. "I want my restaurants to excel. I want to work with food until the day comes when I can't work anymore, and I will try to be better at my job each and every day. It requires an enormous amount of focus and a lot of work."

Phoenix is an unlikely place to find one of the best pizzas in the United States. But, as is the case for many others profiled in this book, Chris has family by his side, and family is at the center of everything. Chris's brother Marco is in charge of making Pizzeria Bianco's dough, by hand, in three daily batches weighing in at 50 pounds each. Family pictures adorn the family's restaurants, lending to the comfy "at-home" atmosphere. The Biancos' father, Leonard, was a painter, and he designed the labels for a tomato project they're involved with. Their mother, Francesca, was a designer, and her influence is apparent throughout the unique interiors of all the Bianco restaurants.

It is, however, the food that draws visitors to the Bianco restaurants. The menu at Pizzeria Bianco is minimalist, offering a small variety of absolutely delicious pizzas. Very few plates cleared from the table have anything left on them, and we found ourselves nibbling on the last bits of crust long after our stomachs' "hunger meters" had hit the full mark.

The Biancos are involved in several other food-related projects, as well. Chris Bianco and Jamie Oliver founded Union Jacks restaurants, a small chain of UK restaurants featuring wood-fired flatbread pizzas using locally sourced ingredients; the Bianco family works with Robert DiNapoli from Los Gatos, California, to produce organic tomatoes called Bianco DiNapoli, which are canned with sea salt and basil; and they work with farmers to produce flour from ancient strains of grain. Anyone serious about pizza should make their way to Phoenix. But be forewarned: After your first visit to Pizzeria Bianco's, you might find yourself looking for excuses for return trips.

CHAPTER 5

CALIFORNIA

CALIFORNIA **Fresh, Healthy, and Tempting** p. 100

QUINTESSENTIAL CALIFORNIA **Alice, Wolfgang, and Ed** p. 103

PIZZERIA MOZZA **À La LA** p. 107

BIG MAMA'S & PAPA'S PIZZERIA **Everything Is Bigger in America** p. 110

GJELINA AND GTA (GJELINA TAKE AWAY) **Pizza in Venice Beach** p. 113

UNA PIZZA NAPOLETANA **From Naples to Jersey to San Francisco** p. 117

TONY'S PIZZA NAPOLETANA **Pizza Extravaganza** p. 123

A16 **Pizza & Wine** p. 126

DEL POPOLO **Minimalist Pleasure on Wheels** p. 129

PIZZERIA DELFINA **Pizza Missionaries** p. 133

FRESH, HEALTHY, AND TEMPTING

It had to happen: The combination of America's most bountiful agriculture areas, creative young chefs focusing on the simple dishes of the Mediterranean, and millions of customers hungry for the next big thing all led, inevitably, to California pizza.

The year was 1980. California's own Prince of Pizza, Ed LaDou, was making pizza for Prego Restaurant in San Francisco, while across the bay in Berkeley, the chefs at Alice Waters's iconic restaurant, Chez Panisse, were also experimenting with pizza. LaDou was a born innovator of Italian-style pizzas topped with unusual ingredients. One evening, he served a thin-crust pizza topped with pâté and red peppers to none other than überchef Wolfgang Puck. The next year, Puck hired LaDou to be head pizzaiolo at his new Beverly Hills restaurant, Spago.

Back at Chez Panisse, Alice Waters and her head chef Jeremiah Tower were preparing to open Chez Panisse Café on the floor above their thriving restaurant. The duo was already credited with inventing California cuisine, and the new addition would give them a chance to offer a simpler menu for their guests. They planned an open kitchen in the café, featuring pizzas topped with the best local ingredients, from fresh herbs to seafood.

Today, California pizza is found all over the Golden State, and chains such as California Pizza Kitchen (CPK) have brought these pizzas to the rest of America and to the world.

The trademarks of California pizza are a certain "Italian-ness" in their appearance and simplicity, combined with the use of ultra-fresh and sometimes exotic ingredients. You might find sausage and peppers and the odd slice of pepperoni on the California pizza, but also ingredients that would shock the hippest of New York slice consumers, such as squash blossoms, smoked salmon, fresh figs, and prosciutto.

The classic California pizza is beautiful, healthy, delicious, and uniquely "Californian." Anyone suggesting that pizza is a poor nutritional choice has never eaten California pizza, which usually means a few choice ingredients in small quantities, with the perfect balance between the tastes and textures of the crust, cheese, sauce, and toppings, with no ingredient getting in the way of the others.

> The trademarks of California pizza are a certain "Italian-ness" in their appearance and simplicity, combined with the use of ultra-fresh and sometimes exotic ingredients.

ALICE, WOLFGANG, AND ED

Alice Waters at Chez Panisse Alice Waters, a New Jersey native, opened the doors of Chez Panisse in Berkeley with a group of friends in 1971. Chez Panisse began as a typical neighborhood bistro. Today, however, the ground-floor bistro functions as a restaurant serving a set menu, while an upstairs café offers a Mediterranean-inspired à la carte menu. Chez Panisse is not a pizzeria, but pizza has graced the menu for more than three decades. The wood-burning oven produces great pizzas featuring locally grown, sustainable, organic ingredients.

Waters has often been called the godmother of California pizza, a direct result of her having essentially invented California cuisine. There was a short period of time when Waters, Wolfgang Puck, and Ed LaDou were all starting to get the California pizza ball rolling, but there is no doubt Waters was instrumental in putting these unique creations on the pizza map once and for all.

Chez Panisse and Waters have won numerous awards. The restaurant was voted Best Restaurant in America by *Gourmet* in 2001, and Waters was named Best Chef in America by the James Beard Foundation in 1992; she was the first woman ever to win this coveted award. Chez Panisse is consistently ranked among the top 50 restaurants in the world.

Wolfgang Puck Wolfgang Puck, born Wolfgang Johannes Topfschnig, the Austrian-born überchef, restaurateur, and television personality, has been cooking since he was a child. Puck's formal training as chef started at the age of 14, and after several years working in Michelin-starred restaurants in France, he moved to the United States at 24 years of age and already a skilled chef.

Today, the Wolfgang Puck restaurant empire spans the globe, but California has been Puck's base since the mid '70s. He established his restaurant, Spago, in Beverly Hills in 1982, and it is at Spago that he pioneered his version of California cuisine, including his first California pizzas.

Even though his culinary background is solidly French, he has always had elements of other Mediterranean foods on his menus, and his culinary expertise does not stop there. Another of his restaurants, Chinois, features an Asian-inspired menu, while Cut is an upscale steakhouse that was recently ranked among America's top three. This acclaimed chef offers a completely different take on Asian cuisine at Five Sixty (Dallas); a modern American approach at Postrio (San Francisco); and, since 1999, spectacular Italian food at Lupo (Las Vegas).

Puck also dishes up quite a lot of pizza. You will find pizza, often from a wood-burning oven, on the menus at his fine dining restaurants as well as casual restaurants, lounges, and bars. His Wolfgang Puck Pizza Bars provide diners in three American cities (Charlotte, NC; Greensboro, NC; and Palm Desert, CA) with traditional and innovative pizzas as well as other Italian specialties. For many of his fans, Puck's iconic pie with smoked salmon, dill cream, salmon roe, red onions, and chives still epitomizes what California pizza is all about.

Ed LaDou   Ed LaDou (1955–2007) was one of the most influential people in the California pizza industry. Not only was he Wolfgang Puck's original pizzaiolo at Spago, he was instrumental in the creation of the original menu for California Pizza Kitchen.

As a vibrant chef in San Francisco in the mid-1970s, LaDou loved experimenting with unusual pizzas. It was LaDou's pizza topped with ricotta,

pâté, red peppers, and mustard that captured Wolfgang Puck's attention and respect. In short order, Ed LaDou was in the Spago kitchen, creating exciting new pizzas for the rich and famous. "It was like being an artist who'd worked with 10 colors all his life, and then got to use 300," LaDou once said.

Before he died, LaDou opened his own restaurant: Caioti in Laurel Canyon (Los Angeles). The restaurant is now in Studio City, where diners can still enjoy LaDou-inspired pizzas as well as his famous Maternity Salad, the dressing of which is said to induce labor. Pregnant California women still visit the restaurant or order the dressing online when the time gets near.

PIZZERIA MOZZA
À LA LA

Pizzeria Mozza must be among the most hyped pizzerias ever. The superstar lineup of owners was the talk of Los Angeles as soon as its opening was announced. Pizzeria Mozza is the perfect combination of an Italian and a California pizzeria. The menu consists of antipasti, sandwiches, and quite a few pizzas, plus some great desserts. There are loads of Italian ingredients, including guanciale (cured pork cheek), anchovies, and finocchiona (fennel salami). The dishes on the menu represent the best of rustic Italian cooking: arancini alla Bolognese, asparagus al forno with speck, and daily specials such as baccalá al forno with tomato, ceci (chickpeas), and rosemary.

The pizzeria is co-owned by Nancy Silverton (of La Brea Bakery), Mario Batali, and Joe Bastianich (restaurateur, winemaker, and son of famous Italian chef Lidia Matticchio Bastianich). If there is an A-team in the world of pizza, this is it.

California cuisine has strong ties to the Italian kitchen, and this connection is apparent in the Mozza menu. You will find wild king salmon with panzanella, chicken wings alla diavola, and little gem lettuces served with dates, red onion, and Gorgonzola cheese. The pizzas are inspired by Italy but are uniquely California.

It's not easy to get a table at Mozza, but we arrived in the late afternoon, before the evening rush, and were seated right away and entertained by the lively chefs manning the open kitchen and its wood-burning oven. We had eaten at other Batali-owned establishments, so

The pizzas are Italian-inspired, but at the same time, they are uniquely California. It is as if someone put Wolfgang Puck and Enzo Coccia in a locked room and didn't let them out until they had agreed on a menu that incorporated the best of what both chefs were able to create.

we knew we had to start with some antipasti and glasses of good, unpretentious Italian wine.

The pizzas we ordered—including the squash blossom, burrata, and tomato pizza that graced the cover of *Saveur* magazine a few years ago—surpassed our expectations. The crust at Pizzeria Mozza was one of the best we had ever tasted—the crispy bottom was a clear favorite— and after devouring their butterscotch budino for dessert, we were ready to move to LA.

What to Drink with Pizza

Most people are particular when it comes to their choice of toppings for their pizzas. If you love pepperoni, there is a good chance pepperoni was on the last pizza you ate and will most likely be on the next one. The same applies to one's choice of beverage with pizza. People who love beer and pizza are seldom found drinking Cabernet or cola with their pizzas. With this logic, we can deduce with almost certainty that pizza toppings and their accompanying beverage are deep-seated, personal choices we all make according to our individual tastes and preferences.

Wine seems to be a natural choice for pizza and is without a doubt an outstanding accompaniment, at least for those who love both pizza and wine. Many of pizza's primary ingredients easily fall into the category of "perfect match with wine," though products such as acidic tomatoes, gooey cheese, and lots of garlic will require a wine that can complement their unique qualities. Beer seems like a natural choice when pizza is on the menu. Beer is also extremely popular at pizzerias in Italy and is possibly even more popular than wine. You would be hard-pressed to find a more loyal pizza lover than those who order an ice-cold beer with their favorite pizza.

Soft drinks are of course extremely popular in the pizza world. For many children, the soft drink of choice is almost as important as the pizza itself. Some adults also prefer soft drinks with their pizzas, even when driving is not an issue. The four of us behind this book have differing opinions regarding what to drink with our pizzas. Here are our comments, proving that there is no singular formula for choosing what to drink with a pizza:

Tore: Well, it depends. Wine is definitely my first choice. Pizzas with an excess of anchovies, or something like a spicy pepperoni pizza, are in a class by themselves, making the choice of what I drink more complicated. With a classic pizza Margherita, I like to drink a Barbera-based wine, possibly a Dolcetto, from the Piedmont region of northern Italy. Chianti Classico is also a good choice, the same with a Montepulciano d'Abruzzo.

If I am going to drink white wine with a pizza, I will often choose a Soave Classico, Greco di Tufo, or even a good dry Riesling. Sparkling wine can also be a fine accompaniment. I love a good Franciacorta and generally end up with one from Ca 'del Bosco.

Beer can also be a good choice with pizza. A hearty India Pale Ale is good if the pizza is richly flavored, but a good pilsner will often do the trick. Right or wrong, I have to admit that an ice-cold glass of cola and a good pizza are great the day after a late night on the town, but that doesn't happen much anymore.

Mats: In the early '90s, red wine from Rioja was what everyone in Sweden drank, even with pizza. I vividly remember terrible pizza with tomato purée, cabbage salad with lots of vinegar, combined with a cheap Rioja wine. It was enough to put one totally off the idea of wine and pizza together. Even now I have a problem with tomatoes and red wine.

I am not big on beer with pizza, but it always tastes good before the pizza arrives. As for the pizza, I prefer a glass of wine or water. If I do choose red wine, I like Zinfandel from California or a Dolcetto-based wine from Piedmont.

I really like pizza bianca and pizza with seafood, and with these, of course I prefer white wine. Campania has some great white wines: Falanghina and Greco di Tufo are favorites. Another great choice is an unoaked Chardonnay or Soave Classico. I also like a sparkling Franciacorta.

One of my favorite pizzas is my Brussels sprouts, pancetta, and pecorino pizza (see page 266). The best wine for this unique creation is Riesling!

Kenneth: Red wine! I also like water but definitely without bubbles. Beer and pizza are great together or Coca-Cola with ice in a paper cup!

Craig: I am ashamed to say it, but I grew up drinking (and thoroughly enjoying) a glass of milk with my pizza. I am happy to report that though old habits die hard, my milk-drinking days have been over for the last few decades. I am not much of a beer drinker, and I have not had a Coke since 1978. (That is another story.)

For me, the best combination for pizza is wine or cold water (senza gas). I am not particularly concerned about which wine, as long as it is good. I am much less particular about finding the correct wine when eating pizza than with, say, a five-course dinner at a fine-dining restaurant. My best tips are "drink local" and even more important "drink something really good." And make sure the wine is served at the correct temperature.

We can deduce with almost certainty that pizza toppings and their accompanying beverage are deep-seated, personal choices we all make according to our individual tastes and preferences.

EVERYTHING IS BIGGER IN AMERICA

Ararat Agakhanyan and his brother Allen started their own pizzeria in 1991. The location was only about 66 square feet, and they baked their pizzas in an old rotisserie oven. Ararat was in high school at the time, and Allen was in junior high. "We were living at home with our mom," says Ararat. "It was a pretty interesting journey." We have to agree. The two young brothers stuck with their passion, and there are now 19 Big Mama's & Papa's locations in the Los Angeles area.

Big Mama's & Papa's Pizzeria's claim to fame is that they hold the Guinness World Record for the largest deliverable pizza in the world: the Giant Sicilian. The pizza is a 54-square-inch pizza—a total of 2,916 square inches. It yields about 200 pieces. If you're thinking of ordering one, you need to do so 24 hours in advance, and there's a limited delivery area. We were lucky enough to get to watch our Giant Sicilian being made.

To put things in perspective: the Giant Sicilian uses 26 pounds of dough, 15 pounds of cheese, and 18 pounds of sauce, plus toppings of your choice. The completed pizza weighs in at about 60 pounds. That's a lot of pizza.

The pizza takes a couple of hours to prepare, assemble, and bake—in a specially designed oven extension to accommodate the pizza's massive size. Watching head pizza chef Ernesto Mote work the enormous mound of dough, and then call in the troops to help roll it out, add the toppings, and guide the monster into the oven, is an unforgettable experience.

The four of us could hardly make a dent in a pizza this size, so we ended up donating our Giant Sicilian to a film production company down the road. The finished pizza was boxed up and delivered in the back of a pickup truck, the only mode of transportation big enough!

"We have about twenty stores, but only three are capable of making the 54-inch pizza," says co-owner Wayne Grigorian. "The company started right here in Burbank. The first store was just a few blocks down the street from here. Our founder and his brother came up with an idea to make a completely unique pizza, so they ended up making a 28-inch (The Big Mama) and

Pizza anyone?

a 36-inch pizza (The Big Papa), which are some pretty big pizzas. Nobody made pizzas like that in those days. The largest pizza available at the time was extra large, which is about 16 to 18 inches wide."

The idea of the larger pizzas was ideal for companies, Wayne explained. If a company had a dozen or more people, they could simply order one of the large pizzas. It was very cost-effective too, cheaper than buying five extra-large pizzas. "After a while, we discovered that other pizzerias were offering 36-inch pizzas. So, our founder came up with something unique again: the largest pizza in the world. Well, at least the largest deliverable pizza in the world."

The interior of the oven measures 54 inches across, with a low ceiling height. The dough is baked first and then removed from the oven, and sauce, cheese, and toppings are added. After a second baking, the pizza is done. Today, Big Mama's & Papa's sells an average of three Giant Sicilians a week, which is about as many as they can manage. One disadvantage with a 54-inch-wide pizza is that the doors in most buildings are no more than 36 inches wide—so most of the gigantic pizzas are eaten outdoors or served from a garage.

PIZZA IN VENICE BEACH

If you're near Los Angeles, Venice Beach is worth a stop—not only for the people-watching but also for the fantastic food you'll find at the tiny Gjelina "empire" of the main Gjelina restaurant and its next-door neighbor, Gjelina Take Away (GTA). It is named after the owner's grandmother, who is Albanian. We tried pizzas from both restaurants and were immediately won over by the fresh approach Gjelina uses in both.

Gjelina pizzas have Italian roots and feature, for the most part, local ingredients. One favorite was a pizza with guanciale (cured pork cheek), green olives, Fresno chiles, and mozzarella di bufala; another, also delicious, was topped with maitake mushrooms, beet greens, and Taleggio. We had the pleasure of chatting with Christopher Norris, the manager at GTA.

What are your unique pizza ingredients?
Our mushroom pizza has garlic confit, smoked mozzarella that we smoke here in-house, Parmesan, and three kinds of mushrooms (baby shiitake, maitake, and king oyster mushrooms) that come from a local mushroom farmer. Next door, they have regular mozzarella, Parmesan, truffle oil, and garlic pizza. Another popular pizza is a pissaladière, which is a traditional Roman pizza with sardines, and a variation that has no sardines but a filling of caramelized onion, Gruyère, and arugula salad.

We actually get our cured meat from an Iowa hog farmer who decided to abandon his traditional hog-raising to learn how to cure meat. He went to Parma, Italy, to learn how to make prosciutto, guanciale, and things like that; he is one of the only Americans to train under the masters in Parma. All of our vegetables come from the local Santa Monica farmers' market, and the produce comes from farmers all around the Southern California area. Our bottarga (cured fish roe) comes from one of the only purveyors of bottarga in the States; he procures his own mullet row in Florida.

How do you make your dough?
The recipe for the dough is based on Neapolitan pizza. We use Caputo flour, which is fine flour from Naples. In addition, we use salt and water, but not oil. The dough is fermented for three days and then put in coolers. We used to take the dough straight from the cooler, but with some experimentation we found that if we take it out and let it sit for a few hours and get it to room temperature, it is easier to work with.

Does the restaurant offer the same pizza as GTA?
There are a few differences. It is mostly the same, but we don't want people saying, "Oh, we don't have to go to the restaurant, because we can get all the same pizzas here." It's the same executive chef, same owner, same investors, but the pizza isn't quite the same.

FROM NAPLES TO JERSEY TO SAN FRANCISCO

Anthony Mangieri grew up in Maplewood, New Jersey, in his grandfather's store, Mangieri Brothers, where they specialized in gelato and candy. He started making pizzas at age 15, and by 19 had started up his own bakery, Sant Arsenio, in Red Bank. In 1996, Mangieri opened the first Una Pizza Napoletana in the ocean-side city of Point Pleasant, and in 2004 he moved the establishment to Manhattan. In 2010, Mangieri moved his pizzeria to San Francisco. The call of the outdoors and a passion for mountain biking prompted the move, and after a short time has become one of the few go-to pizzerias in town.

The San Francisco pizzeria, with its high ceilings and custom-built wood-burning oven from Ferrara, is a stunning example of simplicity and elegance. Mangieri makes all—yes, all—of the pizzas himself, never more than three at a time. All the pizzas are 12-inch rounds; nothing is sold by the slice. Watching Mangieri work is to watch poetry in motion, a must for anyone serious about pizza.

There are only a handful of pizzas on Mangieri's menu, all based on a naturally leavened Neapolitan crust topped with basil, tomatoes, and/or fresh mozzarella. The Margherita is made with buffalo mozzarella, San Marzano

> *There is too much pride behind this pizzeria—its life, heart, and passion—to offer anything less. It is Neapolitan; it is love.*
>
> **ANTHONY MANGIERI**

tomatoes, and no tomato sauce. His Bianca pizza features buffalo mozzarella, extra virgin olive oil, garlic, basil, and a touch of Sicilian sea salt. The Ilaria pizza is made of smoked mozzarella, cherry tomatoes, arugula, extra virgin olive oil, and salt, while the Filetti has cherry tomatoes, regular buffalo mozzarella, garlic, extra virgin olive oil, basil, and sea salt. After so many years, Mangieri has added just one pizza to his original menu, and it is available only on Saturdays. This Apollonia pizza, after Mangieri's daughter, is topped with slightly beaten local eggs, fresh garlic, and a smattering of small pieces of cubed salami. Mangieri is very selective in his choice of ingredients. The garlic and basil are always fresh, and the tomatoes are locally grown (with the exception of the true San Marzano tomatoes featured on some of the pizzas). The mozzarella di bufala is from the Naples region; the flour is, of course, Italian; and, just like in the best pizzerias in Naples, the sea salt is Sicilian. The pizzas created at Una Pizza Napoletana appear surprisingly simple—it's a wonder that so few ingredients, and variations of those ingredients, can work together to create such a mouthwatering effect with every bite.

Anthony Mangieri has dedicated his life to making pizza, and it is a treat to see an American pizzeria preserving a generation-rich pizza tradition from Naples. Mangieri's prices may be on the high end (currently, $25 per pizza), but this is totally irrelevant when considering what lies behind the pizzas he creates.

It's best to make the trip to Una Pizza Napoletana in the early evening before the rush, when there aren't so many guests. The restaurant is hidden behind a roller shutter outside of business hours, but don't worry: When it opens at 5:00 in the evening, you'll walk in and enjoy some of the best pizza you have ever eaten.

The Art of Eating Pizza

There are several ways to tackle eating pizza, and many people are as passionate about their technique as they are about the pizzas.

JoAnne Ling from Scott's Pizza Tours in New York (see page 69) discussed the folding-the-pizza technique so popular in that region: "I prefer a folded slice because of the crispy exterior and the cheesy interior. Scott likes the partial fold; you crease the edges of the crust by putting your finger in the middle and using the fold as a suspension."

In most parts of Italy, it's common to eat pizza slices by hand, but whole pizzas generally mean silverware. The Neapolitans even have a special serrated knife for cutting up their pizzas (generally into quarters), which works well, because classic Neapolitan pizzas are served whole and uncut.

Some like eating slices of pizza unfolded, exactly as they appear on the plate. This technique will give the eater the correct crust-to-topping ratio, and is civilized, fairly tidy, gastronomically correct, but perhaps a tad boring. This technique is more commonly found along the West Coast.

"I think that the most important scene in *Saturday Night Fever*," says JoAnne, "is when John Travolta is walking down Eighty-Sixth Street and he has two slices that he piles up on each other, and he folds them both."

One of the most peculiar approaches to eating pizza is starting from the crust along the slice's outer edge. There are different ways of doing this, including the corn-on-the-cob/typewriter method and the "alternating bites" approach in which you take alternating bites of edge and pizza until the slice is gone. Others prefer to nibble away at the topping, then eat the crust—or leave it, if they are limiting carbs or gluten. The possibilities are limited only by the diners' creativity.

JoAnne says that her all-time favorite technique was deftly demonstrated "by a tiny Italian-American lady on one of my tours. She took her pizza from the pointy end, like what I would call the nose, and she rolled it up to the crust and ate it starting on one end of the thick, rolled-up, cigar-like creation. It was an awesome sight to see, and it's not so easy to do, but she made it look elegant. Apparently, her parents made her eat pizza this way as a child. They had a large family and did not want the crust to go to waste. This way there is crust in every bite."

PIZZA EXTRAVAGANZA

Tony's Pizza Napoletana in San Francisco opened its doors in 2009 on what was, at the time, one of the worst street corners in the area. Everyone went out of business there. The owner, Tony Gemignani, guided us through one of the wildest pizza experiences any of us had ever had. When we met Tony, we had been testing pizza for two and a half weeks, and we were looking forward to getting back home and eating anything but pizza (at least for a week or two). Little did we know that Tony had an extravaganza in mind for us, a fantastic journey in his pizza kingdom.

Tony has seven very different ovens; he uses several different flours, or combinations of flours, and a battery of top-quality ingredients to accomplish what is probably the planet's most ambitious pizza menu. Tony's Pizza

Napoletana is the name of the restaurant, but Naples-style pizza is only one of many styles of pizza they serve. The diverse menu includes authentic Italian pizzas as well as a number of regional Italian pizzas. Here are the 10 pizzas we, the brave culinary foursome, semi-bravely attacked:

- Margherita
- Pizza with white rose potatoes, rosemary, Calabrese peppers, chorizo, guanciale, fromage blanc, quail egg
- Romano: a three-courses-in-one pizza, served on a wooden plank
- Pancetta Porcini: mozzarella, mushrooms, porcini, pancetta, smoked scamorza, fresh thyme
- White Pie: clams and garlic
- New Yorker: mozzarella, tomato sauce, pepperoni, Italian fennel sausage, ricotta, garlic, oregano
- Gigante: garlic, salami, mushrooms, bell peppers, onions, pepperoni, linguica, sausage, green onions, chives, bacon, black olives, cherry tomatoes
- Uncle Vito: pesto, garlic, caramelized onions, smoked pancetta, sweet ricotta
- Red Top: Detroit-style pizza topped with Wisconsin brick cheese, mozzarella, white cheddar, tomato sauce, and corners toasted with garlic butter
- Old Smokey: mozzarella, white cheddar, bacon, house barbecue sauce, Niman Ranch ground beef, fried onions, cilantro

The American-style pizzas range from California to New York but also St. Louis and Detroit. (For those who favor Chicago-style pizzas, Gemignani has now opened a new restaurant called Capo's, specializing in the different styles of Chicago pizza as well as pasta and other dishes.)

At Tony's Pizza Napoletana, they make exactly 73 Margherita pizzas a day—no more, no less. "I won first place in the Standard Traditional Guarantee (STG) category for best Neapolitan pizza at the World Pizza Cup competition in Naples, on San Antonio Day—June 13th," Tony explains. "That is 6-13 so I added the 6 and the 1 together and it became 7-3. I was also born in '73. But the 73 is really to commemorate San Antonio Day."

Tony is also one of the world's leading pizza acrobats (see page 48). He is on a team of American pizza competitors that travels to Italy to compete. "My team is made up of acrobats and pizza makers. I run the world games in Vegas, so I compete and bring the biggest team to Italy, and when they bring people to the United States to compete, my core team organizes everything."

Tony also teaches future pizzaioli the tricks of the trade through his International School of Pizza. If you want to learn how to make pizza like him, you can take one of his courses. He offers a four-day-long course starting every Monday. Tony looks pleased after serving real pizza enthusiasts 10 very different pizzas. His parting words to us are inspiring: "I love what I'm doing. I live and breathe it."

PIZZA & WINE

A16 is named after the highway running from Naples to Canosa in Puglia, and the same region inspires the food and wine served at the restaurant. A16 opened in 2004 with a simple concept: rustic dishes inspired by the cooking of southern Italy, made using the best, most local ingredients possible. At A16, wine is equally important, and their impressive wine list is notably different from those found at other San Francisco restaurants—it's an eclectic and remarkable collection of southern Italian wines rarely found in restaurants in Naples or even Rome. We started with the Cenatiempo Lefkòs Bianco Superiore, from the volcanic island of Ischia in the Gulf of Naples, and finished with an exquisite Montefalco Sagrantino from Còlpetrone in Umbria.

Before we come to the pizzas at A16, it is worth mentioning the delicious appetizers they serve. We started with burrata with olive oil and crostini, as well as Neapolitan tripe with tomato, chiles, white wine, and bread crumbs. We could not resist also trying the house-cured salami and the prosciutto tasting, with speck from Alto Adige and La Quercia Berkshire prosciutto. All starters were skillfully prepared, and the stylish restaurant, excellent staff, and lively atmosphere gave us the uncanny feeling of being in Italy but with everyone speaking a language that even we could understand.

The pizzas at A16 are Neapolitan-style. There are only about 10 pizzas on the menu, but they are, without a doubt, some of California's best. You can, and probably should, try a Marinara or Margherita, but it would be a shame not to try pizzas featuring ingredients such as red radicchio Treviso, kale, fennel sausage, Calabrian chiles, and dandelion greens. We never got further than the pizzas on our visit, but next time we will definitely try the pasta and/or entrées, which also looked delicious.

At A16 you can choose from about 40 wines by the glass, both American wines and regional Italian wines—from Lazio and Calabria to Sardinia and Sicily. Lindgren was selected as Best New Sommelier from Wine & Spirits magazine and Best Wine Director in San Francisco Magazine. The restaurant was also nominated for a James Beard Award for Best Wine Service both in 2010 and 2011.

Wood-fired pizza for lunch at Del Popolo.

MINIMALIST PLEASURE ON WHEELS

In California, food trucks are a daily sight, but Del Popolo takes this concept to a new level. Jon Darsky, a former baseball scout and law student, is the man behind Del Popolo's pizza truck, where you can devour Neapolitan pizza cooked in a wood-burning oven inside of a remodeled 20-foot shipping container.

Del Popolo, meaning "of the people" in Italian, travels to a number of different locations in the San Francisco Bay Area. This restaurant on wheels weighs in at 14 tons (two and one-half of which are the Italian wood-burning oven) and offers really good pizza with a bucket of cold drinks hanging outside.

Jon originally made pizza at San Francisco's Flour + Water but opted for an innovative, modern approach to opening a place of his own. Other restaurants may feature an open kitchen, but at Del Popolo *everything* is open. The entire façade is composed of windows where the oven, work area, and all three employees are on display. Jon and an assistant make all the pizzas, and the third person manages the pick-up window.

The menu at Del Popolo consists of a choice of three or four pizzas. On the day of our visit, our choices were Margherita; Bianca with ricotta, garlic, basil, and mozzarella; and a pizza with pork salami, kale, and mozzarella. Next time you're in San Francisco, stop by Del Popolo. Because they move around the city, check their website (www.delpopolosf.com/location) to find their current location.

Jon Darsky (left), owner of Del Popolo

PIZZERIA DELFINA

PIZZA MISSIONARIES

Pizzeria Delfina in San Francisco's Mission District offers excellent pizzas, and the alfresco dining experience was a perfect complement to the food. We started with fresh-stretched mozzarella and burrata served with homemade grissini. We then tried a few different pizzas, including the delicious Gricia with guanciale, spring onion, panna (Italian cream), and black pepper. We also loved the Napoletana, with tomato, anchovies, capers, hot peppers, olives, and oregano.

The crust of Delfina's pizza is a unique cross between a good Neapolitan dough and a California hybrid dough. One thing is certain: The crust is excellent. Our favorite Italian toppings are strewn about the menu: pecorino, salt-packed anchovies, prosciutto di Parma, and broccoli rabe. The ingredients give the menu a distinctive Italian feel, but these pizzas are more Californian than they are Italian.

The all-Italian wine list at Pizzeria Delfina is exquisite, featuring wines from Sicily, Campania, and Puglia. And if by some chance you still have room, you can end your meal with a Bellwether Farms Ricotta Cannoli or a glass of 10-year-old Marco de Bartoli Marsala.

◄ A tiny kitchen is no hindrance for the great food at Delfina.

Frozen Pizza: A Norwegian Pastime

The first frozen pizzas were introduced in the United States in 1957, marketed by the Celentano Brothers. It did not take long for pizza to become the most popular frozen food in the country.

Frozen pizza has secured its place in the world of Norwegian cuisine, as well. A survey done by AC Nielsen in 2004 found that Norwegians ate the most pizza per capita of any country on Earth. Norway's population just tipped over the five million mark a few years ago, and yet they eat over 50 million frozen pizzas a year.

The frozen pizza with the highest consumption in Norway is called Pizza Grandiosa (Grandis, to its millions of fans). This pizza sensation was created in 1980 and since then nearly half a billion of them have been sold, and Norwegians consume roughly 25 million of them each year. Some say that more than 150,000 Norwegians eat a Grandiosa pizza on Christmas Eve, making it a pretty solid competitor to both *lutefisk* and oven-roasted pork ribs, two more traditional options.

Is frozen pizza good or bad? There's no simple answer. Foodies cry out, "Scandalous!" and fans shout, "Delicious!" Frozen food does not necessarily mean bad food. What is most important with frozen pizza (as with any frozen food) is to start with a good product and then freeze it using the best, most modern methods available. For most of us, this means purchasing a boxed, plastic-wrapped pizza from the freezer section of our local grocery store, coming home, removing the pizza from the box and the plastic, and baking it for 10–15 minutes on the center rack in an oven pre-heated to about 425°F (220°C).

Some experts say that frozen foods, including pizza, could at some point disappear from the marketplace, replaced by technology that previously only existed in the world of science fiction. In fact, NASA's Advanced Food Technology program is working to develop safe, tasty, nutritional food with an extremely long shelf-life. According to an article by Jimmy Daly in *FedTech* magazine (May 2013), a grant has been given to Systems & Materials Research Corporation to make a prototype of a 3D printer that can feed the world. As the article notes, "Pizza could be the first food printed in space. A normal pizza is already made in layers of dough, sauce and cheese, making production with a 3D printer relatively straightforward."

Until the folks at NASA work out the glitches of printing up a steaming slice of pepperoni pie, we'll have to do our best with the familiar—and often delicious—option of frozen pizza when we need a slice or two in a snap.

Leftovers: The Skillet Method

Health authorities surely have opinions about how pizza should be stored, reheated, and eaten, but most leftover pizza comes from the box in which it was purchased, or in the case of homemade pizza, on a covered plate or tray. Hopefully you remembered to put it in the fridge overnight! We recommend taking leftover pizza out of the refrigerator and letting it come almost to room temperature before eating, because really cold pizza loses a lot of flavor.

There are lots of creative uses for leftover pizza. You can make bread crumbs from the remains of the crust or whip up anything from a pizza omelet, pizza pasta, or a pizza salad (using small bits of leftover pizza as croûtons). Most of us just want the simple pleasure of finishing off leftover slices before they dry out.

JoAnne Ling from Scott's Pizza Tours in New York (see page 69), gave us her secret to great leftover pizza: the skillet method for reheating a slice. "Turn the burner up to high to get the skillet really hot. Put your cold slice on the hot skillet and cover it for 90 seconds. The bottom becomes crispy while the top stays gooey. It is the ultimate reheating method, and it works with all kinds of pizza."

Two final tips on JoAnne's method: First, have the lid slightly askew when covering the pizza. This will allow any steam to escape while ensuring the crust will become crispy. Second, it is a good idea to check the pizza after a minute to see how much more time is needed.

THE BEST PIZZA IS MADE FROM THE BEST INGREDIENTS

How do you make a good pizza? The answer is simple, yet not so easy. The best pizza is made from the best ingredients. Good ingredients are essential for making good food. It should always be the goal to use the best ingredients you can get and that you can afford. That being said, it's no big deal if you use the ingredients you have readily available. If you use the correct methods in preparing your pizza, it will still be good, even if the ingredients are not the ones you originally hoped to use.

For years, we have heard how important it is to use good ingredients in cooking. Of course, good ingredients are a wiser choice than bad ingredients, and there is an ever-increasing variety of organic, eco-friendly, and locally sourced food available no matter where you live.

One of the biggest challenges we face today is finding out what foods we should and should not buy. There have been many food scandals in recent years, and there will undoubtedly be more rude awakenings in the future.

From pesticides to carbon footprints, cattle feed to chicken pens, and fish farming to the perils of wild catches, more and more consumers are choosing to learn a little (or a lot) more about the food they eat and how to make better, more ethical choices about ingredients. Although it's easy to be struck with a bad case of information overload, the reward for your research will be not only a clear conscience but some of the tastiest, healthiest food you'll ever eat.

The most important thing is to think about what you are eating. It can be challenging to digest all the information out there about potential problems with the food we buy and consume. We urge you to do as well as you can to choose ingredients that are good for the environment. Think globally, and buy locally, to the extent you can. All truly good eating begins and ends with food that is good, fresh, and safe—for producers and consumers alike.

FLOUR

When it comes to pizza ingredients in Italy, everyone talks about flour, flour manufacturers, and the different types and characteristics of flour. The best pizzaioli all agree: This one ingredient is crucial for quality pizza.

The Mulino Marino flour mill is operated by Felice Marino, his son Ferdinando, and his grandchildren, Fulvio and Fausto. They live in Cossano Belbo in Piedmont, very close to the famed Italian wine region. Mulino Marino is proof that Barolo and Barbaresco are not the only interests in Piedmont today.

The mill itself has existed for approximately 1,000 years; Felice purchased it in 1956. At the time, he and his wife had been selling meat from Piedmont, but mills and milling grain had always fascinated Felice. We sat down with Fausto to learn about the storied flour mill.

Who are your customers?

The majority are professionals, but nowadays there are many people in Italy who make pizza or bake bread at home. They are very interested in using quality flour.

You use both a stone mill and a large industrial mill. What is the difference?

The big difference between a stone mill and an industrial mill is the number of grinding rounds that the flour goes through. The stone mill uses only one round. An industrial mill can have anywhere from 8 to 32 rounds, sometimes up to forty-eight. The nutriments disappear more and more on each round.

In Italy there is a law that regulates how flour is classified. The law focuses on the color of the flour. Tipo 00 is the whitest flour, tipo 0 is a notch darker, and tipo 2—or *tipo integrale*—is whole meal flour.

With the stone mill, we only produce tipos 00 and 0 flour. When the dough needs plenty of time to rise, you need a type of flour with high protein content to get the best dough; tipo 00 is perfect for this.

We have three different stone mills, and in one of them we create only corn meal (polenta flour), which is used for polenta, cookies, and sweet products. In the second stone mill, we produce alternative grains, such as spelt and rye. In the last mill, we make soft and dark wheat, as well as sifted flour. We also use the stone mill to make white flour that contains bran and wheat germ.

The soft wheat flour made in the stone mill is called *farina de grano tenero*: tipo 2. It is not whole wheat flour, but it is not white either. It produces a "blond," but not white, dough. The taste and smell are completely different from tipo 00. We also produce durum wheat flour,

◄ Felice Marino

and we process old-fashioned Italian durum wheat from southern Italy. Durum wheat is used in pasta and bread. Some people also use the flour for pizza, mostly in Neapolitan pizza. In Rome, they use durum wheat to make it easier to press out the dough.

The last type of flour we produce is tipo 0 Dario. This flour is particularly well suited to Neapolitan pizza. Tipo 0 Dario contains 12 percent protein while tipo 00 contains 13.5 percent protein. We do not want our customers, however, to focus too much on protein content or technology, but rather on the taste and smell.

Since 1990, we have only produced organic flour. Organic production allows us to find the best farmers, which helps us have a steady production from year to year.

We produce 150 kilos of flour per hour with a stone mill. It is not possible for big industry to install stone mills, because there are not enough stones. The people who built the type of mill that we have (with real stone, not artificial) no longer exist. We have a French stone mill, like the ones they stopped making in the late 1800s, and the stone we have is harder than iron. A good characteristic of natural stone is that it turns very slowly. You need plenty of time and the right amount of water. The artificial stone does not use the same grinding process. If you use the stone correctly, as my grandfather says, the stone will last 150 years.

Which type of grain do you use?

We still have contact with some of the farmers we have always used here in Piedmont. My father, my brother, and I have decided, however, to start buying grain from other suppliers, as well. Harvested grain from Langhe (in Piedmont) is very high quality in terms of taste and aroma. We need a mixture of organic wheat from Piemonte (Cuneo, Alessandria, and Asti), Lombardia (Pavia), Emilia Romagna (Piacenza and Parma), and Veneto, mostly because we believe that we produce the best panettone, pizza, and bread by mixing the different varieties. It is essential for us to talk to farmers about the cleaning and the sorting processes, just as you would if you were producing grapes for wine. We need time to prepare the wheat—both to process it in the best possible way and to get the best flavor out of the flour.

The pizza recipes often recommend using tipo 00. Can you talk a little bit about that?

All our flour is suitable for pizza. It is the person who makes the pizza, whether he or she is a professional or someone who makes pizza at home, who determines the type of flour to use. I do not know if this answers your question, but for a Neapolitan pizza, I recommend tipo 0. For a Roman pizza, I believe that 00 is the right flour.

Our flour is slightly different in the way that it is used. You have to add water to the dough very slowly. Our bakers and pizza makers say

that they must follow the flour carefully when making dough. Our work is *artigianale*. There is no exact formula to what works best.

Can you explain what you mean by "following the flour" while making the dough?

What I mean by following the flour when mixing dough is that the water must be added very, very slowly after I add flour to the machine. If the flour package says to mix the dough for five minutes, then mix it for five minutes. If it says that the dough should rise for 24 hours, then let it rise for 24 hours. Water quality is also very important, and the same goes for the temperature of the water. The dough must rise at a low temperature, but it is also important that the

Ferdinando Marino

dough is allowed to rest in the warmer temperature—75 to 85°F (24 to 29°C)—at the end of the process, before you put the pizza in the oven. This is extremely important for the right maturation. The dough will smell completely different after resting.

How does the future look for pizza in Italy?

A few years ago, sourdough was the major innovation for pizza. Before that, most people used ordinary yeast. Today, we are seeing the use of a different type of flour as the new innovation: primarily stone-ground flour but also other types of wheat grains. Gabriele Bonci (see page 29) uses only spelt flour in his pizzas. When people order flour from us, they often order three bags of 00 flour and one bag of *enkir* flour (the botanical name of the grain is *Triticum monoccocum*). The pizzaioli have all joined in, and now most people know about it. This is innovation.

We've heard rumors that you're involved in a project in Peru. Please tell us about it.

My father went to Peru with the Slow Food movement to help create a mill that could produce a Peruvian grain. They are struggling to transport grain from 13,000 feet up in the mountains down to the mill in the city. It is very expensive. They do not have cars, so they have to use llamas and other work animals. While in Peru, my father saw a lot of homeless children without parents. When he arrived back home, he told me he wanted to help some of those whose lives were so hard. So

> It is important that you have complete control over the dough, and that will make good pizza. You must let the dough know that you are the boss.
> **FAUSTO MARINO**

we have a friend to whom we have been sending money for the past three or four years so she can buy bread, flour, and T-shirts. We also have a very small stone mill there, where we make flour that we give to the people of Peru. People here in Italy tell us how much they want to contribute, and then we send money to Peru to produce flour for them. For my father, and for us, this is a great experience.

Ferdinando, tell us about your "dream pizza."

We have a very good local onion that I use. It is relatively large, red, sweet, and flat. I also use local black truffles, freshly pressed extra virgin olive oil, a little salt, and maybe some black pepper. It is important that you soak the onions in water for two to three hours before serving, to make them milder. A good Barbaresco is the perfect accompaniment, and this is what I call a great dish.

Would you do anything special with the dough?

Good dough must rest for a long time. It really depends on the flour. Mix the dough and leave it in the fridge for 20 to 24 hours, and then it will be good. Make small balls and let them rise, and then you can make the crust. You can also mix different types of grains in the dough. It is important that you have complete control over the dough, and that will make good pizza. You must let the dough know that you are the boss.

▸ From left: Fulvio, Fausto, Felice, and Ferdinando Marino

TOMATOES

Pomodoro San Marzano dell'Agro Sarnese-Nocerino DOP San Marzano tomatoes are widely considered to be among the best tomatoes produced anywhere in the world. They are standard on many of the best pizzas in Naples and abroad. In season, they are used fresh, and the canned tomatoes are perfect for pizza any time of the year. One of the unique qualities of the San Marzano tomato is its ability to retain its freshness of flavor even after being canned.

In a black-and-white photograph, San Marzano tomatoes look almost like small eggplants, some oblong and pill-shaped, others slightly tapered on the stem end. The flesh of the tomato is meaty, and its bittersweet flavor cannot be found in any other variety of tomato.

True San Marzano tomatoes are grown only in the San Marzano area, where they have been cultivated for the last 150 years. Originally, they came from a combination of three varieties: King Umberto, Fiaschetta, and Fiascona. They are grown in the rich soil created from the eruptions of Mount Vesuvius, and it is this soil that gives the tomatoes their flavor, aroma, and color. The other two important elements are the water in the soil and the people who have cultivated these tomatoes for generations.

Some of the most publicized scandals in the pizza industry have been about illegitimate San Marzano tomatoes that come from other places in Italy and elsewhere in the world. Real San Marzano tomatoes come with the official stamp *Denominazione d'Origine Protetta* (DOP) and the farmer's numbered stamp *Pomodoro San Marzano dell'Agro Sarnese-Nocerino.*

San Marzanos today are cultivated in exactly the same way they always have been. We spoke to Edoardo Ruggiero, head of the Consortium of San Marzano DOP, who told us that it is impossible to modernize the techniques and still keep the true San Marzano flavor. "The techniques have been handed down from father to son," he said, "and each family has its own unique formula for producing the best tomatoes. These techniques cannot be taught in a school. They come from vast experience working the soil."

Pomodorino del Piennolo del Vesuvio DOP Real San Marzano tomatoes are a well-known ingredient, but there is another DOP-protected tomato that is worth noting: *Pomodorino del Piennolo del Vesuvio* DOP. This small, oval tomato has a shell with dimples and a point at one end. This tomato is grown on the hillsides of Mount Vesuvius, at 500 to 1,500 feet above sea level.

The Pomodorino del Piennolo tomato is bright red, with a sweet and sour taste. It also has a slightly bitter aftertaste, which gives the tomato more complexity. You can buy these tomatoes fresh—they're harvested in July and August—or in cans, but what is most special about them is that they are bound together in large bunches on vines and hung to dry. This process causes the tomato to lose much of its water content, intensifying both the sweetness and the acidity.

Most other tomato varieties would rot during this process, but Pomodorino del Piennolo tomatoes have a thick skin and are firmly attached to the vine. This, in combination with the tomato's natural sugar and acid content, enable it to hold up well—often until the following spring. In Italy, you can see bunches of Pomodorino del Piennolo hanging in private kitchens and restaurant kitchens alike. Cooks help themselves to the tomatoes as needed to add delicious flavor to a variety of Italian dishes, including pizza.

We visited Giovanni Marino at Casa Barone, one of the few manufacturers of Pomodorino del Piennolo tomatoes. Giovanni took us up the hillside of Mount Somma, where tomatoes grow in soil that was covered by lava from the eruption of Mount Vesuvius in 1944.

"Everything here is about lava," says Giovanni. "The last eruption was in 1944, and it changed everything. Large parts of the town were covered by it. When the lava flowed down, it pushed the soil down with it and solidified. The lava is about three feet below the surface of the soil, which means that the plant roots reach down to the lava."

Can you tell us about your production process?
We are committed to organic production. Tomatoes have been growing here since 1872, when Francesco Piromallo owned the area. Twelve years ago I bought the site as pieces of land were being sold off. Some areas, however, remain uncultivated. Casa Barone is the largest producer of tomatoes in Vesuvius National Park. When we were deciding what products to cultivate here, we could not focus solely on tomatoes. But tomatoes are something everyone eats and are thus very important, so that became our first choice. We also grow apricots and grapes.

In July and August, we harvest tomatoes in both large and small bunches. Traditionally, the tomatoes are harvested on vines and hung to dry. This is the only cultivation of tomatoes in Italy that lasts until Easter because they are hung up in this particular way. The tomatoes ripen and mature over time, while becoming increasingly flavorful as they lose 20 percent of the water in the process. Good ventilation and air circulation are important in the long dry season. If air circulation is poor, the tomatoes become rotten. The humidity in this region is low. It seldom rains, and when it does rain, the moisture is quickly sucked into the ground. The shell of the tomato is very thick and hard, so it can withstand a lot. Do you see these dimples and the tip on these tomatoes? They are the trademark of the Pomodorino del Piennolo.

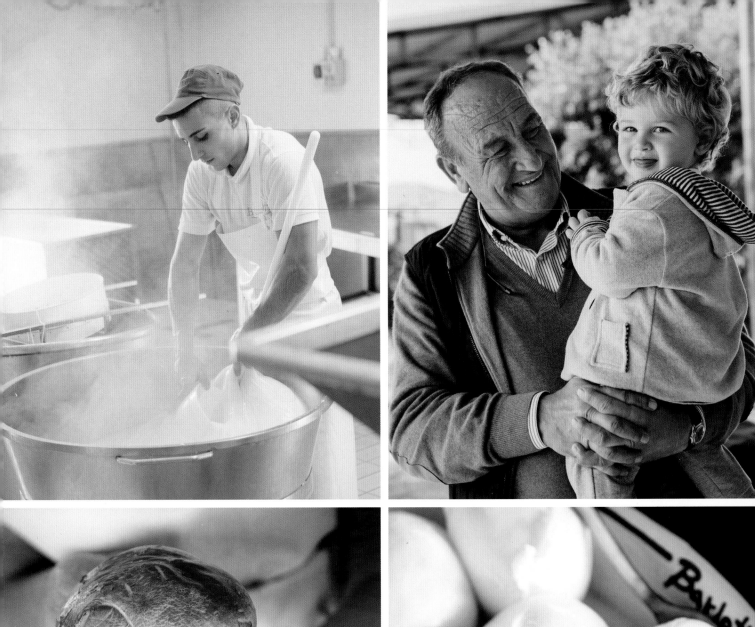

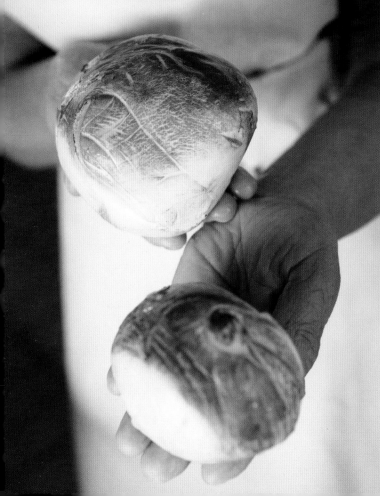

CHEESE

Fresh Mozzarella Although there are a handful of classic pizzas without cheese, such as Italy's famous Marinara pizza, mozzarella is synonymous with pizza. This is particularly true in Italy, but also in the United States and anywhere else pizza is made.

The two famous Italian mozzarellas are fior di latte, made with cow's milk, and mozzarella di bufala, made with milk from the Italian water buffalo (Bubalus bubalis). When ordering mozzarella in Italy, you will generally be given mozzarella di bufala, unless you specifically ask for fior di latte. Both cheeses are native to southern Italy. Campagna, home to Naples, is the primary producer of fresh mozzarella, but the cheese is also produced in Puglia, Sicily, Calabria, and Abruzzo, among other regions. The fior di latte and buffalo mozzarella cheese are sold in bags with a governing liquid. There is also "factory mozzarella," which is made in many countries and sold in blocks or pre-grated. It works well on pizza but can't compete with the flavor of fresh mozzarella.

In addition to fresh mozzarella, the Italian cheese industry produces low-moisture mozzarella, mostly used in the food-service industry. There are also small quantities of smoked mozzarella produced (mozzarella affumicata) and burrata, which is fresh mozzarella filled with cream and chunks of mozzarella.

In the United States, mozarella is made of cow's milk. There have been attempts to produce mozzarella di bufala in America, but none have been successful. Most American mozzarella is the type found on the millions of pizzas baked there every year. The most common type is low-moisture, aged mozzarella, made either from whole milk or part-skim milk. Part-skim mozzarella browns better than whole-milk cheese and is easier to shred. But whole-milk mozzarella is where the flavor is, and equally important, where that great, melty stringiness comes from—due to the cheese's lower moisture content. For most consumers, the longer shelf life of low-moisture mozzarella is also a practical consideration: fresh mozzarella has to be eaten within a few days of its production, and some varieties must be consumed, at the latest, the very next day after they are made.

Buffalo Milk Today, the third and fourth generations of Barlotti family make buffalo milk products: father Nunziante and his three sons. Our visit to Barlotti started with coffee and tea served with the same water buffalo milk used in the world's best mozzarella. Simple and delicious!

We quickly noticed that the milk was exceptionally flavorful. Nunziante told us that milk from water buffalo has two to three times the fat content of regular cow's milk; buffalo milk sometimes contains up to 10 percent fat. The milk is also about three times as expensive as cow's milk.

"We get milk from three farms in the local area," Nunziante explained, "and it is processed within 48 hours of milking. The milk with the lowest fat content comes in September and October, because then the buffalo eat differently, and less, so that affects the fat content. The best period is from December to February, because the milk has a high fat content, making it an extremely rich product. The milk from May to August is also top quality. Although there is less fat in the [summer] milk, the quality is still high. The quality is always high, but if you look at the fat content, the milk in September and October is the thinnest.

Do you notice the difference between cheeses produced in the different seasons?

There are slight differences in taste, but it is not the case that one cheese is any better than any other. It has to do with the *artigianale*, the craftsmanship. We do everything by hand to preserve the flavor. If we use too many industrial processes, we lose something along the way.

Your cheese is a DOP product. Can you tell us more about this system?

DOP is a certification for products that come from a specific area, in our case, Salerno. Everyone who has certification is carefully checked. We must, for example, use 100 percent buffalo milk from this area. We have had DOP certification for 20 years.

Caserta and Salerno are the main areas of mozzarella. In Salerno there are 151 producers, and the majority of them are family run. Here we are nine families. Caserta is a more industrial area, and fewer of the producers there do the work by hand.

Can you tell us about the cows?

We have roughly 185 animals here now. They eat only corn and hay that we mix, and the corn is grown here by us. They eat a little soy, as well. The feeding area is cleaned every other day, something we are very careful about. When the calves are three months old, we release them into the field. On average, the animals live to be 14 or 15 years old, but some live to be 20.

(Barlotti takes us over to the cows.)

These calves are the youngest, 20 days old. This one has been given a number, since he is more than 20 days old. When they are six weeks old, they are moved over here (he points to another pen) and separated, but after a while they are put together with the other animals.

Do you sell cheese to countries other than Italy?

We sell cheese to Japan, Switzerland, England, and Germany, but about 90 percent of our products are sold in Italy. We are privileged that we can deliver to the elite. Food and wine magazine *Gambero Rosso* named us the best producer for the past 25 years, and we have many good customers, such as Enzo Coccia (see page 6).

Please tell us about the smoked mozzarella you make.

We always smoke mozzarella the day after it was made, and it's the first thing we do, at seven o'clock in the morning. We use hay for the smoking. The hay is laid on the ground, while the grate with the cheese is set four and one-half feet above that. The mozzarella is smoked between three and five minutes. The temperature is between 140 and 160°F. It is important that it doesn't get so hot that there are flames.

We were served a lot of good food during the visit, and Nunziante told us about each product that arrived on the table. We had the freshest mozzarella we have ever tasted, with a little more rubbery consistency than cheese that is a few days old. "I prefer to eat mozzarella the day after it is made, totally natural," our gracious host advised.

We also tasted salsiccia, a sausage made of water buffalo meat. Nunziante told us that they are widely known for their salsiccia, which is made from a very old, very secret family recipe. Everyone in the area has their own secret family recipe, every one of which is closely guarded by each successive generation.

We topped off our cheese extravaganza with a fitting dessert: a fabulous buffalo ricotta.

Parmigiano-Reggiano DOP Mozzarella is the most important cheese when it comes to pizza, but the cheese many consider the king of all Italian cheeses is Parmigiano-Reggiano, better known as Parmesan. Truth be told, some celebrated chefs—most notably Mario Batali, who famously calls this cheese "the undisputed king of cheeses"—consider this one of the best cheeses in the world.

But be forewarned: Not everything that says "Parmesan" on the label is true Parmigiano-Reggiano. The powdered "Parmesan" cheese that can be found on the tables of most American pizzerias is nothing like real Parmigiano-Reggiano. The real thing will always be Parmigiano-Reggiano: a hard cheese that is made only in certain areas of Emilia-Romagna in northern Italy. *Parmigiano* is the Italian adjective for *Parma*, and *Reggiano* is the Italian adjective for *Reggio-Emilia*.

Even though mozzarella is the primary pizza cheese, it is very common to use a bit of Parmesan on pizza, too, both in Italy and in other parts of the world. Elsewhere, Parmigiano-Reggiano's "little brother," Grana Padano, is used. Grana

Padano is a good cheese made in the style of real Parmesan, but with a milder flavor. In the United States it is common to find Pecorino Romano on pizza. This cheese is made from sheep's milk and is the standard used in many pizzerias. But nothing compares with the unique flavor of real Parmesan—which, by the way, is also delicious accompanied by almost any type of wine.

Most of the Parmesan we find in stores has been stored for about 18 months, but with some hunting you can find cheese stored for up to three years—sometimes longer. Parmesan's flavor becomes more complex with age, and properly matured Parmesan is something everyone should try.

We have long been advocates of a special Parmesan called Vacche Rosse (red cow), and we had the pleasure of visiting the manufacturer Grana d'Oro, where we got to meet one of the owners Luciana Pedroni.

Why is this breed of cow called Vacche Rosse?

The exact name of this breed is Razza Reggiana, or Red Cows of Reggiana. The name comes from the color of the cow, which is red. Parmesan was originally made 1,000 years ago, and these cows are the original [breed used]. Vacche Rosse arrived here when the barbarians invaded. The first invasion was in approximately 400 AD, when they came here from Eastern Europe, and lived here in Val d'Enza.

In the late 1940s, we had the largest number of Vacche Rosse cows in the region. At that time, another breed of cow arrived here from Northern Europe, specifically from Denmark and Germany. This increased milk production by 30 percent. At that time, there were approximately 130,000 cows of the Reggiana breed in the area. By the

do not want the cows to be there. During the summer the cows get to eat fresh herbs. They do not go out and graze, but we include fresh herbs in their feed twice a day.

Tell us a little about the production of the cheese.
Parmigiano-Reggiano is made with milk from two different milkings—milk from the night before and from the following morning. The milk from the day before stays out all night, and by morning it has separated. We make butter with the cream. Then we mix the partially skimmed milk from the evening and the whole milk from the morning. Each tank holds approximately 265 gallons of milk, which we use to make two wheels. The weight of one large wheel is 220 pounds. Each 220-pound piece is divided into two, and these halves are formed into two wheels of about 110 pounds each. The cheese is then shaped. On the label, you can see the name Parmigiano-Reggiano, and the production year, in addition to the production month and number of this factory. Every cheese factory has a number; ours is 703. After 24 months of storage, the cheese can be approved by the Associazione Nazionale Produttori, which is the consortium that endorses the quality, and it gets its final stamp of Parmigiano-Reggiano Vacche Rosse. It does not become Vacche Rosse until it is stamped.

late 1980s, however, only 40 or 50 years later, the number had dropped to less than 900. Today we are back up to 3,000 cows. We are small, but we are growing. Each year, more than three million wheels of Parmigiano-Reggiano are produced, of which about 10,000 are Vacche Rosse. Here at Grana d'Oro we produce 1,000 wheels per year.

Are the cows indoors all year round, or are they outside during the summer?
During the summer, the barn doors stay open. Our farm is located in a strictly controlled area by the river Enza, and since we grow hundreds of different herbs in the fields, we cannot let the cows out to pasture to graze freely. If we let the cows out, they will destroy the meadow. The herbs are going to be eaten by people, and so we

How does the length of storage time affect the taste of the cheese?
Some stored for 24 months are soft and sweet; a second variety, Stravecchia, is stored more than 30 months and has a strong taste. It is harder than the cheese that is stored for 24 months. The first type is the most common and the one we sell the most of abroad.

What type of salt do you use?

Parmigiano-Reggiano is only made of milk, enzymes, and sea salt. We salt our cheese with a special sea salt. We use the sweet salt from Cervia. Cervia is located on the Adriatic Sea, near Ravenna. The salt is similar to the salt from Trapani in Sicily (see page 34), but milder, sweeter, and not as salty. We found some old papers from a monastery, where it says that the cheese that was made here a long time ago—the first Parmigiano-Reggiano—was salted with the sweet salt from Cervia. And now we are one of the few manufacturers who use it.

How do you tend to serve the cheese?

It is best to eat the cheese by itself, but of course it is used on pasta and other dishes. We eat everything, including the rind, which consists of pure, mature cheese. We clean it with a knife and use it in soup, especially vegetable soup. We also like to grill it. This gives the cheese an absolutely wonderful flavor.

OLIVE OIL

The world of pizza would be a poorer place without olive oil. The use of olive oil on a pizza is second nature to pizzaioli in Naples. There are differing opinions as to when the oil should be applied, which kind of oil is best, and even the correct technique to use when applying the oil. Some American pizzas are also anointed with olive oil, but many are not. The true Neapolitan pizza does not contain oil in the dough, but in the United States it is very common to add some sort of fat to the classic combination of flour, salt, yeast, and water. Olive oil, other types of oil, lard, shortening, and sometimes butter are used in making the dough.

Olive oil can make pizza dough more pliable, and it can be used to dress vegetables used as toppings. Neutral oils are used to oil pizza pans and will occasionally be used in the dough, as well. Some of our favorite toppings—bacon, pancetta, speck, and lardo—also add delicious fats to pizza.

Italy, France, Greece, and Spain are known for their oils, but good oil is also produced in other countries such as Australia, South Africa, and in the United States. Spain produces the most olive oil in the world, but Greece consumes the most olive oil per capita.

Extra virgin olive oil is the gold standard. It contains no more than 0.8 percent acidity, and often less than 0.5 percent. The International Olive Council (IOC) tells us that only about 10 percent of all olive oil produced worldwide is extra virgin, even though in some countries, that percentage is much higher: 45 percent in Italy and a whopping 80 percent in Greece. Virgin olive oil has less than 1.5 percent acidity, and simple "olive oil" has less than 2 percent acidity. The United States is not a member of the IOC, but in late 2010 the US Department of Agriculture established its own voluntary grading system for olive oils produced there; this system closely parallels that of the IOC.

There is an enormous difference in taste from one oil to the next. Some olive oil is described as fruity; others are grassy or peppery. Flavorful oil will affect the taste of a pizza ,and it is worthwhile experimenting with different types of oil to experience how they interact with pizza. We recommend a light, fruity, extra virgin olive oil on top of most pizzas—for example, olive oil from Liguria. This is an oil that enhances the flavors of the pizza without overpowering them. A robust oil—such as some of the oils from Tuscany—can quickly become overbearing, so that the more delicate flavors of cheese, sauce, and toppings are obscured.

CURED MEATS

Salami for Life We met Riccardo Franchi, owner of Edizioni Riccardo Franchi, a company that produces cured meats, in the town of Carpignano Sesia, in Piedmont, Italy, at one of the salami manufacturers Riccardo works with. At that company, Salumificio di Carpignano, we were joined by Matteo Casiraghi, the man responsible for salami production at Salumificio di Carpignano.

Riccardo begins our tour. "In this factory, they produce special salami with truffles and nuts," he explains. "We have a lot of partners. What is important here is that this is a small factory, and it has an owner/partner who works here every day. He controls the raw material he is using and monitors the product through the entire production process. It is a small production facility, but with an owner who oversees everything. He knows every piece of salami inside the factory, and that is so very important."

Matteo elaborates. "This is a very little factory and a family-run business. I am the son, and this is my mother. My father is in the office and goes out to sell and do his work in the marketplace."

"We have only selected partners for our meat," Riccardo adds. "They are all Italian, and they sell pork to us from the same animals they use for prosciutto di Parma. Pork is very important in the market in Italy and in Europe. What we like best in Italy is the leg of the pig. So, when you sell a pig, 60 percent of what you earn comes from the leg. What is particular with this pork is the white fat. It is a very dry fat. When the fat is yellow and very oily it is not good. When the white fat is salted and seasoned it becomes sweet, which produces sweet, delicious salami. That is the reason Italian salami is different than salami from other parts of Europe: They have other kinds of pork. In Germany, Holland, and in the north of Europe, bacon is very important, not the hind leg. They have pigs with very long bodies, which produce a lot of bacon."

How big is your production?
We do about 10 tons a week," Matteo responds, "and about 500 tons per year of salami, sausage, and a product we make here in Italy called cotechino, which is boiled salami.

Do you do any smoked bacon here?
(Riccardo answers as he leads us into the production room with the sausage machine and cutter.) We do only sweet bacon here—no smoked bacon. We mix the spices, salt, and pepper, and then we mix everything together according to our recipes. We use primarily natural casings, and we have 12 people working here in this factory. The first part of the seasoning happens in this room. It is drier here, and the temperature fluctuates between 68 and 77°F. The humidity is low, about 55 to 65 percent. This is a very important part of the process. The small salami stay here about 24 to 26 hours. The larger salami stay roughly 50 hours—about two days. The temperature is very controlled, both here and in the next room. We adjust the conditions every half hour, so the salami is dried properly. The water in the salami has to evaporate very slowly.

◀ Matteo Casiraghi

Riccardo, what is the white coating on the outside of the salami?
It is muffa, or mold. The skin is made of a natural casing as fine as can be eaten, but the taste isn't particularly good and is generally not eaten. The red color of salami comes from the color of the meat. The salt we use comes from Sardinia or Sicily. Another small detail is that we use garlic powder, since fresh garlic is not so easy to work with.

We also make custom salami. If you have a recipe you prefer, you can order it specially made. Every region wants different types of salami. If we sell salami in Milano or Sicily, they want softer salami, but if we sell it in Rome or Naples, they want it hard like a stone. We make it medium for the trip so it arrives not too hard, not too soft. But this does vary. If the client wants harder or softer salami, or medium seasoning, we can customize their order. We also make a lot of pancetta. The most important is the hot pancetta used on pizza, such as the Spianata or Ventricina.

Some people like to put salami on a pizza when it goes in the oven, and some put it on afterwards. What is your opinion on that, Riccardo?
The salami we make here can be put in the oven to cook. The prosciutto cotto and the prosciutto di Parma are normally put on the pizza after it comes out of the oven. The rest should go onto the pizza before it is placed in the oven.

Prosciutto di Parma Parma ham (prosciutto di Parma) has many uses, including being among the most delectable toppings for pizza. We visited Parma ham producer Fontana Ermes, owned by Leonarda Fontana, Beatrice Fontana, and Pier Arnaldo Fontana. It is one of the best-known producers in the region.

Over a mouthwatering lunch laced with prosciutto and Parmesan, we met Roberta Spotti, who works in exporting for Fontana Ermes; Nicola Zileri, son of owner Leonarda Fontana; and Chiara Lasiuolo, press office manager for the Consorzio del Prosciutto di Parma. The organization was established in 1963 to protect the traditional, and only true, Parma ham.

During lunch, we are told that it is important to have the technology in place when making Parma ham and that one must have passion for the meat. The man responsible for selecting hams in Fontana Ermes has been doing it for nearly 30 years and, like our dining companions, can determine if there are any concerns with the product just by looking at it. Is the meat consistent enough? Is there enough fat? Is it too lean? How is the rind and the color of the product? If the ham does not have the correct characteristics to become a Parma ham, it is rejected immediately. There is always the human eye, checking and correcting the small things. This way of working is handcraft—artigianale; the equipment and technology only facilitate the work, although the machines are built to exact standards.

What kind of regulations or requirements do you have regarding fat?
(Roberta Spotti responds.) The Consorzio del Prosciutto di Parma has rules about how much fat is permitted. There has to be at least 0.6 inch of fat to become Parma ham. In Italy, fat is synonymous with taste and quality, and it is a very healthy fat. It is also what gives the aroma to our

product. If you see a nice slice of Parma ham with fat veins in the middle, you buy it, because that is the best product you can get.

To become a Parma ham, the pig must be a minimum of 9 months and not more than 16 months old. It has been established that the meat has the best flavor when the pig is slaughtered during this period. The pig is around 375 pounds when it is slaughtered, so it is a very big pig. If you take the European pigs, they can be slaughtered around 175 to 200 pounds, so there is a big difference in the back legs, where the hams come from. Also, the feed that is given to the pigs destined to be Parma hams is different. It is very controlled, and only certain products are given to the pig.

After lunch, we tour the factory with Roberta and are joined by Fabrizio Basili, the head of production at Fontana Ermes. Fabrizio started in 1963, and he started small, with just 17 hams, in the oldest part of the factory. Today, the company produces approximately 350,000 hams a year. Their main production is Parma ham, and they take in around 4,500 hams a week. In a small area, a whole range of coppa, pancetta, and salami is produced to provide the largest selection of presliced products possible to the large supermarkets. They produce one and one-half tons of charcuterie products per week. The company was among the first to preslice cured meats.

The meat must be of the right cut and is not official Parma ham until it has gone through the process and been approved. "Within the first 15 days of life of the pig, the pig is tattooed with the breeding house tattoo, so we know where the pig was born and from which province. In this way, the consortium guarantees the traceability on the ham, all the way from the breeding house. When the hams arrive, we have to check all the documentation to be sure that the product comes from the correct areas. The letter must correspond to the month in which the pig was born. Every month, we receive documents from Consorzio del Prosciutto di Parma with the list of letters corresponding to the month," Roberta explains.

Fabrizio chimes in, explaining, "At this point, we trim the product to give the ham the Fontana cut. Every factory gives its own trimming to the product. The hams have been slaughtered, more or less, two days before they come into the factory. So they become porous after the slaughtering and after going through the salt-rubbing machine. At this point, the product is wet, which will allow the dry salt to adhere to the ham. In the final stages, we must still have a person put salt on the hams in any places the machine missed, especially around the bone. We use Italian salt from Trapani in Sicily [see page 34]. It is a common sea salt of very good quality. Each factory determines what kind of salt they use and how they are going to use it."

"This is the salting room," Fabrizio continues as we enter the next room. "All of the cells we will be seeing now will have a temperature from 34 to 39°F. The difference between the three different cold rooms is their humidity levels. Here in the first cell, the humidity is very high, as it is necessary to have the salt melt onto the ham. The ham will stay here for about one week. It is then removed, and any remaining salt is blown off of the product. At this point, the product has to be salted for the second time. You can see the color of the product has changed and it has become much flatter. Here, in this second cell, the ham is drying because the humidity in the room has decreased. The salt in this cell will not melt but will conserve the meat.

"This third room is what we call the pre-resting cold room. The product has been worked a lot up to this point, with all of the salt and humidity and drying, so this is a room where the meat can relax. It is very important that the meat not get stressed. The product will remain here for three weeks in a forced ventilation system, which dries out the product. So we can say that the whole resting phase of the product lasts until its 90th or 100th day.

"When the ham has reached its third week in here and has fully dried out, it will enter the trimming phase. You can see the difference here. The ham looks much better aesthetically but continues its resting phase, more or less for 100 days, before the salt is washed away. Now the product has finished the cold phase and will go to the warm phase to begin the curing process. All of the humidity that is still left in the product, which is not a lot, comes out of the product here. That is why the product has a kind of whitish effect to it. Apart from the drying, we also give the ham three hours of warm temperature at 72 to 74°F."

We proceed to another area of the factory, an older building with an entire wall covered by windows. "We are now entering the older part of the factory, which is very narrow and long," Roberta points out. "Here we open the windows to let the air come in. So you see here, the position of the factory is perpendicular to the river.

The air comes from the hills, and the sea is right over those hills. The sea air goes all through the chestnut trees and gets this wonderful malt flavor and captures all of the scents coming in to make the product so mild. In the past, the men who used to work in the factory and open and close the windows all day were called 'the men of the long windows.'

"At this point, the ham has reached its sixth or seventh month since its first day of salting. The exposed part of the meat will be greased to protect it. Pepper and salt are used in the grease only to conserve the pork fat itself, not to add flavor. See how hard and how crusty the surface of the ham has become? This is the reason we have to grease the product, so it can continue breathing, getting rid of moisture without drying and forming a crusty surface.

"It is very important to leave the part of the ham where the bone is ungreased, because all the humidity inside tends to go where the bone is. If we were to close that area around the bone, the humidity would be trapped inside and could cause the ham to spoil.

"Once the product has been greased, it continues its curing phase for up to a minimum of 12 months."

Throughout our tour of the Fontana Ermes factory, it is apparent that each piece of Parma ham is treated with the utmost care to ensure consistent and reliable quality is delivered around the world.

Fontana Ermes allows visitors to the factory by appointment only.

BASIL

Basil, especially when combined with tomatoes, is one of the greatest gifts the Italian kitchen has given us. Yet basil is also the pizza ingredient most taken for granted. Sure, we all know that a pizza Margherita is comprised of mozzarella, tomato, and fresh basil. We know that basil is the herb of choice for green pesto and a good tomato sauce. But if you look carefully, you will see, at the very least, a leaf or two of basil on pretty much any Italian pizza or American pizza with Italian roots. The basil is there; in a way, it simply has to be there, in the same way a suitcase has a handle or a toothbrush has bristles.

Fresh basil has an almost mystical quality, with its pungent and sweet fragrance and delicate flavor. Dried basil cannot compare to the fresh leaves. Dried basil has a grassy flavor that has its culinary place, but it is a flavor almost completely unlike that of the same herb in its fresh form.

It is important to treat fresh basil with care. Basil will bruise and change color if chopped too much or handled roughly. Use a sharp knife or scissors and work quickly. Many chefs recommend stacking five or six freshly washed basil leaves, rolling them into a small cigar shape, and then deftly slicing the bundle into narrow strips; this technique creates attractive, even pieces of the herb and limits the damage and discoloration of the deep green leaves. Overworking the leaves can also give basil a bitter flavor. Cooking or baking basil will reduce the intensity of its flavor, but will produce the desired effect in a sauce or on a pizza. Many pizzaioli top a finished pizza with fresh basil, while others add basil leaves before baking their pizzas, and still others use fresh basil both before and after baking their pizzas. In Italy—a country famous for fantastic herbs—no other herb holds the same power and influence among pizzaioli as basil.

The Fifth Ingredient

Flour, water, yeast, and salt are the building blocks of authentic Neapolitan pizza crust. There is also a fifth ingredient, equally as important, that the pizzaiolo must master: the oven. Stefano Ferrara's grandfather started building ovens in 1930, and today, Ferrara ovens are found worldwide and are the heart of many famous pizzerias.

The Ferraras have never really marketed themselves. They've used no advertising other than word of mouth. The business is a family affair, and the Ferraras feel privileged to have clients who take care of the marketing for them. Stefano Ferrara explains that he is there for the customers 24 hours a day, each and every day. The telephone is always on.

The Ferrara factory and warehouse are nestled in a nondescript industrial area outside of Naples. Once inside the warehouse, we were greeted by Stefano Ferrara and offered a round of small espressos. We met several of Stefano's employees, all busily working on any number of nearly finished ovens, some covered in the local brownish-gray clay, others bedecked in the classic tiny mosaic tiles of the Neapolitan oven. A few of the ovens were enrobed in steel or copper, while others had jagged tiles made of Palladian marble. A few of the ovens displayed the name of the intended owner, while others had the words "Stefano Ferrara Napoli" prominently displayed over the opening of the oven.

The Neapolitan oven has a unique, easily recognizable dome shape. The best of these ovens are handmade, and Ferrara is directly involved in the making of each and every oven he sells. Ferrara's ovens vary from 30 to 60 inches wide and can weigh up to 3,000 pounds. The company's 10 employees build 70 to 100 ovens a year. The ovens are found in many of the most famous pizzerias in Italy and around the world; Ferrara has even delivered one to Honolulu!

There are two basic types of Ferrara ovens: one for bread and the other for pizza. The bread ovens operate at temperatures of up to 480°F, while the pizza ovens operate at more than 750°F.

Stefano built his first oven at the age of 13, when he and his father crafted a wood-burning oven for the famous Pizzeria Brandi in Naples. Ferrara explained that the best ovens are constructed just like the best pizzas: Only the best ingredients are used, and most of them are local. Stefano's father compared each new oven he made to a new son in the family, or a new brother for Stefano.

Stefano recalls that his father used to say that making ovens is all about love and passion, not money. When asked if his profession is more about making ovens or about feeding people, Stefano replied that it is both. "When these two elements join forces, the world is as it is meant to be."

Left: Stefano Ferrara and his wife, Maria Francesca Giangrande

CHAPTER 7

EQUIPMENT

MUST-HAVE TOOLS OF THE TRADE

Except for the oven itself, the equipment needed to make great pizza is not expensive. The following is a list of the most important equipment you will need for making pizza.

Baking Stone If you want to make pizza that stands out from your neighbor's pretty good pizza, or from pizza you have made before, we can't stress the importance of a baking stone enough. A preheated stone will perform miracles for a pizza crust, and today, there are baking stones made of stone (of course), but also of metal (called "baking steel"). There are also baking stones made of salt, but usually they are for uses other than making pizza.

It is important to preheat the baking stone to get the best results. This preheating can take up to an hour, so you'll need to plan ahead. To prepare the baking stone, remove the oven racks and place the stone on the bottom of the oven. Turn the oven up to its maximum baking heat (without the broiler), and give the oven at least half an hour—preferably a full hour—to thoroughly warm up the baking stone.

Pizza Peel There are many different types of pizza peels, which are also known as pizza shovels. Traditional peels are made of wood, but metal, usually aluminum, peels, are also readily available. Pizza peels come in different sizes, lengths, and shapes. Experts use a squarish peel for moving pizzas in and out of the oven and a smaller round peel to rotate the pizza in the oven for even baking.

If you are only going to make pizza at home, on a baking sheet in a conventional oven, then it is not so important to have a pizza peel. If you are going to use a baking stone or a larger oven, however, this tool is essential. When pizza is cooked in a wood-burning oven, a pizza peel is used both to move the pizza in and out of the oven and to move it around inside the oven. With a long peel, you can place a pizza in the back of the oven to cook multiple pizzas at once without burning yourself.

Pizza Wheel Although there are strong opinions in the pizza world about whether or not pizza should be cut into slices, most of us are used to cutting up pizza at home before serving. There are a lot of fun pizza wheels on the market today, some cooler than others. Do a search online, click on the pictures, read the user reviews, and enjoy ingenious solutions to pizza cutting, ranging from strictly utilitarian wheels to those shaped like lobsters to expensive designer models. The cool factor increases by just using a big knife, or better yet, the Italian mezzaluna, which is a large, curved knife with handles at both ends.

Electric Mixer or Food Processor

A sturdy stand mixer is good to have for making pizza dough. It is important to buy a machine with a powerful motor and a large metal bowl so there is plenty of room for the dough.

Knife

No matter what type of food you are making, it is important to own one or two good knives. You'll need them to cut up vegetables, meat, cheese, and other ingredients for making pizza. You can spend a small fortune on knives, but you don't have to; start with just one or two knives of the best quality you can afford, and add to your collection over time. It's also important that you learn how the knife should be sharpened. You can get lots of tips on the web, including detailed videos on sites like YouTube.

The most useful knives to own are a medium-sized chef's knife and a small paring knife for smaller cutting tasks and peeling. A good serrated bread knife, sometimes called a confectionery knife, is also handy.

Using a Pizza Peel

Use sharp, focused movements when using a pizza peel, along with cornmeal or semolina flour (regular flour can also work well) to help the pizza slide off the peel and into the oven. After dusting the peel with the cornmeal, drag the pizza onto the peel. Use your fingers to even up the edges if necessary. The pizza should now slide easily from the peel onto the oven floor or pizza stone. When sliding the pizza peel under the pizza, you must use a single, swift pushing motion.

Working too slowly can result in a pretty messy affair, and practice makes perfect. If the pizza needs a bit of readjustment once you get it onto the peel, just use your fingers to even up the edges. At this point, you can do a couple of short jerks with the peel to see if the pizza moves easily. If it sticks at any point, simply lift the crust carefully and sprinkle a bit more cornmeal or semolina underneath the dough wherever it is sticking to the peel. Excess moisture can also create problems so be sure that both your work surface and peel are completely dry while using.

Now the pizza is ready to be placed on the baking stone. Tip the peel slightly toward the baking stone and give the peel a good jerk to release the pizza, while drawing the peel toward you.

Dough Scraper A dough scraper is an essential tool. It is used to divide the dough into smaller bits but can also be used to scrape off the flour and dough residue from your work area. Dough scrapers can be made of plastic, metal, or wood; none are expensive.

Grater Occasionally, pizza calls for sliced cheese, but when cheese needs to be shredded, you'll need a grater (or a grater blade for your food processor). Some graters have a metal base that collects the cheese inside the grater and can then be removed to sprinkle the cheese over the pizza. There are many different models and sizes, but whichever appeals to you, be sure to purchase one sturdy enough to withstand a lot of use.

Pizza Pans Some types of pizza must be baked in a pan; others do not require it but will be easier to handle if you do. Deep pizza pans are ideal for baking Chicago-style deep-dish pizza. Shallower pans are used for most regular pizzas. We prefer high-quality black steel pans to lightweight aluminum ones, as they conduct heat better and give a crispier crust. Remember to take the finished pizza out of the pan before slicing, so as to avoid damaging the pan. A pizza pan without holes will result in a smoother, softer crust, while pans with holes will result in a crispier crust.

We have found that pizzas made with Neapolitan Dough (see page 192) and Our Favorite Dough (see page 191) are best when placed directly on a baking stone or stone oven floor.

Rolling Pin We prefer to stretch out pizza dough with our hands, but some prefer to roll it out with a rolling pin. Today, there are many different types of rolling pins on the market, but the old-fashioned type, made of wood with handles at both ends, works quite well.

Bowls Most of us have bowls of all sizes and types in the kitchen. To make pizza, you will need bowls for dough, cheese, sauce, and so on. If you want to emulate many of the world's finest chefs, you can measure the flour, yeast, salt, and water

Steel Pans

Steel pans, like cast-iron pans, require just a bit of TLC when it comes to cleaning, or they will rust. After each use, wash the pan in warm water, scrubbing with salt rather than soap if you need an abrasive. Wipe the pan completely dry, then wipe a bit of cooking oil over the entire inside of the pan. (A paper towel works perfectly for this task.) Most good steel pans will come with instructions for this process, which is part of maintaining the "seasoning" of the pan. A well-seasoned pan is easy to maintain and a joy to use.

Measure Consistently for Consistent Results

There are three basic and affordable measuring tools we recommend for any kitchen.

1. A set of dry measuring cups. These are nesting cups that measure one-quarter, one-third, one-half, and one cup of any dry ingredient. They should be loosely filled with the ingredient, then leveled off with the straight, dull edge of a knife. Some measuring cups show both American and metric measures. Heard about killing two birds with one stone?

2. A clear glass liquid measuring cup that holds two cups of liquid. This size is small enough to measure less than a cup of liquid accurately, and large enough to measure even 8 or 10 cups of liquid quickly. To measure liquids accurately, pour the liquid into the measuring cup, set the cup on the counter (or any level surface), and bring your eyes down to the cup's level to check that the liquid is exactly at the level you wanted.

3. A set of measuring spoons. These will be critical for accurately measuring teaspoons, tablespoons, and so on. Liquids can be poured into the appropriate spoon until it is filled, and dry ingredients should be scooped and then leveled with the straight, dull edge of a knife.

before you begin cooking, placing each ingredient in its own bowl in your work area. This makes it easier to follow a recipe accurately, and it means you will never again find yourself without an essential ingredient halfway through a recipe!

Measuring Cups and Measuring Spoons

It is, of course, okay to use visual estimates when making pizza dough, if you are an expert. For most of us, however, measuring the ingredients is critical, especially when it comes to dough, in order for the final product to end up as it should. There are too many home cooks—and even professional chefs, strangely enough—who do

not use measuring cups or spoons. Using these basic tools is easy, quick, and one of the best things you can do to ensure good results every time you bake.

Kitchen Scale

Although home cooks in the United States tend to measure by volume rather than weight, a good kitchen scale is an essential tool. Many recipes, especially those originating anywhere in Europe, require the use of a kitchen scale. Using a scale will greatly increase your reliable success in any baking project.

OVENS

The single most important piece of equipment needed for making pizza is an oven. There are hundreds, if not thousands, of possibilities for both commercial and home use.

Pizza ovens are built on deep-rooted traditions in the world of pizzerias. In Naples, it is common to use a wood-fired oven, and many will say this is the ultimate cooking tool for pizza. Pizzerias in the United States use electric, gas, and coal ovens, although coal-fired ovens are not as prominent today as they were in earlier times.

Most homes feature gas or electric ovens. One of the biggest differences between home ovens and commercial ovens is that most home ovens have a maximum heat of around 500°F—give or take 50°F—far less than the temperatures commercial pizza ovens can reach. Other options for making homemade pizzas are grills and tabletop pizza ovens.

The good news is that any decent oven can produce good pizza, though the type of oven and the maximum temperature it can achieve can drastically alter the final result.

Wood-Fired Ovens All self-respecting pizza fanatics at least wish that they had a wood-burning pizza oven. There have never been more of these ovens found in kitchens and backyards than there are today. There are a number of reasons, however, that most pizza lovers use their kitchen ovens to bake their homemade pizzas; these include a lack of time, space, money—or all three of these!

There is no question that a commercial oven, designed to operate at high temperatures, will deliver a different pizza than one baked in a nor-mal household oven. A wood-burning oven also has the advantage of that slight char flavor we associate with Neapolitan pizza. It is a unique experience to serve and eat pizza from a wood-fired pizza oven.

Let us just say that you, the reader, have a wood-burning oven, construction completed and ready to go. Follow the instructions for breaking in the oven and any other advice the producer may have for installing the oven. This process takes time. The oven must be insulated properly and then embedded with stone, clay, or brick. A wood-burning oven is the most basic of cookers. After all, this oven does not include any moving parts, bits and pieces of rubber and steel or electrical wires. What you actually have is the most advanced oven you could ever imagine.

The location of the oven is also important. It is critical that you have enough space in front for the opening of the oven. There should also be plenty of room behind you (as you stand in front of the oven's opening) for the long shaft of the pizza peel without compromising spectators and breakable fixtures.

The most important step towards becoming a great pizza maker is mastering the temperature inside the oven. In the classical, dome-shaped Italian pizza oven, heat is not just heat. The floor of the oven functions just like a very hot pan on a stove, heating by conduction. It is primarily this heat that gives the pizza crust that delicious, crispy, slightly charred surface. Placement of the pizza on the floor of the oven is paramount for good results. The pizza will need to be moved to different parts of the oven to ensure even cooking. Any oven will have hotter or cooler spots that will affect the final product.

Burning wood in the oven creates a flaming mass that rolls along the inside surface of the domed top. Think of this heat as the equivalent of the broiler element in a household oven. The extreme heat from above will melt the cheese and cook the different toppings on the pizza, caramelizing the flavors in meats and vegetables. The dome of the oven also produces a radiant heat from the intense heat it absorbs from the burning wood. This heat gives the oven consistent warmth and is irreplaceable when baking breads, meats, and other dishes during the long cooling-off period the oven goes through when the pizza baking is finished. No matter how good your pizzas are—and they will be very, very good—there are lots of other dishes that will achieve stunning results from your wood-burning oven.

Lastly, the burning wood and resulting coals are essential components to mastering the oven. The placement of the pizza in connection to the placement of the coal bed is extremely important, as is moving the pizza closer to or farther away from the heat source. The pizzas will also need to be rotated in order to bake evenly. It is often a good idea to use a pizza peel to lift the pizza slightly so that the bed of coals and wood can give a final char to the underside of the crust. A wood-burning oven is a simple oven, but one that requires dedication to master. Many pizzaioli agree: mastering the oven requires patience and practice, but it is very worth the effort.

Extra Equipment

You will need to invest in some basic equipment to use with your wood-burning oven: a long-handled brush for removing ashes, an oven hook, a scraper, and a long-handled peel called a *palino* (used for rotating pizzas in the oven). We also recommend that you have an infrared thermometer to measure the oven's temperature.

It is worth noting that using good-quality hardwood is an absolute must. The wood should also be dried for at least six months, preferably a year or more. Oak is a good example of hardwood, as are hickory, birch, and beech. Fruitwoods, such as apple, cherry, and pear, are also excellent choices; the same goes for pecan or almond, if available. Never use sappy woods such as pine, nor laminated woods such as plywood. Keep to hardwoods that are properly dried, and you will be fine.

As with any type of cooking equipment, cleanliness is very important. A clean oven is a happy oven. Follow the oven maker's advice for caring for your oven to achieve maximum quality and longevity.

Grill a Pizza?

Good ingredients and good techniques produce good pizza. When making pizza at home, one of the biggest challenges is temperature. A normal household oven generally cooks at temperatures up to 475–525°F (250–275°C), while a commercial oven will reach much higher temperatures. This will, of course, affect the baking of the pizza.

Most of us do not have a commercial pizza oven in our home kitchens, but many of us do have a grill. A gas grill can produce great pizza, but a charcoal grill comes the closest to mimicking pizza from a wood-burning oven. A hot grill with a lid, a baking stone, and presoaked wood chips can give you jaw-droppingly good pizza that you never imagined was possible at home.

There are three ways to grill. With the direct-heat method, food is grilled directly over the heat source. Direct grilling is best suited to smaller pieces of meat, vegetables, or fish.

With the indirect-heat method, food is placed next to the heat source (not directly over it). On a gas grill, at least one of the gas burners must be turned off. On a charcoal grill, you must place coal under only half of the grill grate. Indirect grilling is generally used for large pieces of meat and fish. To use indirect grilling, you must have a grill with a lid, which allows you to turn your grill into a type of oven.

The third grilling method is a combination of the direct and indirect methods. In this case, food is initially placed directly over the heat source, which provides a nice charcoal color, and then moved away from the heat source for the bulk of the cooking over indirect heat.

Gas Grilling Grill your pizza crust on direct heat (with the grill lid closed) until it is golden. Remove the crust from the grill and turn it over. Add your pizza ingredients—sauce, cheese, toppings—to the side you just toasted, and place the pizza back on the grill. If you use a pizza stone, you can maintain a high temperature. If not, place the pizza on indirect heat (with the burners under the pizza turned off), at as high a temperature as possible. Bake until the cheese is melted and bubbling and the crust is golden underneath. If the crust is not quite ready, slide the pizza to direct heat, but be vigilant so as to avoid burning the crust. Remember, it is important to keep the lid closed on the grill as much as possible to avoid temperature drops.

Charcoal Grilling There is a lot of pizza equipment on the market today, but none of it is necessary to get great pizzas from your charcoal grill. For great results, soak two or three handfuls of wood chips (hickory chips work well) in water. The soaking will help the chips produce smoke instead of burning up when strewn over hot coals.

Create a layer of hot charcoal or briquettes that covers the entire base of the grill. Place another layer of charcoal or briquettes on top of the hot coals, set the grate carefully on the grill, and place a baking stone on the grate. Close the lid on the grill, and let the baking stone heat for at least half an hour.

Using grill mitts, carefully remove the grate with the baking stone on top. Set the grate on a heat-resistant surface, such as concrete or steel. Add a single layer of charcoal or briquettes, giving them a few minutes to be ignited by the coals underneath. Place the grate (with the baking stone) back on the grill, and close the lid.

Wait 10 minutes to allow the grill to reach maximum temperature. Working quickly, open the lid, dust the baking stone with cornmeal or semolina, and place the prepared pizza on the baking stone. Toss a handful or two of wood chips over the coals, and close the lid. After about 30 seconds, the chips will start smoking, adding a classic smoky flavor to your pizza. Remove the pizza from the grill when the crust is done and the cheese is melted and bubbling.

Note: With the high heat from the grill, the pizza shouldn't need more than 5-6 minutes. Check (quickly) on the pizza after a couple of minutes to see how it is progressing.

RECIPES

It was no easy job choosing the 60 finalists for the recipe section of this book. We knew early on that we hoped to receive recipes from some of the talented people we met on our journey. Several responded and for that we are eternally grateful. Others were too busy running their pizzerias and baking their pizzas. We understand, of course, though there was a glimmer of hope that we would receive even more keys to the magical pizza kingdom.

We knew that classic pizzas such as Margherita, a New Haven Clam Pie, and a really good Cheese Pizza had to be included. The rest of the pizzas are some of our personal favorites. Tore's breakfast pizza, served to him after a long drive from Norway to Italy: check. Mats' near religious experience with Motorino's use of brussels sprouts: check. Kenneth's Bonata and Craig's homage to Pizzeria Bianco: check and check! They are all here.

Ladies and gents, on with the apron and on with the oven. Here are pizzas for the entire family as well as friends and colleagues. There is a whole world of exciting pizzas waiting out there and it's time we get started baking!

CHAPTER 8

LET'S MAKE A PIZZA

BEFORE YOU START

The steps that follow will give the recipes a cleaner appearance, and once you have tried a few of the pizzas in this book, you will be in total control. Remember, there is not a single recipe in this book that you cannot master, whether it is making dough with a starter or trying out a seemingly exotic pizza. We have made every effort to ensure you can make great pizzas at home, using equipment and ingredients accessible to anyone.

A note about the measurements: The recipes were originally developed in Norway, and the metric measurements were used. We converted these measurements to make these recipes accessible to American readers, but some of these measurements are close but not exact. If you are motivated to get the most exact measurements for each of these dough recipes, we encourage cooks to use a scale and measure using the metrics.

The Dough You can relax now. You don't have to throw the dough in the air or twirl it on your fingertips. Although the throw-in-the-air technique works well and can be fun to practice, you get an equally good pizza crust from either rolling or pressing out the dough.

There are other techniques that are essential for good dough, however. The first of these is to "understand" the dough. Your dough will tell you how things are going. If the consistency is too hard or too soft, or if the dough has not finished rising (or does not rise at all), it will let you know.

To make good dough requires a little understanding, a little practice, and a little love. We shall say this only once: everyone—absolutely everyone—can make good dough. This includes even those who think that they cannot do anything in the kitchen.

For detailed instructions on how to make dough, see page 187.

Good Pizza Following a few simple tips will help you avoid the usual pizza pitfalls and make your pizza more beautiful, more delicious, and easier to work with. You will be the master of your pizza's fate.

Please—we beg you!—leave a sauce-and-ingredient-free edge around your pizza. One inch is enough. The Italians even have a name for this lovely part of the pizza, the *cornicione*. This area is holy. Abstaining from putting toppings on the cornicione will also give you a puffier edge, something you will learn to love.

Normally, it is recommended that you top your pizza crust with the sauce first, then the cheese, then any toppings. This process works well with some toppings and not so well with others. Fresh herbs or spinach often work better placed underneath the cheese, or even added raw to the finished pizza. Large pieces of onion or peppers should be sautéed lightly in oil before going on a pizza, but thin pieces of the same can be used raw. Fatty sausage or ground meat can be partially precooked or even poached to reduce some of the fat and avoid making the pizza greasy. Leaner meat products can be used raw, and if you are using cured ham, it should always be placed on top of the pizza after it has been baked.

Don't be afraid to experiment with the order in which ingredients are placed on your pizza. Some of our favorite pizzas reverse the order and achieve wonderful results, such as some of the better Chicago deep-dish pizzas, or one of our New York favorites, the Upside Down Pizza at Pizza Suprema.

We also suggest using less of everything (sauce, cheese, and toppings) in the center of a pizza and more farther out toward the edge. This will help you avoid a soupy center—though some of us actually like that (after all, what are spoons for?).

You will find recipes for dough and sauces on pages 187–199. Of course, if you prefer another type of crust or sauce, use it! In recipes using a different type of sauce, such as the mustard sauce on our Big Easy Pizza (page 252), the sauce recipe will be included with the recipe for the pizza.

Mozzarella In this book we used different types of mozzarella. If the recipe calls for mozzarella we are referring to the "block mozzarella" found in stores. The term fresh mozzarella refers to the Italian fior di latte (fresh cow milk mozzarella). When the recipe calls for mozzarella di bufala we are referring to fresh mozzarella made of water buffalo milk.

When using fresh mozzarella, especially mozzarella di bufala, you may want to remove some of the excess moisture in the cheese. This will also make your pizza less "soupy." Place a mozzarella ball in a towel and squeeze. You can also tear the mozzarella into pieces and lay them on paper towels for a few minutes before topping your pizza.

One last mozzarella tip: We like to use our fresh mozzarella at room temperature instead of right from the fridge. We store the balls of cheese on paper towels inside a bowl. Bringing the cheese to room temperature will also allow time for it to release some of its moisture.

Pecorino Another great pizza cheese is pecorino. There are several varieties of this cheese, but the most common is Pecorino Romano, a hard, grating cheese. Pecorino is made of sheep's milk and is often grated over pizza like Parmesan.

Pizza Composition 101 We cannot say enough about the "less is more" principle. Far too many pizzas have excessive amounts of cheese and toppings on them. In fact, good cheese and your favorite toppings will make a better pizza if used sparingly. The best argument for this is that by now the crust you are making is so unbelievably good that you will want everyone to taste it.

Of course, it's hard to argue with personal preference. If you really love double cheese, then you will probably double up the amount of cheese no matter what these silly authors say. And that is just fine. Even in our little group, there are tendencies toward extra anchovies or a sprinkle of Parmesan no matter what. The key here is to achieve balance in your pizzas. You will be glad you did!

Time and Temperature One of the more complicated aspects of cooking from recipes is the relationship between the cooking time and the oven temperature. The temperature from one oven to another can vary greatly, and any change in oven temperature will also affect the cooking time.

Generally speaking, we will bake a pizza at as high a temperature as we can. For typical home cooks, it is more often the oven itself that limits the maximum temperature. Therefore, it is extremely difficult, and actually a bit risky, to specify exact times and temperatures. Some of the pizza recipes in this book, such as the Pecan Pizza Pie Anno 2013 (page 276), call for a set temperature, and we will use these temperatures (and times) where necessary. Otherwise, we wish to appeal to common sense: maximum

temperature paired with maximum attentiveness. When the crust is golden, the cheese is bubbling, and the top of the pizza has a great color, you should be ready to roll.

Mise en Place One thing French chefs have mastered is the art of being prepared, and in the kitchen, this practice is nonnegotiable. The French even have a term for this called *mise en place* ("putting in place"), and the gist of it is that anything you can do ahead of time should be done ahead of time. This includes washing and cutting vegetables, making sauces and relishes, or checking your cupboards and fridge to make sure all the necessary ingredients are there (and making a list for anything you need to purchase). It means allowing enough time for dough to properly rise and giving ingredients the proper time to marinate. Mise en place will set you up to succeed in any culinary endeavor.

For pizza making, part of the mise en place is having on hand extra virgin olive oil, a small bowl of sea salt, a bowl with flour for your work surface, another bowl for semolina or cornmeal for your pizza peel, and your baking stone.

For those of you using a baking stone and a pizza peel, our advice is to use them and enjoy your inner pizzaiolo. We have not included these two pieces of equipment in each and every recipe. If you have them, use them. If not, do not worry—you will be fine, and so will your pizza.

DOUGH RECIPES

CREATING A GREAT FOUNDATION

Nearly everyone who enjoys pizza can recall that moment when a great pizza spoke to them. Maybe it was the greatest sauce ever; stringy, gooey mozzarella; or an unexpected, to-die-for topping. All of these moments are relevant, but the undeniable key to any great pizza is the crust. Good ingredients on a poorly made crust do not a great pizza make.

It may sound simple: flour, salt, yeast, and water. But making a great crust is more than just these few ingredients. The type and quality of these ingredients is critical. Is the flour low or high in protein? Winter wheat or summer wheat? Italian or American, or maybe Canadian? And what about the yeast: dry or cake, or one of any number of starters—some days old, others decades?

The techniques and equipment used in making the dough are also very important. A hand-kneaded dough will be different from a machine-kneaded dough—not necessarily better, but different.

The type of oven used and the oven's temperature will also affect the finished crust. Add to this the water being used, the manner in which the ingredients were produced, and the myriad small additions of oil or flavorings, and

you begin to understand just how complicated things can get.

There are important other factors to consider, as well: Do you want a thin, Neapolitan crust, or a deep-pan crust for a Chicago-style pizza? How long will you have to wait before the dough is ready to bake? And so on. Making great crust is something anyone with a bit of patience and dedication can master, but you must always use the very best ingredients you can, measure them precisely, and handle them with care to create the best dough possible. After all, all baking is a science as well as an art.

You will find several good dough recipes in this book. Their taste and consistency vary, but all are equally good. The recipes call for a stand mixer, preferably a heavy one with a large motor, which will keep the mixer from overheating during the kneading process. If this happens, stop the mixer and let it cool off before continuing. All dough recipes can also be made by hand, and this kind of working out is rewarding in more ways than one!

Give the dough recipes a try, and feel free to adjust them to your taste. These pizza doughs are wonderful in taste and because they really work. Follow the recipes carefully. If your first attempt isn't quite up to your standards, you will find that your next attempt will be better.

About the Ingredients

None of the ingredients we use are difficult to acquire, although Italian flour may not be a standard item at all grocery stores. Here is some more information about the most important dough ingredients.

Salt

We have witnessed salt's transformation from a kitchen basic to one of the hippest ingredients around. Today, you can purchase a wide range of great salts from all parts of the world. We recommend using a good-quality sea salt in your dough, though normal table salt will also work well. Salt is, without a doubt, one of food's most important ingredients, and even though we are careful about the amount of salt we use in the recipes, salt plays an important role in creating delicious dough. Salt not only adds flavor to the dough, it helps strengthen the gluten, and it assists in the rising process.

Yeast

In some recipes, we use dry yeast, in others, fresh. Both types will work well in all the recipes (after adjusting the amount), but we have specified the type we have found works best with each recipe. Remember to check the expiration date before using any type of yeast.

Flour

We have selected different types of flour for the dough recipes. All-purpose flour is sometimes called for, but in some recipes we have specified using a flour containing a minimum of 12 percent protein. This information is found on the flour's package. The amount of protein is important and, in some recipes, critical for success. In our Chicago Deep-Dish Dough, we also use cornmeal. Our favorite is stone-ground cornmeal.

Water

Some pizzaioli credit their pizza crust's flavor to the local water they use. This may be the case, but in our recipes, tap water will work just fine.

Alternate Doughs

There are other types of dough we want to mention: whole wheat, gluten free, dough with herbs and other flavorings, and others. Working with alternative doughs is exciting, but some may prove to be more difficult to master than others. We have not included alternative doughs in this book; if you are interested, we suggest checking out the wealth of information, tips, and recipes available online.

If you want to make a coarser textured dough, you can replace some of the regular flour with whole wheat flour. This will work well as long as the percentage of whole wheat flour is not too high. A mixture of 80 percent all-purpose flour to 20 percent whole wheat flour should work fine; with any higher percentage of whole wheat flour, the dough can be difficult to work with. In Italy, we met pizza makers who use coarsely ground flour, but they often use specialty flours and more complicated preparation methods.

We also want to mention sourdough, or, in Italian, *lievito madre* or *lievito naturale* (mother yeast or natural yeast). Sourdough uses a starter instead of cake or dry yeast. Making a great sourdough pizza dough requires practice. Sourdough enthusiasts have starters that they feed to keep alive for months, years, or even decades. If you have a dedicated baker somewhere inside of you, you will want to devote some time to mastering this unique type of dough.

Working the Dough, Step by Step

Anyone who has made pizza at home has probably suffered a frustrating moment or two with their dough. Sometimes the dough ends up hard, making it difficult to work with. Other times, it can be sticky or too dry. And what about when the dough you stretch or roll out either tears or springs back, as if saying, "Stop messing with me!"? Is your finished crust crispy and almost cracker-like? Is it pale and soft? Watching talented pizzaioli working their dough makes pizza-making seem simple, but in fact a dough is a living thing, often with a mind of its own.

If there were ever just one essential tip for making pizza dough, it would have to be: Give it time. Some good pizza doughs require little to no kneading; others more. Any dough will be improved by a longer rise, even though a good dough can be made using a shorter rising time.

Some dough recipes require a good 10 minutes of constant kneading, either by machine or by hand, and every minute of this time is necessary for the dough to reach perfection, no matter which kneading method you use.

Here is a step-by-step guide to forming pizza dough once it has finished its rising process. Any deviations from this standard process will be noted in the recipes themselves.

It is important to use a work surface (preferably of stone, steel, or wood) that has been dusted with just enough flour to keep the dough from sticking to the work surface (or your hands). Using too much flour on your work surface will result in too much flour being worked into the dough, and that will change the consistency of your crust.

- Dust flour on the work surface.
- Place the dough on the floured surface. Grip the dough nearest you with one hand, and, with your other hand, press the dough outwards. Turn the dough 90 degrees, and repeat the process.
- Grip the dough with your hands, and make an indentation in the middle of the dough with your thumbs.
- Turn the dough over and form into a ball, drawing the edges of the dough toward the indentation.
- Using a dough scraper, cut the dough into the number of individual balls specified in the recipe.
- Grip one of the small balls of dough and press your thumbs into the center.
- Turn the ball of dough over, drawing the edges of the dough toward the indentation. The dough ball is now ready. Place the dough balls on a floured tray and dust the tops with flour.
- The time has come to turn the balls of dough into a pizza crust. Dust flour on your work surface, and flatten a dough ball on the surface with your hand.
- Stretch the dough slightly with your fingers while rotating it.
- Lay your cupped hand on one side of the dough. Pick up the opposite edge of the dough with your other hand and "slap" this side of the dough over the back of your cupped hand. Rotate the dough, and repeat a few more times to increase the diameter of the dough.
- Lay one hand flat on the side of the dough nearest your other hand. Use the fingers of the other hand to lift the edge of the dough over your flattened hand. Turn the flattened hand upside down with the other side of the dough hanging onto the work surface. Flip the dough over, flat onto the work surface.
- Lay both hands flat on the surface of the dough and work the dough clockwise, slightly stretching and giving the dough its final form.
- You are now ready to add sauce, cheese, and toppings.

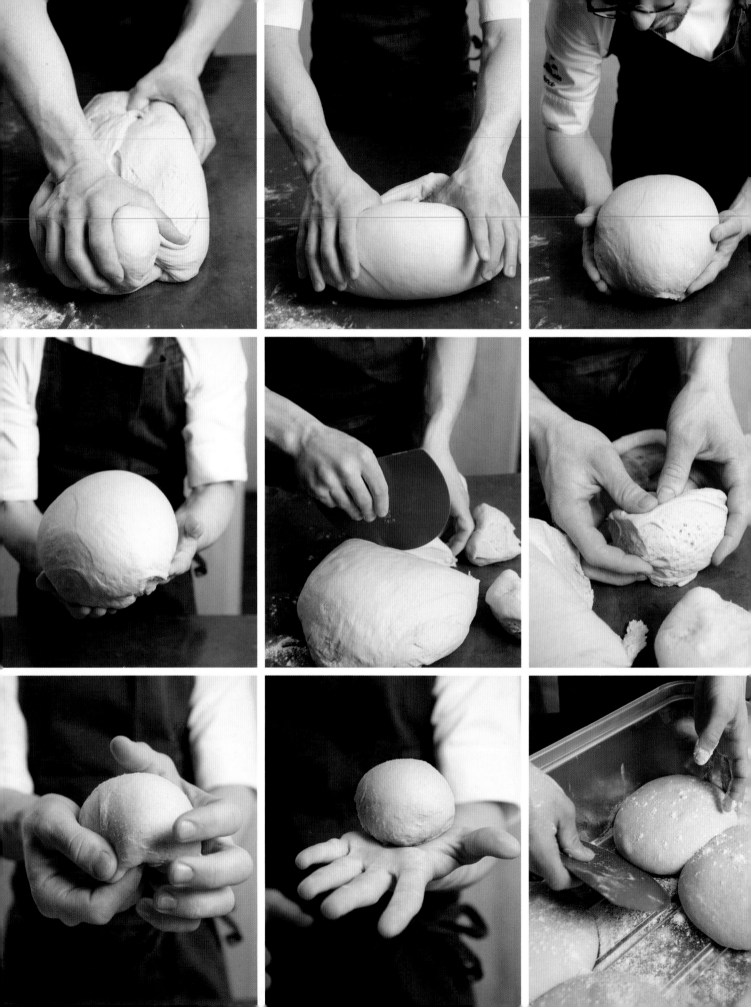

OUR FAVORITE DOUGH

Yield: About 5 9-ounce (260-g) pieces

Easy to work with, this is the perfect pizza dough. We are confident this will become your go-to dough!

Pre-Dough

1 teaspoon (5 g) fresh yeast

⅓ cup plus 1½ tablespoons (100 mL) lukewarm water

⅓ cup plus 1½ tablespoons (1 dl) all-purpose flour

Main Dough

2 teaspoons (10 g) fresh yeast

2 ¼ cups (500 mL) lukewarm water

7 cups (1 kg) all-purpose flour

1 tablespoon (15 g) table salt

Pre-Dough

1. In a small bowl, add the yeast to the water, and stir to dissolve.

2. Add the flour to the yeast mixture and stir.

3. Cover the bowl with plastic wrap and let stand at room temperature for at least 2 hours, preferably as long as 4–5 hours. The mixture should form bubbles on its surface.

Main Dough

1. In a small bowl, add the yeast to the water, and stir to dissolve.

2. Place the flour and salt in the bowl of a stand mixer fitted with a dough hook.

3. Add the yeast mixture and the Pre-Dough to the flour mixture.

4. Run the mixer on its lowest setting until the dough is shiny and smooth (about 15 minutes). If the dough feels a bit dry or hard just add a bit more water (a tablespoon at a time).

5. Pour the dough into another bowl. Cover with plastic wrap and chill in the refrigerator for 24 hours, or up to 48 hours.

6. Remove the dough from the refrigerator. Punch it down to remove air.

7. Divide the dough into 5 or more pieces, depending on how many pizzas you are making. (A 12-inch [30-cm] pizza uses about 9 ounces [260 g] of dough.) Form each piece into a ball and place them on a tray. Cover any dough you are not using right away and store it in the refrigerator for later use, or freeze. Give the dough you are using enough time to reach room temperature. This can take up to 2 hours.

8. Place the dough pieces on a tray and cover with a thin layer of flour.

9. Cover the tray with plastic wrap and let the dough rise to double its original size. It is now ready to use.

Tips

You can make a quicker version of this dough by using 4 teaspoons (20 g) of fresh yeast instead of 2 teaspoons (10 g) in the Main Dough. When you reach step 5, let the dough rise to double its original size. Divide the dough into portions, and use. The shorter time will result in a crust that is less flavorful, but still good.

NEAPOLITAN DOUGH

Yield: About 5 9-ounce (260-g) pieces

This is the classic Neapolitan dough: flour, salt, yeast, and water. It is an incredible dough made from the simplest of ingredients.

¾ teaspoon (3 g) fresh yeast

2¼ cups (500 mL) lukewarm water, divided

1⅛ tablespoons (17 g) table salt

6 cups, 2 tablespoons (950 g) Tipo "00" flour (see Tips) (all-purpose flour will also work)

1. In a small bowl, add the yeast to half of the water, and stir to dissolve.

2. In another small bowl, dissolve the salt in the remaining water.

3. Place the flour in the bowl of a stand mixer fitted with a dough hook.

4. Running the mixer on its lowest setting, add both the yeast mixture and the salt mixture. Mix for a couple minutes until the dough comes together.

5. Increase the mixer's speed to medium, and blend until the dough is shiny and not too sticky (5–6 minutes). If the dough "climbs" up the side of the bowl, turn off the mixer and push the dough down with a wooden spoon.

6. Reduce the mixer's speed to low and continue mixing for 3–4 minutes. The dough should be shiny, and it should come away from the sides of the bowl cleanly.

7. Transfer the dough onto a floured work surface. Sprinkle a bit more flour over the top, turn the dough, and make into a large ball.

8. Divide the dough into 5 or more pieces, depending on how many pizzas you are making. Form each piece into a ball and place them on a tray. Brush the dough pieces with oil. Cover the tray with plastic wrap and refrigerate for 18–24 hours.

Notes

To save time, keep the dough at a cool room temperature for 6–8 hours until the dough has doubled in size.

If the dough has been refrigerated, remove and let stand for 2 hours before using.

Tips

We often prefer using Tipo "0" flour over Tipo "00," although both will make for a great dough. The Tipo "0" is not quite as soft as Tipo "00" and works great for pizza dough. You will need a bit less water if using Tipo "0." Do yourself a favor and try both types of flour to see which one you prefer.

Each of the following pizza recipes has been tagged with an icon indicating which type of dough it requires. Use this key to help determine which pizzas can be prepared with any leftover dough you have on hand.

● Our Favorite Dough

● Neapolitan Dough

● The Wet One Dough

● New York Sicilian Dough

● Classic New York Dough

● Chicago Deep-Dish Dough

THE WET ONE DOUGH

Yield: About 3 9-ounce (280-g) pieces

We love this dough! It contains a lot of moisture, making it more difficult to work with than other dough recipes, but its advantages are that it is amazingly easy to make (a couple of minutes and bang, you're done), and the resulting crust is wonderful. This dough will be easier to master after you have made it a couple of times, so don't miss out on using it for your favorite pizzas.

3¼ cups (500 g) flour (any kind will do)
1 tablespoon (16 g) table salt
¼ teaspoon dry yeast
1½ cups (350 mL) water

1. In a large bowl, combine the flour, salt, and yeast. Add the water, and mix together with a wooden spoon. (Don't worry; the dough is supposed to be this runny.) Cover the bowl with plastic wrap, and let rise at room temperature for 18–24 hours until the dough has doubled in size.

2. Sprinkle a thin layer of flour on a work surface. Use a spatula to carefully transfer the dough from the pan to the floured surface. Divide the dough into 4 balls.

3. Dip your fingers in flour, and carefully lift and fold the sides of each ball of dough toward the middle of the dough.

4. Gently turn each dough ball over so that the seams are underneath. Use more flour as needed to keep it from sticking. The dough can now be used, or you can place the dough balls on a tray and cover them with plastic wrap. (Be sure there is enough flour on top of the dough balls so that the plastic does not stick to them.) You can keep them in the refrigerator for up to 3 days.

Note

> If the dough has been refrigerated, let it stand at room temperature for about 2 hours before use.

NEW YORK SICILIAN DOUGH

Yield: 2 pounds 3 ounces (about 1 kg), enough for 1 12 x 16-inch (30 x 40-cm) baking pan

This Sicilian-inspired dough is often found on menus for pizzerias in the New York area. It is fairly thick and usually baked in a rectangular pan.

3½ cups (500 g) all-purpose flour (preferably with 12–14 percent protein)
⅔ cup (150 mL) extra virgin olive oil, divided
2 teaspoons (10 g) table salt
1 teaspoon dry yeast
1½ cups (350 mL) room-temperature water

1. Place the flour, 3 tablespoons (45 mL) of the olive oil, salt, and yeast in the bowl of a stand mixer fitted with a dough hook.

2. Running the mixer on medium speed, add the water. Mix until the dough comes together (2–3 minutes).

3. Increase the mixer's speed and blend until the dough is shiny (5–6 minutes). The dough should stick to the bottom of the bowl but not to the sides.

4. Line the bottom of a 12 x 16-inch (30 x 40-cm) baking pan with parchment paper.

5. Pour the remaining olive oil onto the parchment-lined pan and spread it over the entire surface with your hands.

6. Transfer the dough onto the baking pan. Turn it over so that the top of the dough is covered in oil.

7. Stretch the dough carefully until it covers the bottom of the baking pan.

8. Let the dough rest for 15–20 minutes, and then stretch the dough again so that it covers the bottom of the entire baking pan.

9. Cover the pan with plastic wrap, and let the dough rise at room temperature for 2 hours.

CLASSIC NEW YORK DOUGH

Yield: About 4 10-ounce (300-g) pieces

This dough is the type that is used for many American pizzas, especially those from, or inspired by, the New York area. This dough is different from the others because it commonly contains sugar or honey and oil. It also uses all-purpose flour, preferably with a minimum of 12 percent protein. Using this type of flour will give you the elastic quality characteristic of a New York–style pizza dough.

2 teaspoons dry yeast

1 cup (250 mL) lukewarm water

1 cup (250 mL) cold water

2 teaspoons honey or sugar

1 tablespoon (17 g) table salt

2 tablespoons extra virgin olive oil

4¾ cups (700 g) all-purpose flour (preferably with 12–14 percent protein)

1. In a small bowl, add the yeast to the lukewarm water, and stir to dissolve.

2. Combine the cold water, honey or sugar, salt, and olive oil in another bowl. Stir well until the salt and sugar or honey are dissolved.

3. Place the flour into the bowl of a stand mixer fitted with a dough hook.

4. Running the mixer on its lowest setting, add both the yeast mixture and the sugar and salt mixture. Mix for a couple minutes until the dough comes together.

5. Turn off the mixer and let the dough rest for 5 minutes.

6. Run the mixer at low speed until the dough is shiny and not too sticky (5–6 minutes). If the dough comes up the side of the bowl, turn off the mixer and push the dough down with a wooden spoon.

7. Transfer the dough onto a floured work surface. Knead the dough until it comes together in a large ball. Use more flour if necessary to ensure that the dough is no longer sticky.

8. Divide the dough into 3 or more pieces, depending on how many pizzas you are making. Form each piece into a ball and place the balls on a tray. Brush the balls of dough with the olive oil. Cover the tray with plastic wrap, and refrigerate for 12–24 hours.

Note

If the dough has been refrigerated, let it stand at room temperature for about 2 hours before use.

CHICAGO DEEP-DISH DOUGH

Yield: 1 14-inch (36-cm) deep-dish pizza

The dough for Chicago's famous deep-dish pizza is unique for many reasons, not the least of which is that it works so well with the other ingredients on this one-of-a-kind pizza. In this recipe, the dough is composed of flour and cornmeal. Not all deep-dish dough recipes use both types of flour, but this one is without a doubt our favorite.

Pre-Dough

2 teaspoons dry yeast

⅓ cup (100 mL) lukewarm water

4 tablespoons all-purpose flour

1 teaspoon sugar

Main Dough

2¾ (400 g) all-purpose flour

½ cup plus 3 tablespoons (150 mL) lukewarm water

⅔ cup (100 g) cornmeal

1 teaspoon (6 g) table salt

5 tablespoons extra virgin olive oil

Pre-Dough

1. In the bowl of a stand mixer, dissolve the yeast in the lukewarm water.

2. Add the all-purpose flour and sugar, and stir with a spatula.

3. Cover the bowl with plastic wrap, and let stand at room temperature for 30 minutes. The mixture should be bubbling on its surface.

Main Dough

1. Place the all-purpose flour, lukewarm water, cornmeal, salt, and olive oil in the bowl with the Pre-Dough.

2. Fit the mixer with a dough hook, and run the mixer on low speed until the dough comes together into a large ball. Add more water if necessary.

3. Turn off the mixer and let the dough rest for 5 minutes.

4. Run the mixer on medium–low speed until the dough is shiny and slightly sticky (2–3 minutes).

5. Transfer the dough onto a floured work surface. Knead the dough for a couple more minutes, until it is a smooth ball.

6. Place the dough in a large bowl, cover with plastic wrap, and let it rise to double its original size (2–3 hours).

7. Punch down the dough and knead again on the work surface for 3–4 minutes. The dough is now ready to use.

Tips

When making the pizza, roll out the dough first and then move it to the baking pan, using your fingers to press the dough up the sides of the pan. Let the dough rise a bit (about 20 minutes) before adding toppings.

CHAPTER 10

SAUCE RECIPES

SAUCES

A good tomato sauce does not need to cook for hours and hours. Many pizzaioli never cook their sauces. With good tomatoes—even canned ones—it is enough simply to enhance them with a pinch of salt.

Here are our two basic sauces, one cooked in the best marinara style, the other uncooked. The recipes in this book refer to the sauce we recommend for each pizza, but feel free to substitute with another of your favorite sauces. And needless to say, fresh, ripe tomatoes are welcome on a great pizza. They can replace the tomato sauce or enhance it.

"SIMPLE IS OFTEN BEST" TOMATO SAUCE

Yield: 28 ounces (800 g)

This simple combination of tomatoes and salt is not really even a sauce, but it is used by pizzaioli the world over, especially in Naples. Simple to prepare and oh so delizioso!

1 (28-ounce [800-g]) can tomatoes (our favorite is the real San Marzano tomato)

½ teaspoon sea salt (less, or possibly none, if the tomatoes are salted)

1. Drain the tomatoes in a colander for a few minutes.

2. Use your fingers to lightly crush the tomatoes, and let them drain for a couple more minutes.

3. Pour the tomatoes into a bowl and crush them thoroughly with your fingers or a potato masher. You can use a food processor, but that will take all the fun out of using your hands to play with the tomatoes.

4. Stir in the salt to taste. Let the tomatoes rest for a few minutes.

5. Taste again and adjust the salt if necessary.

But:

This recipe requires using very good tomatoes (preferably true San Marzano DOP tomatoes). If the tomatoes are very acidic, you might want to add a pinch of sugar to them. If they taste a bit flat, you can add a splash of wine vinegar or lemon juice. After you add the sugar, vinegar, or lemon juice, let the tomatoes rest for a few minutes, and then taste. Adjust if necessary. These added minutes will give you a better sauce.

And finally:

If you wish, you can add some fresh or dried herbs (usually basil and/or oregano) to the sauce. A small amount will give the sauce an extra dimension. You can also try a bit of crushed fresh garlic or freshly ground black pepper, but remember that the sauce is called "Simple Is Often Best," and when you use great tomatoes you do not really need anything other than a pinch of salt.

LA SALSA (COOKED TOMATO SAUCE)

Yield: about 40 ounces (1100 grams)

This sauce is often called "marinara" (not to be confused with the pizza of the same name). The sauce includes classic Italian ingredients such as garlic and basil, and you simmer it just like your grandmother did (or would have done if she were Italian). This great pizza sauce can also be used in pasta dishes, with chicken or fish, or even with baked or grilled vegetables.

1 (28-ounce [800-g]) can tomatoes (the best you can find)

3 tablespoons extra virgin olive oil

1 medium onion, chopped

Pinch sea salt

Pinch freshly ground black pepper

1–2 garlic cloves, minced

Pinch dried oregano

3–4 large fresh basil leaves

1. Strain the tomatoes through a colander placed over a bowl. Reserve the juices.

2. Pour the tomatoes into a large bowl and crush them with your fingers or a potato masher.

3. Warm the oil in a large saucepan over medium heat.

4. Add the onion, salt, and pepper. Cook over medium heat for a couple of minutes.

5. Add the garlic and cook for another minute or so, until the vegetables are soft but not browned.

6. Add the drained tomatoes and the oregano, and stir well. Reduce the heat and simmer for about 15 minutes. Add some of the reserved tomato juice if the sauce is too thick.

7. Add the basil leaves, stir, and season to taste with the salt and pepper. Let the sauce simmer for a few more minutes. Let the sauce cool before using on your pizza.

Variation
SPICY TOMATO SAUCE

Some people like a spicier tomato sauce on their pizza. No problem. Just add a minced chile or two, and cook with the onion and garlic. Another method is to add red pepper flakes or cayenne pepper to the tomatoes. Start with 1 teaspoon and increase the amount to taste.

Tips

This sauce will be even better when it has been allowed to rest for a few hours or overnight. Cover the bowl with plastic wrap and refrigerate.

You can omit the basil leaves if you wish, especially if you plan to use fresh basil on your pizza.

If you have a piece of Parmigiano-Reggiano, you can remove a chunk of the rind and cook it in the sauce. Remove the rind when the sauce has completely cooled, and discard.

Topping Your Pizza

Here are pictures showing a Pizza Margherita La Casa (page 209) being prepared:

- Spread tomato sauce in a circular motion using a tablespoon, or, as in the picture, spread crushed tomatoes over the surface of the dough.
- Spread basil leaves over the pizza if using them before baking. If not, simply add the fresh basil after the pizza comes out of the oven.
- Tear fresh mozzarella into pieces and spread them sparingly and evenly over the tomatoes and basil. Be careful not to have too much cheese in the center of the pizza, or it will have a soupy center.
- Drizzle a small amount of olive oil over the pizza in a circular motion.
- Slide the pizza onto a floured pizza peel, using your fingers to reshape it slightly, if necessary.
- If all goes well, this is the result you can expect when the pizza comes out of the oven!

CHAPTER 11
PIZZA RECIPES

Panna Cucina (p. 234)

Pizza Marinara	p. 205	Kesté's Pistacchio e Salsiccia Pizza	p. 240
Pizza Margherita Veronese	p. 206	Cali-Zone	p. 241
Pizza Margherita La Casa	p. 209	Chicago Deep-Dish Pizza	p. 242
Calzone Fior di Latte	p. 210	Chicago Thin-Crust Pizza	p. 243
Pizza Fritta	p. 211	Tony G's Honey Pizza	p. 245
Verdure Sulla Pizza	p. 212	Norgesvenn Pizza	p. 246
Pizza Quattro Stagioni	p. 214	An Oklahoma Boy's Pizza	p. 249
Focaccia with Cherry Tomatoes	p. 215	Green and Mean Pizza	p. 251
Sfincione	p. 216	The Big Easy Pizza	p. 252
Scampi with Pesto Pizza	p. 218	Rome Antics Pizza	p. 254
BBQ Pizza	p. 218	Grekenland Pizza	p. 255
Pizza with Ham and Mushrooms	p. 219	Blue Pizza	p. 257
Bacon Cheeseburger Pizza	p. 219	Tore's Breakfast Pizza	p. 259
Focaccia with Rosemary	p. 220	Pizza Cipolle e Parmigiano-Reggiano	p. 260
Stefano Ferrara's Pizza with Potato and Ham	p. 221	Spring Swing Pizza	p. 261
Pizza Primavera	p. 222	Pizza Aglio, Olio, e Peperoncino	p. 262
Pizza Lardo, Pepe Nero, e Pecorino	p. 224	New Old El Paso Pizza	p. 262
Pizza Quattro Formaggi	p. 225	Hot Salami Pizza	p. 263
Pizza Caiazzo	p. 226	Pizza al Tonno	p. 263
Pizza Salsiccia e Cipolla	p. 227	Mats's Great Lake Pizza	p. 265
Pizza Imbottita con Salsicce e Friarielli	p. 229	Pizza with Brussels Sprouts	p. 266
Dominick DeMarco's Pizza	p. 230	Bonata	p. 269
New Haven Apizza Tomato Pizza	p. 232	Pissaladière	p. 270
New York–Sicilian Hybrid Pizza	p. 233	Rolled-Up Calzone with Ricotta and Salami	p. 271
Panna Cucina	p. 234	Smokin' Salmon Pizza	p. 273
Cheese Pizza	p. 234	Il Mantuano	p. 274
Pizza Napoletana	p. 234	Pecan Pizza Pie Anno 2013	p. 276
Aloha Pizza	p. 235	Nutella Alla Spacca Napoli	p. 278
New Haven Clam Pie	p. 237	Dessert Pizza with Chèvre	p. 280
"Il Fiore Delle Donne"	p. 239		

PIZZA MARINARA

Yield: 1 (12-inch [30-cm]) pizza

 500° 9oz

Pizza Marinara is one of the two most important Neapolitan pizzas (the other being, of course, Margherita). This pizza is made with garlic, tomato, olive oil, and dried oregano—no cheese. The four simple ingredients combine to give us a pizza with heady aromas and delicious flavors. The toppings are baked on the soft, elastic Neapolitan crust, and the result is one of the best pizzas ever. There are different stories about how this pizza received its name, one of them being that the simple ingredients were easy to store, making it popular with sea folk.

1 Neapolitan Dough (9 ounces [260 g]) (page 192)

3 ounces (90 g) good canned tomatoes, preferably San Marzano DOP, drained

1 clove garlic, peeled and thinly sliced

1 teaspoon dried oregano, divided

Extra virgin olive oil, for drizzling

1. Place a baking stone in the oven, and preheat to 500°F (260°C) or higher for 1 hour.

2. While the oven is preheating, stretch the pizza dough to a diameter of 12 inches (30 cm).

3. Crush the tomatoes with your hands and spread them over the dough, leaving a 1-inch (3-cm) border.

4. Distribute the garlic and half of the oregano over the pizza.

5. Drizzle olive oil over the pizza.

6. Bake the pizza until the crust is golden.

7. Remove the pizza from the oven and place it on a plate. Top with a drizzle of olive oil and the remaining oregano, and serve.

Tip

Some pizzaioli prefer a few leaves of fresh basil on their Marinara, and we would certainly never complain if the pizza were served to us that way!

PIZZA MARGHERITA VERONESE

 500° 10oz

Yield: 1 (12-inch [30-cm]) pizza

This pizza is our version of Simone Padoan's pizza La Bufala Campana (see Pizzeria i Tigli, page 41). Padoan makes his crust from coarsely ground flour and uses an extremely long rising process. We have replaced his dough with one that is simpler to work with. The finished pizza is Padoan's take on a Margherita, and even though it is quite different from the original, it is equally delicious. Make this pizza when you want to impress your boss or your date.

2½ cups (600 g) cherry tomatoes

2 tablespoons extra virgin olive oil, plus more for drizzling

2 cloves garlic, peeled

Sea salt, to taste

3–4 basil leaves

1 The Wet One Dough, 10 ounces (300 g) (page 193)

1 ball mozzarella di bufala, cut into 8 slices

Fresh oregano, to taste

Maldon salt or other flaked salt, to taste

Coarsely ground black pepper, to taste

1. Place a baking stone in the oven and preheat to 500°F (260°C) or higher for 1 hour.

2. Use a small, sharp knife to cut an X in the tops of the tomatoes.

3. Bring a pot of lightly salted water to a boil. When the water boils, add the tomatoes and cook for 1 minute.

4. Drain off the water and place the tomatoes in a bowl of ice water to cool.

5. Remove the tomatoes from the ice water and peel. Cut the tomatoes in half and remove their seeds.

6. Warm the 2 tablespoons of olive oil in a skillet over low heat. Add the garlic and sauté in the oil for 2–3 minutes.

7. Add the tomatoes to the skillet, keeping the heat low, and cook them for about 45 minutes. Season with the sea salt at the end of the cooking time.

8. Remove the pan from the heat, add the basil leaves, stir, and let the sauce cool. Remove the garlic cloves from the sauce and discard.

9. Roll out the dough and place it neatly in the pizza pan. Let the dough rise for 30 minutes.

10. Spread the sauce over the dough.

11. Bake the pizza until the crust is golden, then remove from the oven and place on a heat-resistant surface.

12. Place the mozzarella slices on an oiled baking pan, and bake in the oven just long enough that the cheese is warmed through. (The mozzarella may be baked at the same time as the pizza.)

13. Remove the mozzarella from the oven and place it on a heat-resistant surface.

14. Remove the pizza from the pan and place it on a cutting board. Divide the pizza into 8 wedges.

15. Place a slice of mozzarella on each wedge of pizza.

16. Top with the oregano, Maldon salt, pepper, and olive oil, and serve.

PIZZA MARGHERITA LA CASA

Yield: 1 (12-inch [30-cm]) pizza

 500° 9oz

Bearing the colors of the Italian flag, Pizza Margherita is the world's most famous pizza. In June 1889, Raffaele Esposito from Pizzeria di Pietro e Basta Cosi served his version of the tomato, mozzarella, and basil pizza to Queen Margherita. The queen had never eaten pizza before, but she so loved Esposito's pizza that she sent a letter telling him so. Esposito's pizzeria still exists but is now called Pizzeria di Brandi. The queen's letter still hangs on the restaurant's wall.

This recipe is true to the original, but we have added a bit of Parmigiano-Reggiano (therefore "la casa"). If you are a pizza purist, you can drop the Parmigiano-Reggiano and experience the authentic flavors of long ago.

1 Neapolitan Dough, 9 ounces (260 g) (page 192)

⅓ cup (90 mL) "Simple Is Often Best" Tomato Sauce (page 198)

8–10 fresh basil leaves

4 ounces (110 g) fresh mozzarella di bufala, shredded

Parmigiano-Reggiano, to taste

Extra virgin olive oil, for drizzling

1. Place a baking stone in the oven, and preheat to 500°F (260°C) or higher for 1 hour.

2. While the oven is preheating, stretch the pizza dough to a diameter of 12 inches (30 cm).

3. Spread the sauce over the dough, leaving a 1-inch (3-cm) border.

4. Distribute the basil over the sauce.

5. Spread the mozzarella over the pizza. Grate the Parmigiano-Reggiano over the pizza and drizzle with olive oil.

6. Bake the pizza until the crust is golden and the cheese is bubbling.

7. Remove the pizza from the oven and place it on a plate. Drizzle a bit more of the olive oil over the pizza, and serve.

Tip

You can use fresh tomatoes instead of sauce as long as they are ripe. If you do, sprinkle a little salt on the tomatoes.

CALZONE FIOR DI LATTE

Yield: 1 (12-inch [30-cm]) pizza

The best way to keep a pizza warm for a longer time is to bake it in the form of a calzone. The top is crunchy and the filling deliciously juicy, making it the perfect pizza for a road trip. The original calzone is made with tomatoes and cheese, but this recipe, which comes from our friend Beniamino Bilali, contains artichokes and mushrooms. A wonderful vegetarian pizza!

1 Our Favorite Dough, 9 ounces (260 g) (page 191)

2 ounces (60 g) fresh mozzarella, shredded

2 ounces (60 g) drained canned whole tomatoes, shredded

2 ounces (60 g) cremini mushrooms, thinly sliced

2 ounces (60 g) canned artichokes, thinly sliced

Extra virgin olive oil, for brushing

1. Place a baking stone in the oven, and preheat to 500°F (260°C) or higher for 1 hour.

2. Stretch the pizza dough to a diameter of 12 inches (30 cm).

3. Distribute the cheese, tomatoes, mushrooms, and artichokes over half of the dough, leaving a 1-inch (3-cm) border.

4. Lift the other side of the dough and fold it over the ingredients, making a half-moon shape.

5. Create a border by using a fork to press together the dough at the rounded edge of the pizza.

6. Brush the top of the pizza with olive oil. Bake the pizza on the baking stone until the crust is golden brown.

7. Brush the top of the pizza with more olive oil, and bake it in the oven until it is golden brown, puffed up, and crispy. A few charred spots on the top are a sign that the pizza is ready.

8. Remove the pizza from the oven, place it on a plate, and serve.

Tip

It is important to place this pizza on the middle rack of the oven (or lower). The pizza will puff up, and if it is placed higher in the oven, you risk burning the top.

PIZZA FRITTA

Yield: 1 (12-inch [30-cm]) pizza

For those of you who have never tasted pizza fritta, we can only say, "Do it!" This pizza is a Neapolitan specialty: a deep-fried calzone.

Vegetable oil, for frying

1 Neapolitan Dough, 9 ounces (260 g) (page 192)

3 ounces (90 g) fresh mozzarella di bufala, shredded

2 ounces (60 mL) "Simple Is Often Best" Tomato Sauce (page 198)

1 ounce (30 g) pepperoni or salami, thinly sliced

1 ounce (30 g) ricotta

½ ounce (20 g) Parmigiano-Reggiano, for grating

1. Preheat a deep fryer with the vegetable oil to 360°F (180°C).

2. Stretch the dough to a diameter of 12 inches (30 cm).

3. Spread the sauce, mozzarella, pepperoni or salami, and ricotta over half of the dough, leaving a 1-inch (3-cm) border. Grate the Parmigiano-Reggiano over the other ingredients.

4. Lift the other side of the dough and fold it over the ingredients, making a half-moon shape.

5. Make a nice border by using a fork to press together the dough at the rounded edge of the pizza.

6. Deep-fry the pizza until it has a golden color.

7. Carefully remove the pizza from the oil using metal slotted spoons or spatulas. Place the pizza on paper towels to remove excess oil. Place the pizza on a plate and serve immediately, as the pizza will deflate somewhat after cooking.

Tip

Don't worry; the deflation of the pizza is a part of the cooking process and will not affect the taste of the pizza. You can substitute Sausage (a recipe is on page 283) for the pepperoni or the salami if you wish. You will need to fry the sausage a bit first.

VERDURE SULLA PIZZA

Yield: 1 (12-inch [30-cm]) pizza

This pizza is very different from others we have tried. It is a gift to those who don't eat meat or who want to try a vegetarian alternative. The pizza is made with mozzarella, pan-fried cherry tomatoes, and—of all things—raisins. Making this pizza requires time, but it is, without a doubt, worth it.

1 cup (240 mL) water

2 tablespoons raisins

½ carrot, peeled and thinly sliced

2 ounces (60 g) leeks, cut into ½-inch (1-cm) rings

4 tablespoons extra virgin olive oil, divided, plus more for drizzling

½ head baby romaine (or equivalent amount of romaine hearts)

1 clove garlic, peeled, crushed, and minced

6 fresh cherry tomatoes, cut in half

3–4 basil leaves

1 Our Favorite Dough, 9 ounces (260 g) (page 191)

3 ounces (90 g) fresh mozzarella, shredded

Coarsely ground black pepper

1. Place a baking stone in the oven, and preheat to 500°F (260°C) or higher for 1 hour.

2. Bring the water to a boil in a small saucepan. Add the raisins, reduce the heat, and simmer for 10 minutes. Drain.

3. Fill a large saucepan half full with water, and bring to a boil.

4. Add the carrot slices and leeks to the water, and cook for about 5 minutes, until the carrot slices are just tender.

5. Drain, and transfer the vegetables into a bowl of ice water. Let stand for 5 minutes, and then pour off the water.

6. Warm 2 tablespoons of the olive oil in a skillet over medium heat.

7. Sauté the baby romaine in the oil for 2 minutes. Remove the baby romaine, and place on paper towels to remove excess oil.

8. Warm 2 tablespoons of the olive oil in another skillet over medium heat.

9. Add the garlic to the skillet. Cook for 1 minute and reduce heat to low.

10. Add the cherry tomatoes to the pan and let them cook for 15 minutes, adding 1 to 2 tablespoons of water if necessary. Add the basil leaves for the last 2 minutes of the cooking time.

11. Stretch the pizza dough to a diameter of 12 inches (30 cm).

12. Spread the mozzarella over the dough, leaving a 1-inch (3-cm) border. Distribute the carrot slices, leeks, and baby romaine over the pizza. Drizzle with more olive oil.

13. Bake the pizza on the baking stone until the crust is golden and the cheese is bubbling.

14. Remove the pizza from the oven and place it on a plate. Top with the tomatoes, raisins, and a bit of black pepper, and serve.

Tip

Broccoli, cauliflower, and/or thin slices of onion or fennel also work well on this pizza.

PIZZA QUATTRO STAGIONI

 500° 9oz

Yield: 1 (12-inch [30-cm]) pizza

This classic pizza represents the four seasons, hence the name of the recipe. Artichokes symbolize spring; olives, summer; mushrooms, fall; and cured ham, winter. It is not uncommon to find other types of toppings used on this pizza. You may find other types of cheese used as well, such as fontina or pecorino, in addition to the mozzarella.

1 Our Favorite Dough, 9 ounces (260 g) (page 191)

3 ounces (90 g) drained canned tomatoes

3 ounces (90 g) fresh mozzarella di bufala, shredded

1½ ounces (40 g) canned artichokes, thinly sliced

1 ounce (30 g) cooked ham, thinly sliced

1 ounce (30 g) fresh mushrooms, such as cremini or champignon, sliced

8–10 pitted black olives

Handful baby basil leaves or 3 leaves of regular basil

Extra virgin olive oil, for drizzling

Coarsely ground black pepper, to taste

Tip

Use fresh tomatoes when they are in season, and don't be afraid to try other toppings, such as clams, slices of boiled potato, other types of mushrooms, or grilled red peppers.

1. Place a baking stone in the oven, and preheat to 500°F (260°C) or higher for 1 hour.

2. Stretch the pizza dough to a diameter of 12 inches (30 cm).

3. Crush the tomatoes with your hands and tear them into large pieces. Spread the tomatoes over the dough, leaving a 1-inch (3-cm) border.

4. Spread the mozzarella over the pizza. Distribute the artichokes, ham, mushrooms, and olives over the pizza.

5. Bake the pizza on the baking stone until the crust is golden and the cheese is bubbling.

6. Remove the pizza from the oven and place it on a plate. Top with the basil leaves.

7. Add a drizzle of olive oil and a pinch or two of black pepper, and serve.

FOCACCIA WITH CHERRY TOMATOES

Yield: 1 (12-inch [30-cm]) focaccia

You might think of focaccia as square or rectangular, but that is not always the case. Focaccia can be thin or as thick as a sheet cake. In this case, it is round. No matter how you make it, you will love it!

3 tablespoons extra virgin olive oil

1 clove garlic, peeled

6 cherry tomatoes, cut in half

1 Our Favorite Dough, 9 ounces (260 g) (page 191)

Sea salt, preferably a flaked salt such as Maldon, for sprinkling

6–8 fresh basil leaves

1. Place a pizza pan in the oven, and preheat to 500°F (260°C) or higher for 1 hour.

2. Warm the oil in a saucepan on medium–high heat.

3. Sauté the garlic in the oil for 2 minutes. Turn down the heat to the lowest setting.

4. Add the cherry tomatoes to the pan and let them cook for 10 minutes, stirring occasionally.

5. Remove the tomatoes from the oil with a slotted spoon, and set aside. Discard the garlic, reserving the oil.

6. Stretch the pizza dough to a diameter of 12 inches (30 cm). Place the dough neatly in the pizza pan and let rise for 30 minutes.

7. Distribute the tomatoes over the dough, leaving a 1-inch (3-cm) border. Top with the oil from the saucepan.

8. Sprinkle a couple of pinches of salt over the focaccia, and bake until it is golden brown.

9. Remove the focaccia from the oven and place it on a heat-resistant surface. Top with the basil leaves.

10. Remove the focaccia from the pan, place it on a plate, and serve.

Tip

This focaccia is also good topped with caramelized onions, or even plain, with only a drizzle of extra virgin olive oil and a sprinkle of sea salt.

SFINCIONE

Yield: Enough for 1 (12 x 16 x 2-inch [30 x 40 x 5-cm]) baking pan

🔲 410° ①

Sfincione is a Sicilian pizza. The dough is soft and sponge-like (the word *sfincione* means "sponge"). In days past, this pizza was served on Christmas Eve, New Year's Eve, and Good Friday. Nowadays, the pizza is served year-round, usually warm, but at room temperature during the hottest months. We have chosen a classic Sicilian tomato sauce containing red pepper flakes and anchovies. Sicilians normally use the local caciocavallo cheese, but you can also use other cheeses. Look forward to a new and exciting pizza experience!

Sauce

2 tablespoons vegetable oil

½ onion, chopped

1 clove garlic, peeled and minced

3 anchovies, chopped

14 ounces (400 g) crushed canned tomatoes

½ teaspoon dried oregano

¼ teaspoon red pepper flakes or ⅛ teaspoon cayenne pepper

Sea salt, to taste

Pizza

1 New York Sicilian Dough (page 193)

3 anchovies, chopped

3–4 ounces (90–110 g) caciocavallo cheese, cubed (alternatives: provolone or mozzarella)

Extra virgin olive oil, for drizzling

Dried oregano, to taste

Sauce

1. Warm the oil on medium–high heat in a skillet. Add the onion and sauté until soft (not browned).

2. Add garlic to the skillet. Cook for 1 minute.

3. Add the anchovies to the skillet. Add the tomatoes, oregano, and red pepper flakes, and bring to a boil. Reduce the heat and let the sauce simmer for 15 minutes. Salt to taste.

4. Remove the skillet from the heat and let the sauce cool. (The sauce can be made a day ahead and refrigerated.)

Pizza

1. Place a 12 x 16 x 2-inch (30 x 40 x 5-cm) baking pan in the oven, and preheat to 410°F (210°C) for 1 hour.

2. Stretch the pizza dough to a rectangular shape to fit the pan. Place the dough in the pan and adjust the fit. Cover the pan with plastic wrap and let the dough rise to double in size.

3. Remove the plastic wrap and spread the sauce over the dough, leaving a 1-inch (3-cm) border.

4. Spread the anchovies over the pizza. Spread the cheese over the pizza, and drizzle with olive oil.

5. Bake the pizza for 5 minutes. Reduce the oven temperature to 180°F (80°C) (to avoid burning the top of the pizza), and continue baking for 20–25 minutes until the crust is golden and the cheese is bubbling.

6. Remove the pizza from the oven, and place it on a heat-resistant surface. Sprinkle oregano over the pizza, cut into pieces, and serve.

Tips

You can use whole anchovies if you wish. Anchovies are salty, so be careful if you increase the amount you use. We recommend 3–4 ounces (90–110 g) of cheese, but some may prefer using more on a pizza of this size.

SCAMPI WITH PESTO PIZZA 500° 9oz

Yield: 1 (12-inch [30-cm]) pizza

Pesto is a great sauce for pizza. Try it as an accent on a newly baked pizza or—as in this recipe—as a sauce before baking. The shrimp and pesto combination is a winner every time, but do try pesto on pizzas containing meat or vegetables.

1 Our Favorite Dough, 9 ounces (260 g) (page 191)

2–3 tablespoons Pesto (page 282)

½ pound (230 g) fresh shrimp (or thawed pre-peeled shrimp)

2 tablespoons extra virgin olive oil, plus more for drizzling

Freshly ground black pepper, to taste

Grated or flaked Parmigiano-Reggiano, to taste

1. Place a baking stone in the oven, and preheat to 500°F (260°C) or higher for 1 hour.

2. Stretch the pizza dough to a diameter of 12 inches (30 cm).

3. Spread a thin layer of the pesto over the pizza crust, leaving a 1-inch (3-cm) border.

4. Place the shrimp in a bowl, add 2 tablespoons of the oil, and toss.

5. Distribute the shrimp over the pesto.

6. Bake the pizza on the baking stone until the crust is golden and the shrimp are cooked through.

7. Remove the pizza from the oven, and place it on a plate. Top with black pepper, olive oil, and Parmigiano-Reggiano, and serve.

Tip: Other toppings that work well are salami, fresh mozzarella, or sliced fresh tomatoes.

BBQ PIZZA 500° 10oz

Yield: 1 (12-inch [30-cm]) pizza

California Pizza Kitchen's most famous pizza is their Original BBQ Chicken Pizza, with barbecue sauce, chicken, red onion, smoked Gouda, and cilantro. This is our twist on that famous pizza, and we like it even better than the original. Craig's background from the world of barbecue makes this pizza "more barbecue and less California," he says.

1 chicken breast, sliced into ½-inch (1-cm) slices

2 teaspoons Grill Rub (see following recipe)

1 Classic New York Dough, 10 ounces (280 g) (page 194)

3 ounces (90 mL) BBQ Sauce (see following recipe)

3 ounces (90 g) mozzarella, grated

3 ounces (90 g) cheddar, grated

Chile Oil (page 281), for sprinkling

6–8 pieces Pickled Red Onions (page 282), drained

1. Place a baking stone in the oven, and preheat to 500°F (260°C) or higher for 1 hour.

2. Place the chicken slices in a bowl. Add the Grill Rub, and mix well with a fork.

3. Stretch the pizza dough to a diameter of 12 inches (30 cm).

4. Spread the BBQ Sauce over the dough, leaving a 1-inch (3-cm) border.

5. Distribute both of the cheeses over the sauce. Distribute the chicken slices over the cheese.

6. Bake the pizza on the baking stone until the crust is golden, the cheese is bubbling, and the chicken is cooked through (but not dried out!).

7. Remove the pizza from the oven, and place it on a plate.

8. Sprinkle Chile Oil over the pizza. Top with Pickled Red Onions, and serve.

Tip: Substitute a total of 6 ounces (170 g) Smoked Mozzarella (page 281) for the cheeses in this recipe. Wonderful!

GRILL RUB

1 tablespoon kosher salt

1 tablespoon freshly ground black pepper

1 tablespoon ground sweet paprika

1 tablespoon firmly packed brown sugar

1 teaspoon cayenne pepper

1. Mix all of the ingredients in a small bowl. Leftover rub should be stored in an airtight container for use the next time you grill meat or fish.

BBQ SAUCE

¾ cup (180 mL) ketchup

6 tablespoons firmly packed brown sugar

1 tablespoon apple cider vinegar

2 teaspoons Worcestershire sauce

1 teaspoon Grill Rub (see previous recipe)

1. Combine all of the ingredients in a small saucepan, and bring to a boil. Reduce the heat, and let simmer for 2–3 minutes. Let the sauce cool before use. Leftovers can be stored covered in the refrigerator and used at a later date.

PIZZA WITH HAM AND MUSHROOMS

Yield: 1 (12-inch [30-cm]) pizza

Although canned mushrooms and inferior ham are used by far too many pizzerias, when better ingredients are used, mushroom and ham make one of the great pizza combinations. Our version uses sautéed fresh mushrooms and the best ham you can get your hands on—and wow, what a difference!

2 tablespoons unsalted butter

1 slice bacon, cut into thin strips

3 cloves garlic, chopped

2 ounces (60 g) fresh mushrooms (champignon, porcini, etc.), cleaned and thinly sliced

3 tablespoons finely chopped parsley, divided

1 Our Favorite Dough, 9 ounces (260 g) (page 191)

2 ounces (60 mL) "Simple Is Often Best" Tomato Sauce (page 198)

3 ounces (90 g) fresh mozzarella, shredded

3 ounces (90 g) good-quality ham, cubed or sliced

Parmigiano-Reggiano, to taste

1. Place a baking stone in the oven, and preheat to 500°F (260°C) or higher for 1 hour.

2. Melt the butter on medium–high heat in a large skillet.

3. Fry the bacon in the butter for 2 minutes.

4. Add the garlic, and cook for 1 more minute. Add the mushrooms to the pan, and cook for 2 more minutes.

5. Remove the pan from the heat and drain the fat. Stir in half of the parsley.

6. Stretch the pizza dough to a diameter of 12 inches (30 cm).

7. Spread the sauce over the dough, leaving a 1-inch (3-cm) border. Distribute the cheese over the dough.

8. Distribute the ham and the mushroom mixture over the pizza.

9. Bake the pizza on the baking stone until the crust is golden and the cheese is bubbling.

10. Remove the pizza from the oven, and place it on a plate. Grate Parmigiano-Reggiano over the pizza, top with the remaining parsley, and serve.

Tip: You can use all kinds of mushrooms on this pizza. If you really love garlic, you can add a couple more cloves of chopped garlic to the mushroom mixture.

BACON CHEESEBURGER PIZZA

Yield: 1 (12-inch [30-cm]) pizza

This delicious pizza is the best of both worlds. The crust replaces the bun, and the rest of the toppings are just as at home on a pizza as they are on a burger.

1 Classic New York Dough, 10 ounces (280 g) (page 194)

3 ounces (90 mL) "Simple Is Often Best" Tomato Sauce (page 198)

5 ounces (140 g) mozzarella, grated (alternative: cheddar, grated)

3 ounces (90 g) ground beef with a bit of added salt

2–3 bacon slices

½ small red onion, thinly sliced

Yellow mustard or another favorite mustard, for drizzling

1. Place a baking stone in the oven, and preheat to 500°F (260°C) or higher for 1 hour.

2. Stretch the pizza dough to a diameter of 12 inches (30 cm).

3. Spread the sauce over the dough, leaving a 1-inch (3-cm) border.

4. Distribute the cheese over the sauce.

5. Top the cheese with small, flattened bits of the ground beef. Distribute the bacon and red onion over the pizza.

6. Bake the pizza on the baking stone until the crust is golden and the cheese is bubbling, and the meat is cooked through.

7. Remove the pizza from the oven, and place it on a plate.

8. Drizzle mustard over the pizza, and serve.

Tip: You can substitute the tomato sauce with BBQ Sauce (page 218) if you like. Why not use other burger favorites, such as pickles or crispy lettuce, on top of your pizza? These ingredients should be added to the pizza after it is finished baking.

FOCACCIA WITH ROSEMARY

 500° 9oz

Yield: 1 (12-inch [30-cm]) pizza

This is a classic focaccia, topped with fresh rosemary!

2 tablespoons extra virgin olive oil

1 clove garlic, peeled

1 generous sprig of rosemary

1 Our Favorite Dough, 9 ounces (260 g) (page 191)

Couple pinches of sea salt, preferably flaked salt such as Maldon

1. Place a pizza pan in the oven, and preheat to 500°F (260°C) or higher for 1 hour.

2. Warm the oil in a saucepan on medium–high heat.

3. Sauté the garlic in the oil for 2 minutes. Turn down the heat to the lowest setting, then add the rosemary and cook for 3–4 minutes. Remove the pan from the heat, and let it cool.

4. Discard the garlic, reserving the oil and rosemary.

5. Stretch the pizza dough to a diameter of 12 inches (30 cm). Place the dough neatly in the pizza pan and let rise for 30 minutes.

6. Use your fingertips to gently "dimple" the dough. Pour the oil mixture over the dough, leaving a 1-inch (3-cm) border. Redistribute the rosemary leaves if necessary.

7. Sprinkle salt over the focaccia, and bake until golden brown.

8. Remove the focaccia from the oven, and place it on a heat-resistant surface.

9. Remove the focaccia from the pan, place it on a plate, and serve.

Tip

For a thicker focaccia, let the dough rise for 45 minutes or longer.

STEFANO FERRARA'S PIZZA WITH POTATO AND HAM

 500° 9oz

Yield: 1 (12-inch [30-cm]) pizza

We met Stefano Ferrara and his wife at his oven factory outside of Naples. We asked what his favorite pizza was, and although he felt it was difficult to choose just one, he finally landed on this potato, ham, and cheese concoction. This is a pizza the whole family will love. Give it a try.

1 Neapolitan Dough, 9 ounces (260 g) (page 192)

3–4 tablespoons heavy cream

3 ounces (90 g) boiled potatoes, sliced and then crushed or grated

3 ounces (90 g) fresh mozzarella, shredded

1 ounce (30 g) cooked ham, sliced

1 ounce (30 g) scamorza cheese, cubed (alternatives: provolone or Smoked Mozzarella [page 281])

1 ounce (30 g) Parmigiano-Reggiano, grated

Extra virgin olive oil, for drizzling

Sea salt, to taste

Coarsely ground black pepper, to taste

1. Place a baking stone in the oven, and preheat to 500°F (260°C) or higher for 1 hour.

2. Stretch the pizza dough to a diameter of 12 inches (30 cm).

3. Pour a thin layer of the cream on the dough, leaving a 1-inch (3-cm) border.

4. Distribute the potatoes and mozzarella over the pizza. Distribute the ham, scamorza, and Parmigiano-Reggiano over the pizza.

5. Bake the pizza on the baking stone until the crust is golden and the cheese is bubbling.

6. Remove the pizza from the oven, and place it on a plate.

7. Drizzle olive oil over the pizza, add salt and pepper, and serve.

PIZZA PRIMAVERA

Yield: 1 (8-inch [20-cm]) pizza

  500° 9oz

Grilled vegetables are the main attraction of this pizza. The range of colors and textures makes for a beautiful pizza, and with a sauce of only crushed cherry tomatoes, this is one of our healthiest and tastiest pizzas. Just what the doctor ordered!

2–3 thin slices zucchini

1–2 thin slices eggplant

½ head baby romaine lettuce (or an equivalent amount of romaine heart leaves)

¼ yellow bell pepper, thinly sliced

1 Our Favorite Dough, 9 ounces (260 g) (page 191)

2 ounces (60 g) canned cherry tomatoes, drained

3–4 fresh basil leaves

Extra virgin olive oil, for drizzling

¼ avocado, peeled and thinly sliced

2 pinches Maldon salt (or other flaked salt)

1. Place a baking stone in the oven, and preheat to 500°F (260°C) or higher for 1 hour.

2. Grill the zucchini, eggplant, romaine, and bell pepper on a grill or in a grill pan until just soft.

3. Stretch the pizza dough to a diameter of 8 inches (20 cm). (This will be a fairly thick pizza.)

4. Use your hands to lightly crush the cherry tomatoes. Spread them over the dough, leaving a 1-inch (3-cm) border.

5. Place the basil leaves on the pizza, and drizzle olive oil over the pizza.

6. Bake the pizza on the baking stone until the crust is golden.

7. Remove the pizza from the oven, and place it on a plate. Top the pizza with the grilled vegetables and the avocado slices.

8. Drizzle a little more olive oil over the pizza, add salt, and serve.

Tip

You can use other vegetables instead of, or in addition to, the ones in the recipe. Some favorites are broccoli, onion, asparagus, and cauliflower.

PIZZA LARDO, PEPE NERO, E PECORINO

Yield: 1 (12-inch [30-cm]) pizza

This pizza is topped with lardo (spiced and cured fatback), black pepper, and pecorino. The lardo might be hard to find, but it is well worth seeking out to create this delicious pizza.

We use mozzarella and Pecorino di Fossa from Sogliano al Rubicone in the Emilia-Romagna area of northern Italy. This sheep's milk (occasionally a mixture of cow's and sheep's milk) cheese is aged in *fossae*—naturally occurring underground pits. The pits are lined with straw that is charred to keep a low moisture level. You can substitute a different type of pecorino if Pecorino di Fossa is not available in your area.

1 Our Favorite Dough, 9 ounces (260 g) (page 191)

4 ounces (110 g) fresh mozzarella, shredded

2 ounces (60 g) Pecorino di Fossa or another good pecorino cheese, crumbled

1 ounce (30 g) lardo, thinly sliced

Handful of basil leaves

Extra virgin olive oil, for drizzling

Freshly ground black pepper, to taste

1. Place a baking stone in the oven, and preheat to 500°F (260°C) or higher for 1 hour.

2. Stretch the pizza dough to a diameter of 12 inches (30 cm). Spread the mozzarella over the dough.

3. Bake the pizza on the baking stone until the crust is golden and the cheese is bubbling.

4. Remove the pizza from the oven, and place it on a plate. Distribute the pecorino, lardo, and basil over the pizza.

5. Drizzle olive oil over the pizza, add black pepper, and serve.

PIZZA QUATTRO FORMAGGI

Yield: 1 (12-inch [30-cm]) pizza

  500° 9oz

It is hard to beat a great crust topped with four great cheeses. We recommend the stronger-flavored Gorgonzola piccante when available—this is the original Gorgonzola, a wonderful cheese to melt on top of a pizza. The word *piccante* refers not to the cheese being spicy but to the fact that it is extra flavorful.

The milder Gorgonzola dolce will also work well.

1 Our Favorite Dough, 9 ounces (260 g) (page 191)

4 ounces (110 g) fresh mozzarella di bufala, shredded

2 ounces (60 g) Gorgonzola piccante, thinly sliced

1 ounce (30 g) Taleggio, thinly sliced

1 ounce (30 g) Parmigiano-Reggiano, thinly sliced

2–3 fresh basil leaves

Coarsely ground black pepper, to taste

1. Place a baking stone in the oven, and preheat to 500°F (260°C) or higher for 1 hour.

2. Stretch the pizza dough to a diameter of 12 inches (30 cm).

3. Spread the mozzarella over the dough, leaving a 1-inch (3-cm) border.

4. Bake the pizza on the baking stone until the mozzarella has melted and the crust is a light golden color, and remove from the oven. Place the pizza on a heat-resistant surface.

5. Distribute the Gorgonzola and Taleggio over the pizza, return the pizza to the oven, and continue baking until the crust is golden and the cheese is bubbling.

6. Remove the pizza from the oven, and place it on a plate.

7. Distribute the Parmigiano-Reggiano and basil leaves over the pizza, add coarsely ground black pepper, and serve.

Tips

You can add the Parmigiano-Reggiano to the pizza before baking if you like. We prefer topping the freshly baked pizza with the Parmigiano-Reggiano. You can also try other cheeses on this pizza. Some favorites are provolone, Fontina, ricotta, Asiago, and caciocavallo. You can also substitute pecorino for the Parmigiano-Reggiano.

PIZZA CAIAZZO

 500° 9oz

Yield: 1 (12-inch [30-cm]) pizza

Franco Pepe (page 37) makes some of the most exciting pizzas in Italy. This is an homage to his Sole nel Piatto pizza. Pepe uses local ingredients from the best producers to be found: Pomodorino del Piennolo del Vesuvio tomatoes (page 147), local olives, anchovies from Cetara, and oregano from Alto Casertano. Visit your favorite shops and markets to search out the best olives and tomatoes you can find, and put together your own version of Franco Pepe's pizza.

1 Our Favorite Dough, 9 ounces (260 g) (page 191)

3 ounces (90 mL) "Simple Is Often Best" Tomato Sauce (page 198)

10 fresh cherry tomatoes

2 ounces (60 g) fresh mozzarella di bufala, shredded

10 pitted olives

2 teaspoons anchovies

Extra virgin olive oil, for drizzling

Dried oregano, to taste

Freshly ground black pepper, to taste

Maldon salt (or other flaxed salt), to taste

1. Place a baking stone in the oven, and preheat to 500°F (260°C) or higher for 1 hour.

2. Stretch the pizza dough to a diameter of 12 inches (30 cm).

3. Spread the sauce and tomatoes over the dough, leaving a 1-inch (3-cm) border.

4. Spread the cheese over the pizza. Distribute the olives and anchovies over the pizza.

5. Drizzle olive oil on top of the pizza, and sprinkle with oregano.

6. Bake the pizza on the baking stone until the crust is golden and the cheese is bubbling.

7. Remove the pizza from the oven, and place it on a plate. Top with freshly ground black pepper, salt, and another drizzle of olive oil. Serve.

PIZZA SALSICCIA E CIPOLLA

Yield: 1 (12-inch [30-cm]) pizza

It is hard to argue with the "simple is best" principle. The crust of this pizza is topped with three ingredients: mozzarella, sautéed onions, and Italian sausage—and that's it. The interaction among these simple ingredients results in one of the best dishes an oven ever baked.

2 tablespoons butter

½ onion, peeled and thinly sliced

1 Our Favorite Dough, 9 ounces (260 g) (page 191)

2 ounces (60 g) fresh mozzarella, shredded

2 ounces (60 g) Salsiccia (page 283), sliced into small, flat pieces

1. Place a baking stone in the oven, and preheat to 500°F (260°C) or higher for 1 hour.

2. Melt the butter in a skillet on medium heat.

3. Sauté the onion in the butter until it is soft, about 5 minutes. Remove from the heat, and let cool down.

4. Stretch the pizza dough to a diameter of 12 inches (30 cm).

5. Spread the mozzarella over the pizza dough, leaving a 1-inch (3-cm) border. Distribute the Salsiccia and onion over the pizza.

6. Bake the pizza on the baking stone until the crust is golden and the cheese is bubbling.

7. Remove the pizza from the oven, and place it on a plate. Serve.

Tip

You can replace the onion with thin slices of fennel or, even better, use a bit of both. The fennel will need a bit more time to soften, but those extra minutes are well worth the wait.

PIZZA IMBOTTITA CON SALSICCE E FRIARIELLI

Yield: 1 (12-inch [30-cm]) pizza

In Naples, this type of pizza is called *ripiena*, or stuffed. We were given this recipe by oven-maker Stefano Ferrara (page 168). This pizza resembles a tart or a quiche in appearance, but it is definitely a pizza. It contains no cheese, only sausage and *friarielli*, which is the Neapolitan word for "rapini" (broccoli rabe). The pizza is baked in a pan and has crusts both under and over the filling.

3 ounces (90 g) rapini or broccolini

4 tablespoons extra virgin olive oil, divided, plus more for brushing

1 clove garlic, peeled and thinly sliced

½ red chile with seeds, minced (use more if you want a spicier pizza)

Pinch sea salt

7 ounces (200 g) good-quality Italian sausage, sliced into ½-inch (1-cm) thick slices (alternative: Salsiccia [page 283])

2 Our Favorite Doughs, 6 ounces (170 g) each (page 191)

1. Place a 2-inch (5-cm) deep pan in the oven, and preheat to 500°F (260°C) or higher for 1 hour.

2. Bring a saucepan of lightly salted water to a boil. Cook the rapini in the boiling water for about 30 seconds.

3. Use a slotted spoon to transfer the rapini from the saucepan to a bowl of ice water. Let stand for a couple of minutes to cool, and then drain off the water. Wrap the rapini in paper towels, and squeeze gently to remove excess water.

4. Warm 2 tablespoons of the olive oil in a skillet over medium–high heat. Sauté the garlic and chile in the oil for 1 minute.

5. Add the rapini to the pan, add the salt, and cook for 2 more minutes.

6. Pour off the excess oil, and place the rapini mixture on paper towels to remove excess oil.

7. Warm the remaining 2 tablespoons of the olive oil in another skillet over medium–high heat.

8. Fry the sausage or Salsiccia in the skillet until browned but not cooked through. Pour off the excess oil, and transfer the sausage to a bowl.

9. Roll out one of the pieces of dough on a floured work surface to a diameter of about 15 inches (38 cm). Lay the dough carefully in the pan so that it covers the bottom and sides evenly. Spread the rapini and sausage over the dough in the bottom of the pan.

10. Roll out the other piece of dough to a diameter of just over 12 inches (30 cm). Lay the dough evenly over the pan.

11. Pinch the edges of the bottom and top dough pieces together to seal, and use your fingers or a fork to make an attractively sealed edge. Brush the top pizza dough with olive oil.

12. Bake the pizza until the crust is golden. Remove the pizza from the oven, and place it on a heat-resistant surface. Let the pizza cool slightly, cut in slices, and serve on plates.

Tips

For a spicier pizza, you can sprinkle red pepper flakes on the pizza right before eating. Another alternative is to serve it with Chile Oil (page 281).

DOMINICK DeMARCO'S PIZZA

 410° ①

Yield: Enough for 1 (12 x 16 x 2-inch [30 x 40 x 5-cm]) baking pan

Domenick DeMarco, son of the famous Domenico DeMarco at Di Fara Pizza in Brooklyn, told us of his fondness for salami: "My favorite filling is a combination of pepperoni and garlic, especially on square pizza. The crust is thick, and the flavors of the garlic and salami meld perfectly with the melted cheese and tomato sauce. Amazing!" Ladies and gentlemen, here is the recipe.

1 New York Sicilian Dough (page 193)

1½ cups (350 g) La Salsa (page 199)

4 ounces (110 g) mozzarella, grated

4 ounces (110 g) pepperoni, sliced

3 cloves garlic, peeled and minced

Extra virgin olive oil, for drizzling

Dried oregano, to taste

1. Place a 12 x 16 x 2-inch (30 x 40 x 5-cm) baking pan in the oven, and preheat to 410°F (210°C) for 1 hour.

2. Stretch the pizza dough to a rectangular shape to fit the pan. Place the dough in the pan, and adjust the fit. Cover the pan with plastic wrap, and let the dough rise to double its original size.

3. Remove the plastic wrap, and spread the sauce over the dough, leaving a 1-inch (3-cm) border.

4. Spread the mozzarella over the pizza. Distribute the pepperoni slices and garlic over the pizza. Drizzle olive oil over the pizza.

5. Bake the pizza for 5 minutes. Reduce the oven temperature to 350°F (180°C) (to avoid burning the top of the pizza), and continue baking for 20–25 minutes until the crust is golden and the cheese is bubbling.

6. Remove the pizza from the oven, and place it on a heat-resistant surface.

7. Sprinkle oregano over the pizza, cut into pieces, and serve.

Tip

Domenick's father, Domenico DeMarco, is famous for using basil on his pizzas. He uses scissors to cut the fresh basil right over the top of the pizza. You might just want to do the same!

NEW HAVEN APIZZA TOMATO PIZZA

 500° 10oz

Yield: 1 (12-inch [30-cm]) pizza

New Haven, Connecticut, is one of the premier stops on any journey through the world of American pizza. This dish, which the locals call "apizza," features a crust topped with tomato sauce, dried oregano, and Pecorino Romano. If you add mozzarella ("mutz"), the cheese is considered a topping, along the lines of onions, peppers, or sausage. This is a great pie, a pie you will want to make often.

1 Classic New York Dough, 10 ounces (280 g) (page 194)

3 ounces (90 mL) La Salsa (page 199) (a bit of extra garlic in the sauce will give you that authentic "apizza" flavor)

1½ ounces (40 g) Pecorino Romano, grated

2 teaspoons dried oregano, divided

Extra virgin olive oil, for drizzling

1. Place a baking stone in the oven, and preheat to 500°F (260°C) or higher for 1 hour.

2. Stretch the pizza dough to a diameter of 12 inches (30 cm).

3. Spread the sauce over the dough, leaving a 1-inch (3-cm) border.

4. Sprinkle the Pecorino Romano and half of the oregano over the pizza. Drizzle olive oil over the pizza.

5. Bake the pizza on the baking stone until the crust is golden. Remove the pizza from the oven, and place it on a plate.

6. Drizzle a bit more olive oil over the pizza, and top with the remaining oregano. Serve.

Tips
Sausage is another example of a great topping for New Haven–style pizza. And, if you get a chance, take a trip to Pepe's or Sally's in New Haven for some of America's greatest pizza.

NEW YORK–SICILIAN HYBRID PIZZA

Yield: Enough for 1 (12 x 16 x 2-inch [30 x 40 x 5-cm]) baking pan

The large, round New York pizza is familiar to all, but there is another important pizza in "The City." It has Sicilian roots but is different from the original Sicilian pizzas. In New York, it is common to use mozzarella or Pecorino Romano, or even make the pizza with no cheese. In Sicily, caciocavallo is the cheese of choice. This hybrid pizza is like a greatest-hits version of both the Sicilian and New York varieties. You can also prepare this pie with other toppings, such as salami, chiles, and garlic.

1 New York Sicilian Dough (page 193)

1½ cups (350 g) La Salsa (page 199)

2–3 anchovies, chopped

2 ounces (60 g) caciocavallo cheese, grated or cubed (alternative: mozzarella)

1 cup (280 g) bread crumbs

Dried oregano, to taste

Extra virgin olive oil, for drizzling

Pecorino Romano, to taste

Handful arugula

1. Place a 12 x 16 x 2-inch (30 x 40 x 5-cm) baking pan in the oven, and preheat to 410°F (210°C) for 1 hour.

2. Stretch the pizza dough to a rectangular shape to fit the pan. Place the dough in the pan, and adjust the fit. Cover the pan with plastic wrap, and let the dough rise to double its original size.

3. Remove the plastic wrap, and spread the sauce over the dough, leaving a 1-inch (3-cm) border.

4. Spread the anchovies over the pizza. Spread the caciocavallo over the pizza.

5. Cover the pizza with a thin layer of the bread crumbs and a sprinkle of oregano.

6. Drizzle olive oil over the pizza.

7. Bake the pizza for 5 minutes. Reduce the oven temperature to 350°F (180°C) (to avoid burning the top of the pizza), and continue baking for 20–25 minutes until the crust is golden and the cheese is bubbling.

8. Remove the pizza from the oven, and place it on a heat-resistant surface.

9. Sprinkle Pecorino Romano over the pizza, top with the arugula, cut into pieces, and serve.

PANNA CUCINA

 500° 9oz

Yield: 1 (12-inch [30-cm]) pizza

Jonathan Goldsmith from Chicago's Spacca Napoli pizzeria introduced us to this pizza. He uses fresh shrimp, and in our Norwegian version, we have used saltwater crayfish tails. The sweet shrimp are the perfect foil for the tomatoes and slightly bitter arugula. Pictured on page 202.

1 Neapolitan Dough, 9 ounces (260 g) (page 192)

3 ounces (90 g) fresh mozzarella, shredded

¼ pound (110 g) fresh shrimp, peeled and deveined (or thawed pre-peeled shrimp)

6 cherry tomatoes, cut in half

Extra virgin olive oil, for drizzling, plus 2 tablespoons, divided

Handful of arugula

Fresh-squeezed lemon juice from ½ lemon

1. Place a baking stone in the oven, and preheat to 500°F (260°C) or higher for 1 hour.

2. Stretch the pizza dough to a diameter of 12 inches (30 cm).

3. Spread the mozzarella over the dough, leaving a 1-inch (3-cm) border.

4. Distribute the shrimp and cherry tomatoes over the pizza. Drizzle olive oil over the pizza.

5. Bake the pizza on the baking stone until the crust is golden.

6. Place the arugula in a large bowl. Add 2 tablespoons olive oil and lemon juice, and toss lightly.

7. Remove the pizza from the oven, and place it on a plate. Top with the arugula, and serve.

CHEESE PIZZA

 500° 10oz

Yield: 1 (12-inch [30-cm]) pizza

Crust, sauce, and cheese: the pizza that everyone loves. The key to success with this pie is choosing the best ingredients available and finding the proper balance among them. We like using both regular and fresh mozzarella, and we add Parmigiano-Reggiano to the finished pizza. Other cheeses will work well, but don't go crazy with the amount of cheese on top.

1 Classic New York Dough, 10 ounces (280 g) (page 194)

3 ounces (90 mL) La Salsa (page 199) or "Simple Is Often Best" Tomato Sauce (page 198)

3 ounces (90 g) mozzarella, grated

2 ounces (60 g) fresh mozzarella, grated

Dried oregano, to taste

Extra virgin olive oil, for drizzling (or Garlic Oil [see Tip on page 281])

Parmigiano-Reggiano, grated, to taste

1. Place a baking stone in the oven, and preheat to 500°F (260°C) or higher for 1 hour.

2. Stretch the pizza dough to a diameter of 12 inches (30 cm).

3. Spread the sauce over the dough, leaving a 1-inch (3-cm) border.

4. Distribute both of the cheeses over the sauce.

5. Sprinkle oregano over the cheeses, and bake the pizza on the baking stone until the crust is golden and the cheeses are bubbling.

6. Remove the pizza from the oven, and place it on a plate. Sprinkle more oregano over the pizza, and drizzle with olive oil. Grate Parmigiano-Reggiano over the pizza, and serve.

Tips: It's up to you how much cheese you want on your pizza. And don't be afraid to try other types, such as Gouda or caciocavallo. As far as the sauce goes, we love them both, so it is really hard to decide which one is best. You can also use fresh tomatoes when they are in season, instead of the sauce.

PIZZA NAPOLETANA

 500° 9oz

Yield: 1 (12-inch [30-cm]) pizza

Until 2010, La Marinara and La Margherita were the only pizzas classified as true Neapolitan pizzas by the Verace Pizza Napoletana organization. In 2010, Pizza Napoletana (sometimes called Pizza Romana) also received its accreditation. Making this pizza requires that one follows the rules for both preparation of the dough and the required toppings, although the pizza is sometimes served without capers.

1 Neapolitan Dough, 9 ounces (260 g) (page 192)

2 ounces (60 g) drained canned tomatoes, preferably San Marzano DOP

2 ounces (60 g) fresh mozzarella di bufala, shredded

2 anchovies, diced

6–8 pitted black olives

1 tablespoon capers

Extra virgin olive oil, for drizzling

Sea salt, to taste

Coarsely ground black pepper, to taste

Extra virgin olive oil, for drizzling

1. Place a baking stone in the oven, and preheat to 500°F (260°C) or higher for 1 hour.

2. Stretch the pizza dough to a diameter of 12 inches (30 cm).

3. Use your hands to lightly crush the tomatoes, and spread them over the dough.

4. Spread the mozzarella over the pizza. Distribute the anchovies, olives, and capers over the pizza.

5. Top the pizza with a drizzle of olive oil, and bake on the baking stone until the crust is golden.

6. Remove the pizza from the oven and place it on a plate. Add the salt, pepper, and a drizzle of olive oil, and serve.

ALOHA PIZZA

Yield: 1 (12-inch [30-cm]) pizza   500° 9oz

If there is one pizza that polarizes pizza lovers, it's this one. This pie divides families, brings uncertainty to long-term friendships, and has probably started a war or two. Some will say that this Hawaiian-inspired pie is the godfather of all pizza, while others are disgusted by the idea of putting pineapple anywhere near a pizza.

We are sure that some readers, or even critics, will say that this pizza should never have been included in a book like this. Others will surely consider us heroes for taking their favorite pizza seriously. Ham and pineapple—check! We also use chicken breast marinated in pineapple juice. Here is our take on the ultimate pizza homage to the Aloha State.

1 chicken breast, sliced into 1-inch (3-cm) cubes

Aloha Marinade (see recipe below)

1 Classic New York Dough, 9 ounces (260 g) (page 194)

2 ounces (60 mL) "Simple Is Often Best" Tomato Sauce (page 198)

6 ounces (170 g) mozzarella, grated

½ small red onion, sliced into thin rings

4 ounces (110 g) good-quality ham, cut into ½-inch (1-cm) cubes

4 ounces (110 g) fresh pineapple, cut into ½-inch (1-cm) cubes

1 red chile with seeds, diced (optional)

1. Place the chicken breast cubes in a bowl with the Aloha Marinade and stir to combine. Cover with plastic wrap, and allow to marinate in the refrigerator for 2–6 hours.

2. Place a baking stone in the oven, and preheat to 500°F (260°C) or higher for 1 hour.

3. Remove the bowl of marinated chicken from the refrigerator, drain and pat dry with paper towels.

4. Warm a 10-inch skillet over high heat. Cook the chicken pieces in the pan just until browned. (You do not want to cook them through, because they will top the pizza before going into the oven.) Stir occasionally, making sure the chicken pieces do not burn. (The marinade contains sugar and can easily burn.) Remove the pan from the heat, place the chicken pieces in a small bowl, and set aside.

5. Stretch the pizza dough to a diameter of 12 inches (30 cm).

6. Spread the sauce over the dough, leaving a 1-inch (3-cm) border.

7. Distribute the cheese over the sauce. Top the pizza with the chicken, onion slices, ham, pineapple, and chile.

8. Bake the pizza on the baking stone until the crust is golden, the cheese is bubbling, and the chicken pieces are cooked through (but not dried out!).

9. Remove the pizza from the oven, place it on a plate, and serve.

Tips: Surgical gloves are a wise choice when working with raw chicken. Avoid contact with other ingredients, and be sure to wash your cutting board and other utensils when you are done working with the raw chicken.
For a twist, you can substitute a cured ham, such as Parma, for the regular ham. The cured ham should be placed on the pizza after it comes out of the oven.

For a simpler version of this pizza, you can substitute the marinated chicken with precooked chicken, again after the pizza is fully baked.

ALOHA MARINADE

2 cloves garlic, peeled and minced

1 red chile, with seeds, minced

1 cup (240 mL) pineapple juice

½ cup (120 mL) vegetable oil

3 tablespoons soy sauce

2 tablespoons sugar

1. Mix all of the ingredients together in a bowl.

NEW HAVEN CLAM PIE

 500° 10oz

Yield: 1 (12-inch [30-cm]) pizza

New Haven is famous for this pizza. You will find it prepared with both canned and fresh clams. We prefer fresh, simply because they both look and taste better. The other ingredients are bacon and Pecorino Romano, and boy, what a pizza this is!

6 slices bacon, each cut into 2 or 3 smaller pieces

2 tablespoons extra virgin olive oil, plus more for drizzling

1 clove garlic, peeled and minced

1 tablespoon minced onion

½ cup (120 mL) dry white wine

1 tablespoon minced parsley

10 clams in their shells

1 Classic New York Dough, 10 ounces (280 g) (page 194)

1 teaspoon dried oregano, divided

2 cloves garlic, peeled and thinly sliced

Pecorino Romano, grated, to taste

1. Place a baking stone in the oven, and preheat to 500°F (260°C) or higher for 1 hour.

2. Fry the bacon until crisp, and then place on paper towels to absorb excess grease.

3. Warm 2 tablespoons of the oil in a large nonreactive pan. Add the garlic and onion to the pan, and let cook for 1 minute over medium–high heat.

4. Add the white wine and parsley, and bring to a boil.

5. Add the clams, place a lid on the pan, and steam until the clam shells have opened. Remove the pan from the heat, and move the lid a bit so that the steam can escape. Throw away any clams that do not open.

6. Stretch the pizza dough to a diameter of 12 inches (30 cm).

7. Cover the pizza with half of the oregano. Distribute the 2 thinly sliced garlic cloves over the pizza, leaving a 1-inch (3-cm) border.

8. Grate Pecorino Romano over the pizza, and drizzle with olive oil.

9. Bake the pizza on the baking stone until the crust is golden. Remove the pizza from the oven, and place it on a plate.

10. Use a slotted spoon to remove the clams from the pan, and distribute them over the pizza. Spread the bacon pieces over the pizza.

11. Drizzle a couple tablespoons of the liquid from the pan over the pizza. Add the rest of the oregano and a bit more Pecorino Romano, and serve.

Tips

Some people like to use mozzarella on this pizza. If using mozzarella, spread the cheese over the dough before you add the oregano and sliced garlic. Bake in the oven until the cheese is bubbling, and then follow the last steps of the recipe.

Some also use tomatoes on this pizza for a variation known as Red Clam Pie. To make this variation, simply add tomatoes instead of the mozzarella.

"IL FIORE DELLE DONNE"

 500° 9oz

Yield: 1 (12-inch [30-cm]) pizza

One of our favorite pizzas on our US trip was the tomato, burrata, and squash blossom creation from Pizzeria Mozza in Los Angeles. It is also one of the most beautiful pizzas to be found anywhere. The taste is California fresh and reminds us of summer. Beniamino Bilali (page 45) created this as his own tribute to summer and to the woman he most wanted to impress. Summer is the season for squash blossoms, and the unusual addition of cinnamon makes for a unique pizza you will not soon forget.

1 Our Favorite Dough, 9 ounces (260 g) (page 191)

3 ounces (90 g) drained canned tomatoes, preferably San Marzano DOP

2 ounces (60 g) ricotta

3 squash blossoms, stamens removed and sliced in half lengthwise

3–4 whole anchovies (or chopped, if you prefer)

Extra virgin olive oil, for drizzling

4–5 sprigs fresh oregano

Pinch ground cinnamon

Pinch freshly ground black pepper

1. Place a baking stone in the oven, and preheat to 500°F (260°C) or higher for 1 hour.

2. Stretch the pizza dough to a diameter of 12 inches (30 cm).

3. Crush the tomatoes with your hands, and distribute over the pizza.

4. Distribute the ricotta over the pizza. Distribute the squash blossoms over the pizza.

5. Spread the anchovies over the pizza, and drizzle the pizza with olive oil.

6. Bake the pizza on the baking stone until the crust is golden. Keep an eye on the pizza so that the squash blossoms do not burn.

7. Remove the pizza from the oven, and place it on a plate. Top with fresh oregano, cinnamon, and freshly ground black pepper. Drizzle with olive oil, and serve.

Tip

Sometimes squash blossoms are sold with small squash attached. Slice right through both the blossom and the squash, and use them both on the pizza. Just remember to remove the stamen.

KESTÉ'S PISTACCHIO E SALSICCIA PIZZA

 500° 9oz

Yield: 1 (12-inch [30-cm]) pizza

Roberto Caporuscio (page 57), the man behind Kesté Pizza and Vino in New York City, is proof that great Neapolitan pizza doesn't only exist in Naples. His restaurant offers classical pizzas, in addition to a couple with unusual toppings. The first of these unusual pizzas is Pizza Sorrentina, topped with lemon slices, smoked mozzarella, and fresh basil. The other, which we have created a version of here, features pistachios, sausage, mozzarella, and Pecorino Romano.

3 ounces (90 g) shelled pistachios

1 ounce (30 g) Parmigiano-Reggiano, cut in large pieces

2 tablespoons extra virgin olive oil, plus more for drizzling

Sea salt, to taste

3 ounces (90 g) Salsiccia (page 283)

2 tablespoons red wine

1 Neapolitan Dough, 9 ounces (260 g) (page 192)

4 ounces (110 g) fresh mozzarella, shredded

4–5 fresh basil leaves

1 ounce (30 g) Pecorino Romano, grated

1. Place a baking stone in the oven, and preheat to 500°F (260°C) or higher for 1 hour.

2. Purée the pistachios, Parmigiano-Reggiano, and 2 tablespoons of the olive oil in a food processor to a smooth sauce. Salt to taste.

3. Fry the Salsiccia in a little oil over medium–high heat until browned but not cooked through.

4. Add the red wine, and let the wine cook in completely.

5. Stretch the pizza dough to a diameter of 12 inches (30 g). Spread the pistachio cream over the dough, leaving a 1-inch (3-cm) border.

6. Distribute the Salsiccia, mozzarella, and basil leaves over the dough.

7. Spread the Pecorino Romano over the pizza. Drizzle a little more olive oil over the pizza.

8. Bake the pizza on the baking stone until the crust is golden and the cheese is bubbling.

9. Remove the pizza from the oven, place it on a plate, and serve.

CALI-ZONE

Yield: 1 (12-inch [30-cm]) pizza

Franco Pepe (page 37) has a version of this calzone that could make even the most carnivorous of us a vegetarian. This pizza would be as much at home in sunny California as in Caiazzo, Italy, where Pepe's pizzeria is located.

1 Our Favorite Dough, 9 ounces (260 g) (page 191)

2–3 anchovies, chopped

10 pitted Gaeta or Ligurian olives

1 ounce (30 g) frisée lettuce, rinsed, dried, and torn into large pieces

1 tablespoon capers

1 tablespoon extra virgin olive oil

1. Place a baking stone in the oven, and preheat to 500°F (260°C) or higher for 1 hour.

2. Stretch the pizza dough to a diameter of 12 inches (30 cm).

3. Mix the anchovies, olives, frisée, capers, and olive oil in a bowl. Toss lightly.

4. Spread the frisée mixture over half of the dough, leaving a 1-inch (3-cm) wide border.

5. Lift the other side of the dough, and fold it over the ingredients, making a half-moon shape.

6. Make a nice border by using a fork to press together the dough at the rounded edge of the pizza.

7. Bake the pizza on the baking stone until the crust is golden brown.

8. Remove the pizza from the oven, and place it on a cutting board. Cut the pizza in half, place it on a plate, and serve.

CHICAGO DEEP-DISH PIZZA

 500° 1

Yield: 1 (14-inch [36-cm]) deep-dish pizza

Our trip to Chicago was life-changing for Tore. He had always been skeptical of the deep-dish pizzas Chicago is famous for, but after eating at several Chicago pizzerias, something happened. And after visiting both Lou Malnati's Pizzeria and Burt's Place in less than 12 hours, he felt like he had come home.

With this recipe, you can make tremendous deep-dish pizza at home. You will need a 14-inch-wide (36-cm) deep-dish pizza pan, available in kitchen stores or online. It is a good idea to also purchase a pan gripper for removing the pizza from the oven.

We have topped this pie with sausage and onions, but you should also give peppers and mushrooms a try. We recommend that the toppings be softened in a pan because they are placed inside the pizza.

3 tablespoons extra virgin olive oil, divided

1 Chicago Deep-Dish Dough (page 195)

½ onion, peeled and chopped

14 ounces (400 g) Sausage (page 283)

7 ounces (200 g) mozzarella, sliced

1½ cups (300 mL) La Salsa (page 199) or "Simple Is Often Best" Tomato Sauce (page 198), at room temperature

7 ounces (200 g) mozzarella, grated

2 ounces (60 g) Parmigiano-Reggiano, grated

1. Place a baking stone in the oven, and preheat to 500°F (260°C) or higher for 1 hour.

2. Grease a 14-inch-wide (36-cm) deep-dish pizza pan with 1 tablespoon of the olive oil.

3. Roll out the dough to a width of 16 inches (40 cm). Place the dough neatly in the bottom and up the sides of the pizza pan.

4. Cover the pan with plastic wrap, and let the dough rise for 20 minutes.

5. Warm the remaining 2 tablespoons of the olive oil in a large skillet over medium heat.

6. Add the onion to the skillet, and cook for about 2 minutes until the onion is soft but not browned.

7. Add the Sausage to the pan, and fry until it has a nice color but is not completely cooked through. Drain off the excess oil, and place the onion and Sausage mixture on paper towels to soak up any remaining fat.

8. Remove the plastic wrap from the pan. If the dough on the sides of the pan has sunk down, gently press it back in place.

9. Line the dough on the bottom of the pan with the sliced mozzarella, making sure that the slices overlap each other.

10. Distribute the onion and Sausage over the cheese slices in the pan. Spread the tomato sauce gently over the pizza.

11. Distribute the grated mozzarella and Parmigiano-Reggiano over the pizza.

12. Place the pizza in the oven, reduce the heat to 400°F (200°C), and bake until the crust is golden and the cheese is bubbling (about 30 minutes).

13. Remove the pizza from the oven, and place it on a heat-resistant surface. Let the pizza cool for 6–8 minutes. Cut in slices, and serve.

Tips

Another popular version of this pizza has the tomato sauce on top. Simply reverse the placement of the tomato sauce and the grated mozzarella, and distribute the grated Parmigiano-Reggiano on top of the sauce.

Our favorite Chicago deep-dish pizza is known for its famous caramelized crust. To get this effect, place slices of mozzarella between the edge of the dough and the pan before letting the dough rise (between steps 3 and 4).

CHICAGO THIN-CRUST PIZZA

Yield: 1 (12-inch [30-cm]) pizza

 500° 8oz

This thin-crust pizza is made in a pizza pan instead of being placed directly on the oven's stone floor. The toppings take us back to our visits to places like Pequod's Pizza, Pizano's, and Burt's Place. Sauté the onions and the peppers slightly before putting them on the pizza to bring out the sweetness of the vegetables. It is also traditional to place the vegetables under the cheese, with only the sausage going on top.

1 tablespoon vegetable oil, plus more for greasing pan

1 Classic New York Dough, 8 ounces (230 g) (page 194)

3 ounces (90 g) La Salsa (page 199)

3–4 thin strips red bell pepper

3–4 thin strips green bell pepper

3–4 thin rings onion

6 ounces (170 g) mozzarella (or fresh mozzarella), grated

4 ounces (110 g) Sausage (page 283)

1. Place a pizza pan in the oven, and preheat to 500°F (260°C) or higher for 1 hour.

2. Warm 1 tablespoon of the oil in a skillet on medium–high heat. Sauté the peppers and onions just until tender. Remove the vegetables with a slotted spoon and place them on kitchen paper to absorb any excess oil.

3. Grease a pizza pan with the additional vegetable oil.

4. Stretch the pizza dough to a diameter of 12 inches (30 cm). Lay the dough in the pizza pan, and adjust to fit the pan.

5. Spread the sauce over the dough, leaving a 1-inch (3-cm) border.

6. Distribute the peppers and onions over the sauce. Distribute the mozzarella over the pizza.

7. Top the cheese with small, flattened bits of the Sausage.

8. Bake the pizza until the crust is golden, the cheese is bubbling, and the meat is cooked through.

9. Remove the pizza from the oven, and place it on a plate. Let it cool down a bit, then slice and serve.

Tip

There are a lot of toppings that will work on this pizza: pepperoni, mushrooms, olives, spinach, and anchovies, to name a few.

TONY G'S HONEY PIZZA

Yield: 1 (12-inch [30-cm]) pizza

 500° 9oz

Tony Gemignani (page 123) is pizza's Renaissance man. His restaurants serve very good pizza across a wide range of styles: Neapolitan, Roman, and other Italian classics, in addition to American favorites like California-style, New Haven clam pizza, and Detroit- and St. Louis–style pizzas.

This pizza is inspired by one of Tony's favorites, which features unique ingredients such as deep-fried caramelized onion rings and honey from bees kept on the roof of his San Francisco restaurant, Tony's Pizza Napoletana. You can sample the original, with Piave cheese and Calabrian chilies, the next time you visit him in San Francisco.

3 tablespoons unsalted butter

½ onion, peeled and sliced into ½-inch (1-cm) rings

6 ounces (170 g) flour

2 ounces (60 g) cornstarch

4 tablespoons coarsely chopped bacon

1 Our Favorite Dough, 9 ounces (260 g) (page 191)

7 ounces (200 g) mozzarella, grated

Vegetable oil, for frying

1 tablespoon finely chopped spring onions

Sea salt, to taste

Freshly ground black pepper, to taste

½ teaspoon red pepper flakes

½ teaspoon finely chopped jalapeño pepper

6–8 slices Parmigiano-Reggiano, sliced into flakes with a potato peeler

1 tablespoon good liquid honey

1. Place a baking stone in the oven, and preheat to 500°F (260°C) or higher for 1 hour.

2. Melt the butter in a skillet over low heat.

3. Fry the onion rings in the butter until they are caramelized (about 30 minutes). Add a bit more butter during the frying if necessary. Remove the skillet from the heat.

4. Mix the flour and cornstarch together in a bowl, and set aside.

5. Fry the bacon in another skillet over medium heat for 3 minutes. Drain off the fat, and place the bacon pieces on paper towels to soak up any excess grease.

6. Stretch the pizza dough to a diameter of 12 inches (30 cm).

7. Spread the mozzarella over the dough, leaving a 1-inch (3-cm) border.

8. Bake the pizza on the baking stone for 5 minutes. While the pizza is baking, fill a large pot with 2 inches (5 cm) of the vegetable oil. Heat the oil to 350°F (180°C).

9. While the oil is heating, remove the pizza from the oven, and place it on a heat-resistant surface. Distribute the bacon pieces over the pizza, and put it back in the oven. Bake until the crust is golden and the cheese is bubbling. Then remove the pizza from the oven, and place it on a heat-resistant surface.

10. When the oil has heated to 350°F (180°C), dip the caramelized onion rings in the flour mixture, and fry them in the oil until golden. Place the onion rings on paper towels to soak up excess oil and season with salt and pepper.

11. Distribute the spring onions, red pepper flakes, jalapeño, and Parmigiano-Reggiano over the pizza. Top the pizza with the onion rings, drizzle the honey over the pizza, and serve.

Tips

Tony uses Piave cheese instead of Parmigiano-Reggiano. If you can access this great cheese, you should try it. He also uses serrano chiles instead of jalapeño peppers, and Calabrian chiles instead of red pepper flakes. Our version of the pizza is delicious—Tony's is magical!

NORGESVENN PIZZA

Yield: 1 (12-inch [30-cm]) pizza

 525° 9oz

A Norgesvenn is a non-Norwegian who loves Norway enough that he or she can be called a friend (venn). This pizza is one of the most popular pizzas served at pizzerias in Norway, and eating it will no doubt make you a Norgesvenn. The featured ingredients are bacon, ground beef, and shallots, so how could you possibly go wrong?

2 shallots

Extra virgin olive oil, for drizzling

Salt, to taste

1 Our Favorite Dough, 9 ounces (260 g) (page 191)

4 ounces (110 g) canned cherry tomatoes, drained

4 ounces (110 g) Jarlsberg, grated

5–6 slices bacon

2 ounces (60 g) ground beef

5–6 flatleaf parsley leaves

Few pinches coarsely ground black pepper

1. Place a baking stone in the oven, and preheat to 350°F (180°C) for 1 hour.

2. Place the shallots, peels on, on a baking sheet. Cover the shallots with a thin layer of olive oil and salt. Bake for about 15 minutes, until they are soft and caramelized. Remove the shallots from the oven, let them cool, and then peel them.

3. Increase the oven temperature to 525°F (275°C) or higher if possible.

4. Stretch the pizza dough to a diameter of 12 inches (30 cm).

5. Use your hands to lightly crush the cherry tomatoes. Spread them over the pizza dough, leaving a 1-inch (3-cm) border.

6. Cover the pizza with the cheese.

7. Top the cheese with small, flattened bits of the ground beef.

8. Cut the shallots in half, and distribute them over the pizza.

9. Bake the pizza on the baking stone until the crust is golden, the cheese is bubbling, and the meat is cooked through.

10. While the pizza is cooking, fry the bacon in a pan until crispy. Remove from the heat, and set aside.

11. Remove the pizza from the oven, and place it on a plate.

12. Distribute the bacon slices and parsley leaves over the pizza. Drizzle a little more olive oil over the pizza. Add the black pepper, and serve.

Tips

You can substitute curly leaf parsley for the flatleaf if you wish, and you might want to try other cheeses or combinations of cheeses. Mozzarella, for instance, works great on this pizza.

We like to use one of our sausage recipes (page 283) instead of the ground beef for an even more flavorful pizza.

AN OKLAHOMA BOY'S PIZZA

Yield: 1 (12-inch [30-cm]) pizza

 500° 9oz

One of Craig's favorite pizzas anywhere is Pizzeria Bianco's famous Wiseguy, with smoked mozzarella and fennel sausage made by a local Phoenix butcher. This recipe is an homage to Chris Bianco and his crew. As Craig says, "I would never consider copying the Wiseguy, and I know my version could never top his, but for anyone brought up with smoke and meat, this pizza is way beyond good!"

1 Classic New York Dough, 9 ounces (260 g) (page 194)

5 ounces (140 g) Smoked Mozzarella (page 281), shredded

3 ounces (90 g) Italian sausage or Salsiccia (page 283), sliced

2 Grilled Red Peppers (page 283), sliced

3 ounces (90 g) bacon, cooked and chopped

1 shallot, peeled and diced

1 clove garlic, peeled and thinly sliced

Parmigiano-Reggiano, to grate over pizza

Extra virgin olive oil, for drizzling

Chopped fresh parsley or fresh oregano, to taste

Freshly ground black pepper, to taste

1. Place a baking stone in the oven, and preheat to 500°F (260°C) or higher for 1 hour.

2. Stretch the pizza dough to a diameter of 12 inches (30 cm).

3. Distribute the Smoked Mozzarella over the dough, leaving a 1-inch (3-cm) border.

4. Distribute the Italian sausage or Salsiccia over the pizza, if using. Distribute the Grilled Red Peppers and bacon over the pizza.

5. Spread the shallot and garlic over the pizza. Grate Parmigiano-Reggiano over the pizza, and top with a little extra virgin olive oil.

6. Bake the pizza on the baking stone until the crust is golden and the cheese is bubbling.

7. Remove the pizza from the oven, place it on a plate, and top it with chopped parsley or oregano. Add some freshly ground pepper and serve.

Tips

Feel free to try the Smoked Mozzarella (page 281) on other pizzas. It is simple to make, and it is great on pizza or as a snack. You can also replace the bacon with pancetta or pepper bacon.

To make things perfectly clear, this Oklahoma boy is equally happy using dried oregano as he is using fresh.

GREEN AND MEAN PIZZA

 500° 9oz

Yield: 1 (12-inch [30-cm]) pizza

This pizza, inspired by our trip to California, is simple, healthy, and tasty. There are few ingredients, and freshness is essential. This is an example of just why California pizza is so important.

1 The Wet One Dough, 9 ounces (260 g) (page 193)

3 ounces (90 g) mozzarella di bufala, shredded

3 cloves garlic, peeled and thinly sliced

Extra virgin olive oil, for drizzling

¼–⅓ cup (1½–2 ounces) fresh watercress (alternatives: baby spinach, pea shoots, or other baby greens)

Fresh-squeezed lemon juice from ½ lemon

Sea salt, to taste

Coarsely ground black pepper, to taste

Parmigiano-Reggiano, to taste

1. Place a baking stone in the oven, and preheat to 500°F (260°C) or higher for 1 hour.

2. Stretch the pizza dough to a diameter of 12 inches (30 cm).

3. Distribute the mozzarella and garlic over the dough, leaving a 1-inch (3-cm) border. Drizzle some extra virgin olive oil over the pizza.

4. Place the watercress in a large bowl. Drizzle with more olive oil and lemon juice, and toss lightly.

5. Bake the pizza on the baking stone until the crust is golden and the cheese is bubbling. Remove the pizza from the oven, and place it on a plate.

6. Top the pizza with the greens. Sprinkle with salt and pepper. Grate Parmigiano-Reggiano over the pizza, and serve.

Tips

You might want to use a mandoline or Microplane to achieve the thinnest slices of garlic, but you can also use a sharp knife.

THE BIG EASY PIZZA

Yield: 1 (12-inch [30-cm]) pizza

 500° **9oz**

Some of the most exciting food anywhere comes from southern Louisiana, where local seafood and vegetables are featured in dozens of Cajun and Creole dishes. This pizza celebrates New Orleans, also known as The Big Easy. It's spicy and unlike any pizza you've ever eaten.

2 tablespoons vegetable oil

⅓ green pepper, minced

1 shallot, minced

2 fresh jalapeño chilies, minced

3 cloves garlic, minced

3 live saltwater crawfish (or large shrimp; if using shrimp, skip steps 3–5)

2 teaspoons Cajun Seasoning (see recipe on next page)

1 Classic New York Dough, 9 ounces (260 g) (page 194)

2 ounces (60 g) Cajun Mustard Sauce (see recipe on next page)

4 ounces (110 g) cheddar, grated

Tabasco or another hot sauce, for serving

1. Place a baking stone in the oven, and preheat to 500°F (260°C) or higher for 1 hour.

2. Heat the oil in a skillet over medium–high heat. Sauté the vegetables in the oil for about 1 minute. Pour off the oil, and place the vegetables on paper towels to absorb excess oil.

3. Place the crawfish, one at a time, facing you on a cutting board.

4. Hold a large, sharp knife so that the tip is right above the crawfish's head. Place the tip of the knife right on top of the head. Carefully press the knife's tip hard and quickly right between the crawfish's eyes and down to the cutting board. This will immediately kill the crawfish.

5. Reverse the knife so that the sharp edge is pointing toward the tail. Slice the crawfish in half lengthwise. Lay the two crawfish halves with the shell side down. Remove the meat from the 2 tail pieces, and cut each of these in 2–3 pieces.

6. Coat the crawfish pieces lightly with the Cajun Seasoning, and set aside.

7. Stretch the pizza dough to a diameter of 12 inches (30 cm). Place the dough in a pizza pan and adjust the edges.

8. Spread the Cajun Mustard Sauce over the dough, leaving a 1-inch (3-cm) border.

9. Distribute the vegetable mixture over the pizza. Spread the cheese over the pizza.

10. Distribute the crawfish or shrimp pieces over the pizza, and press them gently into the cheese.

11. Bake the pizza on the baking stone until the crust is golden and the cheese is bubbling.

12. Remove the pizza from the oven, and place it on a heat-resistant surface. Let it cool a bit, cut in slices, and serve with the Tabasco on the side.

Tips

In Louisiana, it is common to use seafood and meat in the same dish, such as in the famous dishes gumbo and jambalaya. You can place thin slices of Andouille sausage on top of this pizza right before baking. A good smoked ham or tasso will also work well.

CAJUN SEASONING

Yield: About 6 tablespoons (90 g)

1 tablespoon salt
1 tablespoon ground paprika
2 teaspoons onion powder
2 teaspoons garlic powder
2 teaspoons cayenne pepper
2 teaspoons ground black pepper
1 teaspoon ground white pepper
1 teaspoon dried thyme
1 teaspoon dried oregano

1. Mix all of the ingredients together in a small bowl. Any leftover seasoning should be stored in an airtight container for later use.

CAJUN MUSTARD SAUCE

Yield: About 1½ cups (360 mL)

1¼ cups (300 mL) crème fraîche
3 tablespoons whole grain mustard
1 teaspoon Dijon mustard
1 teaspoon horseradish cream
1 teaspoon Worcestershire sauce
1 teaspoon Cajun Seasoning (see recipe to the left)

1. Place all of the ingredients in a small saucepan. Stir together, and bring to a boil. Reduce the heat, and simmer just until the sauce starts to thicken. Refrigerate leftover sauce in a covered container for later use.

ROME ANTICS PIZZA

500° · 9oz

Yield: 1 (12-inch [30-cm]) pizza

One of our favorite pizzas in Rome is not found on any menu. We ate lunch at Salumeria Roscioli (page 23), where slices of long rectangular pizzas are lunch staples for Romans and tourists alike. We, of course, tried all the pizzas they had, and after gorging on pizza slices and porchetta sandwiches, we were served a house specialty: a baked crust filled with delicious mortadella. Our version is a bit more embellished, but it still features mortadella in the starring role.

1 ounce (30 g) shelled pistachios

1 Our Favorite Dough, 9 ounces (260 g) (page 191)

3 ounces (90 g) mortadella, cut into cubes

Extra virgin olive oil, for drizzling

4 ounces (110 g) ricotta

6–8 slices Parmigiano-Reggiano, sliced with a potato peeler

Coarsely ground black pepper, to taste

1. Place a baking stone in the oven, and preheat to 500°F (260°C) or higher for 1 hour.

2. Toast the pistachios in a dry skillet, stirring frequently, just until they are slightly browned and aromatic. Transfer them immediately to a small bowl.

3. Stretch the pizza dough to a diameter of 12 inches (30 cm).

4. Spread the mortadella over the dough, leaving a 1-inch (3-cm) border.

5. Drizzle a little olive oil over the pizza, and bake the pizza on the baking stone until the crust is golden.

6. Remove the pizza from the oven, and place it on a plate.

7. Distribute the pistachios and ricotta over the pizza. Top the pizza with the Parmigiano-Reggiano and black pepper, and serve.

Tip

You can use slices of mortadella if you wish, but if so, it is better to add the mortadella slices to the pizza after baking.

GREKENLAND PIZZA

Yield: 1 (12-inch [30-cm]) pizza

This pizza is inspired by some of the well-known ingredients from the Greek kitchen—the kitchen some say invented pizza. Let's save that discussion for another day. In the meantime, enjoy a Mediterranean-inspired pizza with olives, tomatoes, lamb, and oregano.

1 Our Favorite Dough, 9 ounces (260 g) (page 191)

3 ounces (90 mL) "Simple Is Often Best" Tomato Sauce (page 198)

1 small green bell pepper, thinly sliced

2 ounces (60 g) feta cheese, cubed or thinly sliced

15 grams (½ ounce) pitted olives

2–3 ounces (60–90 g) Lamb Sausage (see recipe below)

Extra virgin olive oil, for drizzling

Fresh oregano, for garnish

1. Place a baking stone in the oven, and preheat to 500°F (260°C) or higher for 1 hour.

2. Stretch the pizza dough to a diameter of 12 inches (30 cm).

3. Spread the sauce over the dough, leaving a 1-inch (3-cm) border.

4. Distribute the bell pepper, feta, and olives over the pizza. Distribute the Lamb Sausage in small, flattened bits over the pizza, and drizzle with extra virgin olive oil.

5. Bake the pizza on the baking stone until the crust is golden.

6. Remove the pizza from the oven, and place it on a plate. Garnish with fresh oregano, and serve.

Tips

Store the remaining Lamb Sausage covered in the refrigerator. Use later for pasta or tacos. You can also freeze it for later use.

LAMB SAUSAGE

Yield: About 2 pounds, 2 ounces (940 g)

2 pounds (910 g) ground lamb (alternative: ground beef)

3 cloves garlic, minced

2 teaspoons salt

2 teaspoons minced fresh rosemary

1 teaspoon coarsely ground black pepper

1 teaspoon minced fresh mint

½ teaspoon dried oregano

1. Mix all of the ingredients together in a bowl.

BLUE PIZZA

Yield: 1 (12-inch [30-cm]) pizza

 500° 9oz

You probably either love blue cheese or prefer not having to look at it or smell it, let alone eat it. We love the stuff, and one of our favorites is Italy's own Gorgonzola. This cheese is made in Lombardy in northern Italy. There are two types: the well-known dolce, which is softer and milder flavored, and Gorgonzola piccante, with its sharp, more pronounced taste.

1 tablespoon unsalted butter

10–12 thin slices red onion

**1 Our Favorite Dough, 9 ounces (260 g)
(page 191)**

3 ounces (90 g) fresh mozzarella

2 ounces (60 g) Onion Jam (see recipe on the right)

2 ounces (60 g) Gorgonzola piccante, crumbled

2 tablespoons Parmigiano-Reggiano, grated

Extra virgin olive oil, for drizzling

1 ounce (30 g) pecans, roughly chopped

1. Place a baking stone in the oven, and preheat to 500°F (260°C) or higher for 1 hour.

2. Warm the butter in a medium skillet over medium heat.

3. Add the red onion slices, and cook for about 2 minutes. The onion slices should be soft but not browned.

4. Stretch the pizza dough to a diameter of 12 inches (30 cm).

5. Tear the mozzarella, and distribute over the dough, leaving a 1-inch (3-cm) wide border.

6. Distribute the Onion Jam over the pizza. Spread the Gorgonzola over the pizza.

7. Spread the Parmigiano-Reggiano over the pizza, and drizzle olive oil over the pizza. Distribute the pecans and red onion slices over the pizza.

8. Bake the pizza on the baking stone until the crust is golden and the cheese is bubbling.

9. Remove the pizza from the oven, place it on a plate, and serve.

ONION JAM

Yield: About 3½ cups

2 tablespoons unsalted butter

1 tablespoon vegetable oil

2 large onions, peeled and chopped

2 cloves garlic, peeled and minced

4 tablespoons balsamic vinegar

1 tablespoon tightly packed brown sugar

1 teaspoon fresh thyme, chopped

Sea salt, to taste

1. Warm the butter and oil in a large pan over medium–low heat.

2. Add the onions and garlic to the pan, and cook until the onions are soft (not brown). Stir well a few times during this process. The cooking will take time, but the slow-cooking really brings out the sweetness of the onions.

3. Add the balsamic vinegar, brown sugar, thyme, and stir well.

4. Stir constantly until the balsamic has cooked into the onions and they have a deep brown color. Salt to taste.

Tips

You only need 2 ounces (60 g) of the Onion Jam for one pizza, but there are plenty of other uses for the rest of it. Store covered in the refrigerator and use on sandwiches, with grilled fish or meat, on a cheese plate, or on toast for a tasty breakfast.

TORE'S BREAKFAST PIZZA

 500° 9oz

Yield: 1 (12-inch [30-cm]) pizza

Several years ago, Tore drove nonstop from Norway to Italy for a vacation. When he finally arrived, it was morning. He was in a small village near Lake Garda just in time for breakfast. The smell of bacon drew him toward a local trattoria and his first meeting with a breakfast pizza featuring egg and bacon. Here is the recipe.

2 tablespoons vegetable oil

4 cherry tomatoes, cut in half

½ shallot, peeled and cut into wedges

3 tablespoons unsalted butter, divided

1 Neapolitan Dough, 9 ounces (260 g) (page 192)

2 ounces (60 mL) "Simple Is Often Best" Tomato Sauce (page 198)

2 ounces (60 g) fresh mozzarella, shredded

4 quail eggs

4 slices bacon

Flatleaf parsley, for garnish

1. Place a baking stone in the oven, and preheat to 500°F (260°C) or higher for 1 hour.

2. Heat the oil in a skillet over medium heat.

3. Place the tomatoes, cut side down, in the oil. Remove after the cut side of the tomatoes has gotten a nice char.

4. Place the shallot wedges in the hot oil, reduce the heat to low, add 1 tablespoon of the butter, and stir.

5. Place a lid on the skillet, and let the shallot wedges cook for 10 minutes.

6. Stretch the pizza dough to a diameter of 12 inches (30 cm).

7. Spread the sauce over the dough, leaving a 1-inch (3-cm) border. Spread the mozzarella over the pizza.

8. Bake the pizza on the baking stone until the crust is golden and the cheese is bubbling.

9. While the pizza is baking, melt the remaining 2 tablespoons of butter in a clean skillet over medium heat. Fry the quail eggs (sunny-side up) in the butter.

10. In another skillet, fry the bacon until crisp. Pour off the excess oil.

11. Remove the pizza from the oven, and place it on a heat-resistant surface. Distribute the fried eggs, bacon, shallot wedges, and tomatoes over the pizza.

12. Garnish with parsley, cut in slices, and serve.

Tip

You can replace the quail eggs with 2 chicken eggs if you like.

PIZZA CIPOLLE E PARMIGIANO-REGGIANO

 350° 9oz

Yield: 1 (12-inch [30-cm]) pizza

Beniamino Bilali created this pizza in honor of the popular combination of onion and fior di latte. He has added Parmigiano-Reggiano to the sweet-baked onion and the creamy mozzarella. These flavors unite in a mouthwatering delight of a pizza. Beniamino prefers a sourdough crust, but we have found that pretty much any crust works fine.

1 medium onion

Extra virgin olive oil, for drizzling

Sea salt, to taste

**1 Our Favorite Dough, 9 ounces (260 g)
    (page 191)**

4 ounces (110 g) fresh mozzarella

**1½ ounces (40 g) Parmigiano-Reggiano, broken
    into small pieces**

Coarsely ground black pepper, to taste

1. Place a baking stone in the oven, and preheat to 350°F (180°C) for 1 hour.

2. Place the whole onion, peel on, on a baking sheet. Cover the onion with a thin layer of olive oil and salt.

3. Bake the onion for about 30 minutes until it is soft and caramelized.

4. Remove the onion from the oven, let it cool, and remove the skin.

5. Raise the oven temperature to 500°F (260°C), or higher if possible.

6. Stretch the pizza dough to a diameter of 12 inches (30 cm).

7. Tear the mozzarella, and distribute it over the dough, leaving a 1-inch (3-cm) border. Slice the onion into 8 wedges, and distribute them over the pizza.

8. Bake the pizza on the baking stone until the crust is golden and the cheese is bubbling.

9. Remove the pizza from the oven, and place it on a plate.

10. Spread the Parmigiano-Reggiano over the pizza, and drizzle with more olive oil. Sprinkle with more salt and pepper, and serve.

SPRING SWING PIZZA

Yield: 1 (12-inch [30-cm]) pizza

Call this dish fine-dining pizza: fresh green asparagus, spinach, bacon, and truffles. This gathering of ingredients is perfectly suited to the crispy crust and soft, creamy mozzarella.

2 spears green asparagus

1 Our Favorite Dough, 9 ounces (260 g) (page 191)

3 ounces (90 g) fresh mozzarella, shredded

5 slices bacon, cooked and chopped

10–15 baby spinach leaves

Few slices of truffle

1. Place a baking stone in the oven, and preheat to 500°F (260°C) or higher for 1 hour.

2. Fill a wide saucepan with water, and bring to a boil. Cook the asparagus spears in the boiling water for 1–2 minutes (depending on their thickness), until just tender.

3. Drain off the water, and place the asparagus spears on a plate to cool. Slice the asparagus spears into 1-inch pieces, then set aside.

4. Stretch the pizza dough to a diameter of 12 inches (30 cm).

5. Spread the mozzarella over the dough, leaving a 1-inch (3-cm) border.

6. Bake the pizza on the baking stone until the crust is golden and the cheese is bubbling. Remove the pizza from the oven, and place it on a plate.

7. Distribute the asparagus, bacon, and spinach leaves over the pizza.

8. Shave thin slices of the truffle over the pizza, and serve.

Tip

To make another version of this pizza that we also like, replace the mozzarella with a thin layer of béchamel sauce.

PIZZA AGLIO, OLIO, E PEPERONCINO

 500° 9oz

Yield: 1 (12-inch [30-cm]) pizza

The inspiration for this pizza is a famous Roman pasta dish. The olive oil, garlic, and red pepper flakes do wonders, not only to a pasta but to a pizza crust. This is a great snack for an evening in front of the TV, or you could even grill the pizza and serve small pieces to hungry guests while they eagerly wait to taste your other masterfully grilled delicacies.

1 Our Favorite Dough, 9 ounces (260 g) (page 191)

Extra virgin olive oil, for drizzling

3 cloves garlic, peeled and thinly sliced

2 teaspoons red pepper flakes (or 1 minced red chile)

2 tablespoons minced parsley

Sea salt, to taste

1. Place a baking stone in the oven, and preheat to 500°F (260°C) or higher for 1 hour.

2. Stretch the pizza dough to a diameter of 12 inches (30 cm).

3. Drizzle olive oil over the dough, leaving a 1-inch (3-cm) border.

4. Spread the garlic and red pepper flakes over the pizza.

5. Bake the pizza on the baking stone until the crust is golden. Remove the pizza from the oven, and place it on a plate.

6. Top the pizza with the parsley. Drizzle a little more oil over the pizza, add salt, and serve.

Tip: It is uncommon to use Parmigiano-Reggiano or pecorino on this pizza in Italy, but the pizza tastes great with a bit of grated cheese on top. It's your call!

NEW OLD EL PASO PIZZA

 500° 9oz

Yield: 1 (12-inch [30-cm]) pizza

It is not at all uncommon to find Mexican ingredients on an American pizza. Here, we use cheddar in addition to mozzarella. Jalapeños and a squeeze of lime juice over the finished pie give it a Southwestern flair.

2 tablespoons vegetable oil

½ small onion, thinly sliced

½ small green bell pepper, thinly sliced

2 ounces (60 g) jalapeño pepper, finely chopped (or more if you wish)

6 ounces (170 g) steak (rib eye, sirloin, or tenderloin)

Sea salt, to taste

Coarsely ground black pepper, to taste

1 Classic New York Dough, 9 ounces (260 g) (page 194)

3 ounces (90 g) La Salsa, or the spicy variation (page 199)

3 ounces (90 g) mozzarella, grated

3 ounces (90 g) cheddar, grated

Chile Oil, for drizzling (page 281)

1 lime, cut into wedges

Your favorite hot sauce, for serving

1. Place a baking stone in the oven, and preheat to 500°F (260°C) or higher for 1 hour.

2. Warm the oil in a skillet on medium–high heat. Fry the onion and bell pepper in the oil for 1 minute. Add the jalapeño pepper to the pan, and fry for 30 seconds more.

3. Remove the pan from the heat, drain the oil, and place the vegetables on paper towels to absorb excess grease.

4. Season the steak to taste with salt and pepper, and cook to medium-rare on a grill or in a skillet with a bit of oil.

5. Place the steak on a plate, and cover with a loosely tented piece of aluminum foil to keep it warm.

6. Stretch the pizza dough to a diameter of 12 inches (30 cm).

7. Spread the sauce over the dough, leaving a 1-inch (3-cm) border.

8. Distribute both of the cheeses over the sauce.

9. Bake the pizza on the baking stone until the crust is golden and the cheese is bubbling. Remove the pizza from the oven, and place it on a plate.

10. Thinly slice the steak, and distribute over the pizza.

11. Drizzle Chile Oil over the pizza. Serve with the lime wedges and hot sauce.

Tips: You can use chicken breast or pork loin instead of the steak if you wish. We also like to serve this pizza with some freshly made salsa on the side.

HOT SALAMI PIZZA

 500° **10oz**

Yield: 1 (12-inch [30-cm]) pizza

We like it hot! Some days, nothing works quite as well as a spicy pizza, topped with chiles or hot sauce. This pizza is covered with spicy soppressata, though you could also use a hot chorizo or ventricina piccante salami. We also use homemade Chile Oil to spice things up a bit, and if that's not enough, some chopped fresh or canned chilies should do the trick.

1 Classic New York Dough, 10 ounces (280 g) (page 194)

3 ounces (90 mL) La Salsa, or the spicy variation (page 199)

10–12 thin slices hot soppressata or other spicy salami

4 ounces (110 g) mozzarella, grated

1 Grilled Red Pepper, sliced thin (page 283)

Dried oregano, to taste

Chile Oil (page 281), for drizzling

10–12 fresh basil leaves

1. Place a baking stone in the oven, and preheat to 500°F (260°C) or higher for 1 hour.

2. Stretch the pizza dough to a diameter of 12 inches (30 cm).

3. Spread the sauce over the dough, leaving a 1-inch (3-cm) border.

4. Distribute the salami over the sauce. Spread the mozzarella over the sauce.

5. Top the pizza with the Grilled Red Pepper and dried oregano, and bake on the baking stone until the crust is golden and the cheese is bubbling.

6. Remove the pizza from the oven, and place it on a plate.

7. Sprinkle the Chile Oil over the pizza, top with the basil leaves, and serve.

Tip: Sometimes nothing can beat a spicy pizza, but as with any pizza, a balance among all the ingredients is important. The basil gives this pizza a fresh taste, which goes well with the spice.

PIZZA AL TONNO

 500° **9oz**

Yield: 1 (12-inch [30-cm]) pizza

"Tuna on a pizza? And canned tuna, at that? You have got to be kidding." No, we are not kidding. As a matter of fact, you wouldn't have to look far to find this pizza being served in the middle of Naples. Delizioso!

6 ounces (170 g) good-quality canned tuna (in oil)

Extra virgin olive oil, for drizzling

2 cloves garlic, peeled and minced

½ small onion, sliced in thin rings

1 Neapolitan Dough, 9 ounces (260 g) (page 192)

8 cherry tomatoes, sliced in half

2 ounces (60 g) fresh mozzarella di bufala, shredded

1 Grilled Red Pepper (page 283), sliced in thin strips

Red pepper flakes, to taste

Parmigiano-Reggiano, to taste

Fresh thyme, for garnish

1. Place a baking stone in the oven, and preheat to 500°F (260°C) or higher for 1 hour.

2. Drain 2 tablespoons of the oil from the tuna into a skillet. If you do not have enough, add a bit of the extra virgin olive oil.

3. Warm the oil over medium heat. Add the garlic and onion to the skillet and cook for 3–4 minutes. Remove the pan from the heat.

4. Stretch the pizza dough to a diameter of 12 inches (30 cm).

5. Distribute the cherry tomatoes over the dough, leaving a 1-inch (3-cm) border.

6. Spread the mozzarella over the pizza. Top the pizza with the Grilled Red Pepper strips and tuna, then pour the oil from the pan over the pizza.

7. Bake the pizza on the baking stone until the crust is golden and the cheese is bubbling.

8. Remove the pizza from the oven, and place it on a plate.

9. Drizzle a little more olive oil over the pizza, and add red pepper flakes to taste. Grate Parmigiano-Reggiano over the pizza, top with fresh thyme, and serve.

Tip: In Italy, you will also find versions of this pizza using other ingredients, and excluding tomatoes.

MATS'S GREAT LAKE PIZZA

 500° **9oz**

Yield: 1 (12-inch [30-cm]) pizza

This is another of Mats's favorites, inspired by the pizzas Nick Lessins (page 93) prepared for us at his now-closed restaurant, Great Lake, in Chicago. One of the pizzas contained goat's milk cheddar and oyster mushrooms, and this is Mats's version of it. If mushroom pizza is your thing, look no further!

1 The Wet One Dough, 9 ounces (260 g) (page 193)

2 ounces (60 g) fresh mozzarella di bufala, shredded

1 ounce (30 g) baby spinach leaves (or regular spinach leaves)

2 ounces (60 g) mushrooms, cleaned (porcini, portobello, or other types)

1 ounce (30 g) ricotta

1 ounce (30 g) Pecorino Romano, crumbled

1 clove garlic, peeled and minced

Extra virgin olive oil, for drizzling

Freshly ground black pepper, to taste

1. Place a baking stone in the oven, and preheat to 500°F (260°C) or higher for 1 hour.

2. Stretch the pizza dough to a diameter of 12 inches (30 cm).

3. Spread the mozzarella over the pizza.

4. Distribute the spinach leaves over the pizza. Distribute the mushrooms over the pizza. Using a spoon, distribute the ricotta over the pizza.

5. Top the pizza with the Pecorino Romano, garlic, and a drizzle of olive oil. Bake the pizza on the baking stone until the crust is golden and the cheese is bubbling.

6. Remove the pizza from the oven, and place it on a plate. Top with black pepper and another drizzle of olive oil, and serve.

Tip

Other types of mushrooms will also work well on this pizza.

PIZZA WITH BRUSSELS SPROUTS

Yield: 1 (12-inch [30-cm]) pizza

 500° 9oz

This is Mats's favorite pizza, inspired by one he ate at Motorino Pizza in New York City. The star ingredient is Brussels sprouts, and for Mats, they opened a world of new possibilities for pizza ingredients. This was also the pizza that introduced him to white pizza (pizza bianca). He, like many of us, grew up with tomato sauce on all pizzas, but today his pizza of choice is always tomato-free.

1 teaspoon sea salt

2 ounces (60 g) Brussels sprouts

1 Our Favorite Dough, 9 ounces (260 g) (page 191)

2 ounces (60 g) fresh mozzarella, shredded

1 ounce (30 g) fresh ricotta

1 ounce (30 g) Pecorino Romano, crumbled

1 ounce (30 g) smoked pancetta, thinly sliced (alternatives: bacon or unsmoked pancetta)

1 clove garlic, peeled and thinly sliced

Parmigiano-Reggiano, for grating

Coarsely ground black pepper, to taste

Extra virgin olive oil, for drizzling

1. Place a baking stone in the oven, and preheat to 500°F (260°C) or higher for 1 hour.

2. Bring 1 quart water with sea salt to a boil in a 2-quart saucepan.

3. While the water is heating, rinse the Brussels sprouts in cold water, and remove any wilted leaves. Place the Brussels sprouts in the boiling water, and cook for 2 minutes.

4. Remove the Brussels sprouts with a slotted spoon, and place them in a bowl of ice water for a few minutes to cool. Pour off the water.

5. Stretch the pizza dough to a diameter of 12 inches (30 cm).

6. Distribute the mozzarella, ricotta, and Pecorino Romano over the pizza. Distribute the pancetta and garlic over the pizza.

7. Peel the leaves from the Brussels sprouts, and place them on the pizza.

8. Bake the pizza on the baking stone until the crust is golden and the cheese is bubbling.

9. Remove the pizza from the oven, and place it on a plate. Top with coarsely ground black pepper and a bit of olive oil, and serve.

Tip

Mats prefers fresh Brussels sprouts on this pizza but says that frozen will work fine. This will also give you the opportunity to make this pizza year-round.

BONATA

 400° 9oz

Yield: 1 (12-inch [30-cm]) pizza

The word *bonata* is Sicilian, and it means both "generous" and "good bread." Normally, the bonata is a bread dough that is filled and rolled up before baking. This version, a close relative of stromboli, is filled with anchovies, sausage, garlic, and Parmesan. Other ingredients are also welcome, and no doubt this is a pizza you will soon prepare again.

2 ounces (60 g) spinach leaves

2 ounces (60 g) Hot Italian Sausage (page 283)

1 Our Favorite Dough, 9 ounces (260 g) (page 191)

4 (preferably) Italian anchovies, minced

2 cloves garlic, peeled and minced

3 tablespoons grated Parmigiano-Reggiano

Extra virgin olive oil, for brushing

1. Preheat the oven to 400°F (200°C) for 1 hour.

2. Place the spinach in boiling water for 30 seconds. Pour off the water, and let the spinach cool. Wrap the spinach in paper towels, and squeeze to remove excess moisture.

3. Fry the sausage in a skillet over medium–high heat until brown but not cooked through. Transfer the sausage to paper towels to absorb excess grease.

4. Roll out the dough to a fairly thin rectangle with the long side facing you at the countertop.

5. Distribute the spinach, sausage, anchovies, garlic, and Parmigiano-Reggiano over the dough, leaving a 1-inch (3-cm) border.

6. Starting with the long side, carefully roll up the dough. Tuck the ends of the dough under the rolled-up pizza.

7. Brush a baking sheet with extra virgin olive oil. Brush the top of the pizza roll with oil, and make 3–4 slices in the top with a sharp knife.

8. Use two spatulas to move the pizza onto the baking sheet, and bake the pizza in the oven until golden brown.

9. Remove the pizza from the oven, and let it cool for 10 minutes. Cut into slices, and serve.

Tips

You can also use the same ingredients to make a calzone or regular pizza. If you like, you can also add grated mozzarella to the pizza before rolling it up.

It is not necessary to let the pizza rise after filling and rolling it up, but if you do, let it rise for about a half hour to get a more bread-like pizza.

PISSALADIÈRE

Yield: 1 (12-inch [30-cm]) pizza

🔲 500° ⬤9oz

France has made a strong contribution to the world of pizza. This dish originates in Provence, which borders Italy. The filling is composed of caramelized onions, anchovies, and olives, and it is called *pissaladière*. This pizza makes a wonderful appetizer with a glass of white or sparkling wine.

3 tablespoons extra virgin olive oil, plus more for drizzling

2 large onions, peeled and sliced into thin rings

2 teaspoons fresh thyme leaves, plus more for garnish

Pinch sea salt

1 The Wet One Dough, 9 ounces (260 g) (page 193)

15–20 pitted black olives

8 anchovies

2 tablespoons Parmigiano-Reggiano, grated

1. Place a baking stone in the oven, and preheat to 500°F (260°C) or higher for 1 hour.

2. Warm 3 tablespoons (45 mL) of the oil in a wide pan over low heat.

3. Add the onions, 2 teaspoons of the thyme, and salt to the pan, and stir well. Cook until the onions are soft and have a nice nutty brown color. When the onions are done, transfer them to a bowl to cool.

4. Stretch the pizza dough to a diameter of 12 inches (30 cm).

5. Spread the onions over the dough, leaving a 1-inch (3-cm) border.

6. Spread the olives and anchovies over the pizza. Spread the Parmigiano-Reggiano over the pizza, and drizzle with more olive oil.

7. Bake the pizza on the baking stone until the crust is golden.

8. Remove the pizza from the oven, and place it on a plate. Garnish with more fresh thyme, and serve.

Tips

Cooking at a low temperature for a longer period of time are the secrets for the most flavorful—and never bitter—onions.

This pizza can be served both warm and cold, and it is also good at room temperature.

ROLLED-UP CALZONE WITH RICOTTA AND SALAMI

  500° 9oz

Yield: 1 (12-inch [30-cm]) pizza

What is this? A calzone? Maybe a stromboli? Or is this a bonata? Think of it as a new way to form your pizza, an alternative to flat and round. This is one of the few pizzas where we prefer to roll out the dough with a rolling pin, and whatever you decide to call it, you are going to love it.

1 Our Favorite Dough, 9 ounces (260 g) (page 191)

4 ounces (110 g) ricotta

1 large canned tomato (preferably San Marzano DOP), sliced in thin strips

1 ounce (30 g) salami, sliced in thin strips

1 ounce (30 g) pitted olives, chopped

Extra virgin olive oil, for brushing

1. Preheat the oven to 500°F (260°C) or higher for 1 hour.

2. Roll out the dough to a fairly thin rectangle with the long side facing you at the countertop.

3. Distribute the ricotta, tomato, salami, and olives over the dough, leaving a 1-inch (3-cm) border.

4. Starting with the long side, carefully roll up the dough. Tuck the ends of the dough under the rolled-up pizza.

5. Brush a baking sheet with oil. Brush the top of the pizza roll with oil.

6. Use two spatulas to move the pizza onto the baking sheet, and bake the pizza until golden brown.

7. Remove the pizza from the oven, and let it cool for 10 minutes. Cut into slices, and serve.

Tip

You can, and should, try other ingredients in this pizza. Other cheeses and cured meats will work well.

SMOKIN' SALMON PIZZA

Yield: 1 (12-inch [30-cm]) pizza

 500° 9oz

In Norway, we eat a lot of salmon: poached, oven-baked, grilled—you name it. We also eat a lot of gravlax (cured salmon) and, of course, smoked salmon. Asparagus is a vegetable we often serve with salmon, and we also use it on this delightful pizza.

1–2 teaspoons trout roe or other type of roe

2–3 tablespoons soy sauce

3 asparagus spears (a combination of green and white is good)

1 Our Favorite Dough, 9 ounces (260 g) (page 191)

5 ounces (140 g) mozzarella di bufala, shredded

2 ounces (60 g) smoked salmon, thinly sliced

7–8 baby spinach leaves (alternative: 3–4 regular spinach leaves)

Sorrel leaves or any baby lettuce leaves

1 tablespoon Dill Oil (see recipe below)

Extra virgin olive oil, for sprinkling

Freshly ground black pepper, to taste

1. Place a baking stone in the oven, and preheat to 500°F (260°C) or higher for 1 hour.

2. Place the roe in a small bowl, and cover with the soy sauce. Let stand for 30 minutes.

3. Use a potato peeler to trim the root ends of the asparagus, and cut each piece in half.

4. Fill a saucepan with water, and bring to a boil. Cook the root ends of the asparagus in the boiling water for 2 minutes (less if the pieces are on the thin side). Add the asparagus tops, and cook about a minute more, until just tender. Pour off the water, and let the asparagus cool.

5. Slice each piece of asparagus in half lengthwise. Set aside.

6. Stretch the pizza dough to a diameter of 12 inches (30 cm).

7. Spread the mozzarella over the dough, leaving a 1-inch (3-cm) border.

8. Bake the pizza on the baking stone until the crust is golden and the cheese is bubbling.

9. Remove the pizza from the oven, and place it on a plate. Distribute the asparagus, smoked salmon, spinach, and sorrel leaves over the pizza.

10. Drain the soy sauce from the roe, and distribute the roe over the pizza.

11. Sprinkle the Dill Oil and extra virgin olive oil over the pizza. Add black pepper, and serve.

Tips

Another idea is to slice the raw asparagus on a mandoline. If you do this, your cooking time will be reduced to just a few seconds.

You can make this pizza without the Dill Oil. Replace the oil with some fresh dill.

DILL OIL

Yield: About 1 cup

4 ounces (110 g) fresh dill

½ cup (110 mL) vegetable oil

1. Place the ingredients in a blender, and purée until smooth. Pour the mixture into a saucepan, and warm to 165°F.

2. Pour the Dill Oil back in the blender, and purée for 1 more minute.

3. Pour the Dill Oil back in the saucepan, and warm over medium heat, until just starting to boil.

4. Remove from the heat, pour through a fine sieve, and let cool.

IL MANTUANO

Yield: 1 (12-inch [30-cm]) pizza

Jonathan Goldsmith from Spacca Napoli in Chicago (page 86) gave us this recipe. He uses guanciale (cured pork jowl) and rapini, just as one would in Italy. You can substitute pancetta or bacon for the guanciale and broccolini for the rapini if they are not available in your area. The combination works extremely well, and with the addition of red pepper flakes, you might find yourself craving this pizza when you least expect it!

3 ounces (90 g) rapini (broccoli rabe) (alternative: broccolini)

2 tablespoons extra virgin olive oil, plus more for drizzling

2 cloves garlic, peeled and roughly chopped

Pinch sea salt

1 Our Favorite Dough, 9 ounces (260 g) (page 191)

3 ounces (90 g) fresh mozzarella, shredded

6 slices guanciale (cured pork jowl) (alternatives: pancetta or bacon)

Red pepper flakes, to taste

1. Place a baking stone in the oven, and preheat to 500°F (260°C) or higher for 1 hour.

2. Bring a pot of salted water to a boil. Add the rapini, and let it cook for 30 seconds.

3. Remove the rapini from the boiling water with a slotted spoon, and transfer it to a bowl of ice water. Let it cool in the water for a couple minutes, then drain.

4. Wrap the rapini in paper towels. Gently squeeze to remove most of the moisture.

5. Warm the 2 tablespoons of olive oil in a skillet. Add the garlic and cook over medium–high heat for 1 minute. Add the rapini and sea salt, and cook for about 2 more minutes.

6. Remove from the heat, pour off the oil, and place the rapini and garlic on paper towels.

7. Stretch the pizza dough to a diameter of 12 inches (30 cm).

8. Spread the cheese over the dough, leaving a 1-inch (3-cm) border.

9. Distribute the rapini, garlic, and guanciale over the pizza. Add the red pepper flakes and a drizzle of olive oil.

10. Bake the pizza on the baking stone until the crust is golden and the cheese is bubbling.

11. Remove the pizza from the oven, and place it on a plate. Top the pizza with a bit more olive oil and, if you like, more red pepper flakes. Serve.

PECAN PIZZA PIE ANNO 2013

 400° 9oz

Yield: 1 (10-inch [25-cm]) pie or several portion-sized dessert pizzas

In 1998, Tore, Craig, and a Norwegian chef named Trond Moi won first place for their dessert pizza at the International Pizza Expo in Las Vegas. There were a few challenges that had to be overcome, and the trio made many failed attempts before landing on the winning recipe. All entries had to include cheese, not the most common ingredient in this pizza's inspiration: pecan pie. The pizzas had to be baked in a pizza oven at a high temperature, also unusual in pecan pie baking.

The winning entry was based on a classic pecan pie but with the addition of a thin layer of sweetened cream cheese spread over the crust. The challenge of a high baking temperature was met by using flour in the filling so that it would set quickly enough. This recipe is the revised version, 15 years in the making, and we are sure you will enjoy it.

1½ cups (350 g) pecans

3 eggs, beaten for 1 minute

1 cup (240 g) sugar

1 cup (240 mL) light corn syrup or maple syrup

2 tablespoons melted unsalted butter

2 tablespoons flour

Seeds from ½ vanilla bean (alternative: 1 teaspoon vanilla extract)

⅛ teaspoon salt

1 Classic New York Dough, 9 ounces (260 g) (page 194)

Caramel Sauce, for serving (see recipe on next page)

1. Preheat the oven to 400°F.

2. Place the pecans on a baking sheet, and bake for 3–4 minutes, until they just become aromatic.

3. Remove the pecans from the oven, and let them cool. Pulverize half the pecans in a food processor or spice mill.

4. Combine the pecans and all the remaining ingredients, except the dough and Caramel Sauce, in a large bowl.

5. Stretch the pizza dough to a diameter of 12 inches (30 cm). Place the dough neatly in the bottom and sides of a 10-inch (25-cm) pie form or pizza pan. You can also make portion-sized pies if you wish.

6. Pour the filling over the dough in the pan, about ⅔ full.

7. Bake the pie in the middle of the oven until the filling is just set and the surface of the filling is no longer shiny.

8. Remove the pie from the oven, and let it cool completely down on a wire rack. Serve with Caramel Sauce.

Tips

No matter how much you really want to eat the pie after it comes out of the oven, wait! The pie needs to cool down, and this process also helps the pie set. Serve with vanilla ice cream or whipped cream.

Our original version of this pie had a layer of sweetened cream cheese covering the crust before the filling was poured in. If you would like to give it a try, you can mix one package of Philadelphia cream cheese with 1 tablespoon of sugar and ½ teaspoon vanilla extract. The cooking process is the same.

CARAMEL SAUCE

Yield: About 1¼ cups

1 cup (240 mL) heavy cream
3½ ounces (100 g) light brown sugar
4 tablespoons unsalted butter

1. Warm the cream over medium–low heat in a saucepan. (Do not bring to a boil!) Remove from the heat.

2. Melt the brown sugar in another saucepan over medium heat. Stir gently once in a while.

3. Dip a pastry brush in cold water. Brush the sides of the pan with the brown sugar so that the sugar does not crystallize.

4. Pour the warm cream, a little at a time, into the pan of melted sugar, stirring constantly.

5. Stir the butter into the sauce a little at a time.

6. Bring the sauce to a gentle boil, and let simmer for about 3 minutes.

7. Strain the sauce into a metal bowl, and stir once in a while as it cools.

NUTELLA ALLA SPACCA NAPOLI

 500° 9oz

Yield: 1 (10-inch [25-cm]) pizza

This is the dessert pizza Jonathan Goldsmith of Spacca Napoli (page 86) gave to us as we left his pizzeria in Chicago. We shared the pizza with the others on the bus, and it was, needless to say, a big hit.

1 Our Favorite Dough, 9 ounces (260 grams) (page 191)

4 tablespoons Nutella

Powdered sugar, for sprinkling

1. Preheat the oven to 500°F (260°C) or higher for 1 hour.

2. Stretch the pizza dough to a diameter of 10 inches (25 cm), and place it neatly in a pizza pan.

3. Fill a saucepan with about 2 inches (5 cm) of water. Bring to a boil, and reduce the heat.

4. Pour the Nutella into a bowl large enough to rest inside the edge of the saucepan without the bottom of the bowl touching the boiling water.

5. Stir until the Nutella is soft and spreadable.

6. Bake the pizza crust until it is golden. The dough should puff up during the baking.

7. Remove the crust from the oven, and place the pan on a heat-resistant surface.

8. Slice the dough in half horizontally as if it were a hamburger bun, leaving an edge around the bottom half of the crust.

9. Spread the Nutella over the bottom crust, then lay the top crust over the Nutella.

10. Sprinkle powdered sugar over the pizza, carefully cut into slices, and serve.

Tip

This pizza is perfect for dessert or as a sweet snack with a cup of coffee.

DESSERT PIZZA WITH CHÈVRE

 500°

Yield: This pizza can be made in any size you like and is traditionally shared with others.

Think of this dish as your cheese course, preceding or replacing dessert. There is no sauce on this pizza, just chèvre (goat cheese), fresh rosemary, and honey. We like serving this pizza in small individual portions, but serving slices from the larger pie will work just fine.

1 Our Favorite Dough (page 191)
Chèvre, thinly sliced
Fresh rosemary leaves
Acacia honey or any other good honey

1. Place a baking stone in the oven, and preheat to 500°F (260°C) or higher for 1 hour.

2. Roll out the dough so that it is very thin.

3. Distribute the cheese and rosemary leaves over the pizza.

4. Bake the pizza on the baking stone until the crust is golden brown and the cheese is melted and starting to brown.

5. Remove the pizza from the oven, and place it on a plate. Drizzle honey over the pizza, cut into small pieces, and serve.

 Tip

Chèvre is goat cheese. There are many types of chèvre, and most of them will work on this pizza. Two of our favorites are Bucheron and Sainte-Maure de Touraine.

SMOKED MOZZARELLA

Ingredients
1 8- or 9-ounce (250-gram) ball fresh mozzarella
Vegetable oil

Equipment
Grill
Wood chips (hickory or apple)
Cheesecloth
String
Sharp knife
Small aluminum tray
Aluminum foil

1. Place a couple handfuls of wood chips in water about an hour before using them. The moisture will help the chips smoke instead of just burning up.

2. Fire up the grill. With a gas grill, it is enough to use one burner, and the temperature should be about 150°F (65°C). If you are using a charcoal grill (it is important that you use a grill with a lid), it is enough to have a small amount of lighted charcoal or briquettes in a corner of the grill.

3. Lay a piece of cheesecloth on the counter, and brush it with oil. Brush the mozzarella with oil as well. Wrap the mozzarella in the cheesecloth, and fasten with a piece of string.

4. Use a sharp knife to make several small holes in the bottom of an aluminum tray. Place the cheese in the tray.

5. (If using a gas grill, skip to the next step.) If using a charcoal grill, place the aluminum tray with the cheese over indirect heat, away from the heat source. Grab a handful of wood chips, let the water drip off them a bit, and place them right on top of the charcoal or briquettes. Close the lid of the grill.

6. (If using a charcoal grill, skip to the next step.) If using a gas grill, make a double layer of aluminum foil, about 12 x 12 inches (30 x 30 cm). Place the foil on the counter, and add a couple of handfuls of the wood chips. Wrap the chips in the foil, creating a rather thick round disc (2 x 6 inches [5 x 15 cm]). Use the knife to make several slits in the top of the foil package. Carefully place the foil package with the chips directly on the lit burner you are using. Close the lid, and wait until you see smoke escaping from the edges of the lid. Raise the lid, and use tongs to move the foil package with the wood chips from the burner to the grill's grates. Place the aluminum form with the cheese on the grates, away from the heat source, and immediately close the lid.

7. Turn down the heat to about 100 degrees. Let the cheese smoke for 10–15 minutes, until both the cheese and cheesecloth have a brownish-yellow color. Remove the aluminum tray with the cheese from the grill, and place it on a heat-resistant surface. Let the cheese cool completely before removing it from the tray so that the cheese, softened during the smoking process, can firm up again. The cheese is now ready to use.

CHILE OIL
Yield: About 1 cup

3–4 fresh or dried chiles, sliced in half lengthwise

¾ cup (180 mL) vegetable oil (sunflower oil works well)

1. Place the chiles in a small saucepan. Add the oil, and warm over medium–low heat for about 5 minutes. Do not let boil.

2. Pour the oil and chiles into a heat-resistant bowl, and cover with plastic wrap. Let the Chile Oil stand for 1–2 hours.

3. Strain the oil through a cheesecloth into a bottle or another bowl.

Tips: You can use any type of chiles you prefer. This and the number of chilies will affect the flavor and the heat of the final product.

You might also try adding a clove or two of garlic to this oil or even omitting the chilies to make garlic oil. For garlic oil, use 5–6 cloves of garlic, sliced in half. Another twist is to use a handful of fresh herbs, with or without the garlic, and extra virgin olive oil instead of the sunflower oil.

SOUR CREAM DIP

Yield: 1¼ cup

Dip your favorite pizza slice in this delicious dip for a new twist on your favorite pizza. This dip can be used on pretty much any pizza—a method that is very common in Norway.

1 cup (240 mL) sour cream or crème fraîche
Grated rind of ¼ lemon
1 clove garlic, pressed
1 tablespoon mayonnaise
1 tablespoon finely chopped parsley
2 teaspoons finely chopped scallions
1 teaspoon horseradish cream
1 teaspoon lemon juice
1 teaspoon sugar
¼ teaspoon freshly ground black pepper
Pinch salt

1. Mix the sour cream, lemon rind, garlic, mayonnaise, parsley, scallions, horseradish cream, lemon juice, and sugar in a bowl.

2. Season with the pepper and salt, and taste to see whether you need to adjust with a bit more lemon juice or sugar.

Tip: This dip also works well with chips or raw vegetable slices.

PIZZA SEASONING

Yield: About 4½ ounces

Grated Parmesan and chile flakes are popular at many American pizzerias. Try this seasoning mix to give your pizzas a new taste dimension.

4 tablespoons (60 g) salt
1½ tablespoons sugar
1 tablespoon coarsely ground black pepper
1 tablespoon garlic powder
1 tablespoon onion powder
1 teaspoon ground fennel seeds
1 teaspoon dried oregano
1 teaspoon dried thyme
¼ teaspoon cayenne pepper

1. Mix all of the ingredients together in a small bowl. Store in an airtight container, preferably in a dark cabinet.

PICKLED RED ONIONS

Yield: About 1 cup using a medium red onion

1 red onion, peeled and thinly sliced
½ teaspoon dried oregano
¼ teaspoon freshly ground black pepper
¼ teaspoon ground cumin
¼ teaspoon salt
2 cloves garlic, peeled and sliced in half
¼ cup (60 mL) apple cider vinegar

1. Cook the onion slices in boiling water for about 45 seconds. Pour off the water, and place the onion slices in a bowl.

2. Add the oregano, black pepper, and cumin to the onions.

3. Sprinkle the salt over the garlic, and crush the garlic cloves with the flat side of a large knife. Add the garlic to the onion mixture.

4. Pour the vinegar over the onion mixture, and top with just enough water to cover the onions. Let the onions stand until ready to use.

PESTO

Yield: About 1½ cups

4 ounces (110 g) fresh basil
4 tablespoons (60 g) pine nuts
1 clove garlic, peeled
Salt, to taste
2 tablespoons Parmigiano-Reggiano, finely grated
¾ cup (180 mL) extra virgin olive oil

1. Rinse the basil in cold water, and dry with a kitchen towel.

2. Place the basil, pine nuts, garlic, and salt in a mortar, and crush the ingredients with the pestle.

3. Add the grated Parmigiano-Reggiano a little at a time, mixing the cheese into the mixture with the pestle.

4. Transfer the basil mixture to a bowl. Drizzle the oil, first a few drops at a time, then in a thin drizzle, while stirring with a wooden spoon. Add a bit more oil if necessary.

GRILLED RED PEPPERS

Yield: About 4 cups

These red bell peppers can be grilled or baked in the oven. If using the oven, set the temperature at 400°F (200°C), and bake for about 30–40 minutes. Turn them once in a while during baking.

4 (or more) red bell peppers
2–3 tablespoons (28–45 mL) extra virgin olive oil

1. Grill the peppers over the heat source of the grill. The skin will turn black.

2. Remove the peppers, and place them in a heatproof bowl. Cover with plastic wrap, and let cool for about 30 minutes.

3. Remove the plastic wrap, and remove the stems, seeds, and blackened skin from the peppers.

4. Drizzle the olive oil on the peppers, cover the bowl with plastic film, and store in the refrigerator. Slice or serve as desired.

SALSICCIA

Yield: About 2½ pounds

1 tablespoon fennel seeds
2¼ pounds (1 kg) coarsely ground pork
2 cloves garlic, crushed and finely chopped
1 tablespoon minced parsley
2 teaspoons salt
1 teaspoon coarsely ground black pepper
½ teaspoon dried oregano

1. Toast the fennel seeds in a dry skillet just until you can smell the fennel aroma.

2. Mix all of the ingredients together in a bowl.

Tip: Leftovers can go into the freezer for later use. Pack smaller amounts, roughly 3 ounces (90 g) each, in plastic bags.

SAUSAGE

Yield: About 2½ pounds

2 teaspoons fennel seeds
2¼ pounds (1 kg) coarsely ground pork
2 cloves garlic, crushed and finely chopped
2 teaspoons salt
1 teaspoon sugar
1 teaspoon freshly ground black pepper
½ teaspoon dried marjoram
¼ teaspoon cayenne pepper

1. Toast the fennel seeds in a dry skillet just until you can smell the fennel aroma.

2. Mix all of the ingredients together in a bowl.

Tip: Leftovers can go into the freezer for later use. Pack smaller amounts, roughly 3 ounces (90 g) each, in plastic bags.

HOT ITALIAN SAUSAGE

Yield: About 2½ pounds

1 tablespoon fennel seeds
2½ pounds (1 kg) ground pork
1 clove garlic, crushed and finely chopped
1 tablespoon finely chopped parsley
2 teaspoons kosher salt
1 teaspoon coarsely ground black pepper
½ teaspoon red pepper flakes (or more if desired)
¼ teaspoon cayenne pepper (or more if desired)

1. Toast the fennel seeds in a dry skillet just until you can smell the fennel aroma.

2. Mix all of the ingredients together in a bowl.

Tip: Leftovers can go into the freezer for later use. Pack smaller amounts, roughly 3 ounces (90 g) each, in plastic bags.

RESOURCES

Italy

00100
Via Giovanni Branca, 88
Rome
Featured on page 27

Antica Focacceria San Francesco
www.anticafocacceria.it
Featured on page 32

Antico Forno Roscioli
Via dei Chiavari, 34
Rome
www.anticofornoroscioli.it/en
Featured on page 23

Forno Campo de' Fiori
Campo de' Fiori, 22
Rome
www.fornocampodefiori.com
Featured on page 24

Il Pizzaiolo del Presidente
Via dei Tribunali, 120
Naples
Featured on pp. 12 and 19

La Figlia del Presidente
Via Grande Archivio, 23
Naples
www.lafigliadelpresidente.it
Featured on page 12

L'Antica Pizzeria da Michele
Via Cesare Sersale, 1/3
Naples
www.damichele.net
Featured on page 11

L'Antica Pizzeria Port'Alba
Via Port'Alba, 18
Naples
www.anticapizzeriaristoranteportalba.com
Featured on page 19

Panificio Graziano Salvatore
Via del Granatiere, 11/13
Palermo
www.panificiograziano.it
Featured on page 31

Panificio Pasticceria Tossini
Via Roma, 15
Recco
www.tossini.it
Featured on page 43

Pepe in Grani
Vico S. Giovanni Battista, 3
Caiazzo
www.pepeingrani.it
Featured on page 37

Pizzaria La Notizia
Via Michelangelo da Caravaggio, 53
Naples
www.enzococcia.it
Featured on page 6

Pizzarium
Via della Meloria, 43
Rome
Featured on page 29

Pizzeria Brandi
Salita Sant'Anna di Palazzo, 1-2
Naples
www.brandi.it
Featured on page 19

Pizzeria Di Matteo
Via dei Tribunali, 94
Naples
www.pizzeriadimatteo.com
Featured on page 5

Pizzeria Gino Sorbillo
Via dei Tribunali, 32
Naples
www.sorbillo.it/en
Featured on page 8

Pizzeria i Tigli
Via Camporosolo, 11
San Bonifacio
www.pizzeriaitigli.it
Featured on page 41

Pizzeria Starita a Materdei
Via Materdei, 27/28
Naples
www.pizzeriastarita.it
Featured on page 14

Pizzeria Trianon da Ciro
Via Pietro Colletta, 44/46
Naples
www.pizzeriatrianon.it
Featured on page 19

Ristorante Ettore di Napoli
Via Santa Lucia, 56
Naples
www.ristoranteettore.it
Featured on page 19

Ristorante Mattozzi Europeo
Via Marchese Campodisola, 4
Naples
www.mattozzieuropeo.com
Featured on page 19

Ristorante Umberto
Via Alabardieri, 30/31
Naples
www.umberto.it
Featured on page 18

Salumeria Roscioli
Via dei Giubbonari, 21
Rome
www.salumeriaroscioli.com
Featured on page 23

Sforno
Via Statilio Ottato, 110/116
Rome
www.sforno.it
Featured on page 27

Tonda
Via Valle Corteno, 31
Rome
Featured on page 27

New York

Bari Restaurant & Pizza Equipment
240 Bowery
Manhattan
www.bariequipment.com
Featured on page 75

Di Fara Pizza
1424 Avenue J
Brooklyn
www.difara.com
Featured on page 58

Don Antonio by Starita
309 West Fiftieth Street
Manhattan
www.donantoniopizza.com
Featured on page 67

Eataly NYC
200 Fifth Avenue
Manhattan
www.eataly.com/nyc
Featured on page 77

(Famous) Joe's Pizza
www.joespizzanyc.com
Featured on page 66

Forcella
334 Bowery
East Village
www.forcellaeatery.com
Featured on page 66

John's of Bleecker Street
278 Bleecker Street
West Village
www.johnsbrickovenpizza.com
Featured on page 67

Kesté Pizza & Vino
271 Bleecker Street
West Village
www.kestepizzeria.com
Featured on page 57

Lombardi's
www.firstpizza.com
featured on page 54

Lucali
575 Henry Street
Brooklyn
www.lucali.com
Featured on page 67

Motorino
www.motorinopizza.com
Featured on page 66

New York Pizza Suprema
413 Eighth Avenue
Manhattan
www.nypizzasuprema.com
Featured on page 63

Pizza a Casa Pizza School
371 Grand Street
Lower East Side
www.pizzaschool.com
Featured on page 73

Sam's Restaurant
238 Court Street
Brooklyn
Featured on page 65

Totonno's
1524 Neptune Avenue
Brooklyn
Featured on page 61

Chicago

Burt's Place
8541 Ferris Avenue
Morton Grove
Featured on page 91

Coalfire Pizza
1321 West Grand Avenue
www.coalfirechicago.com
Featured on page 88

Lou Malnati's Pizzeria
www.loumalnatis.com
Featured on page 85

Spacca Napoli Pizzeria
1769 West Sunnyside Avenue
www.spaccanapolipizzeria.com
Featured on page 86

Arizona

Pizzeria Bianco
www.pizzeriabianco.com
Featured on page 97

California

A16
2355 Chestnut Street
San Francisco
www.a16sf.com
Featured on page 126

Big Mama's & Papa's Pizzeria
www.bigmamaspizza.com
Featured on page 110

Chez Panisse
1517 Shattuck Avenue
Berkeley
www.chezpanisse.com
Featured on page 103

Del Popolo
San Francisco
www.delpopolosf.com
Featured on page 129

Gjelina and GTA (Gjelina Take Away)
1429 Abbot Kinney Boulevard
Venice
www.gjelina.com
Featured on page 113

Pizzeria Delfina
3621 Eighteenth Street
San Francisco
www.pizzeriadelfina.com/mission
Featured on page 133

Pizzeria Mozza
641 North Highland Avenue
Los Angeles
www.pizzeriamozza.com
Featured on page 107

**Tony Gemignani's International
School of Pizza**
www.internationalschoolofpizza.com
Featured on page 123

Tony's Pizza Napoletana
1570 Stockton Street
San Francisco
www.tonyspizzanapoletana.com
Featured on page 123

Una Pizza Napoletana
210 Eleventh Street
San Francisco
www.unapizza.com
Featured on page 117

People

Beniamino Bilali
www.beniaminobilali.it
Featured on page 45

Monica Piscitelli: Campania Che Vai
www.campaniachevai.blogspot.com
Featured on page 16

Tony Gemignani
www.tonygemignani.com
Featured on page 123

Wolfgang Puck
www.wolfgangpuck.com
Featured on page 103

Groups/Associations

Chicago Pizza Tours
www.chicagopizzatours.com
Featured on page 82

Scott's Pizza Tours
www.scottspizzatours.com
Featured on page 69

Squadra Nazionale Acrobati Pizzaioli
www.nazionaleacrobatipizzaioli.it
Featured on page 48

ACKNOWLEDGMENTS

First, we want to thank the wonderful and talented people we have met along the way, both in the United States and Italy. You inspire us every day, and we are very sure that you will inspire even more people in the coming years. Grazie mille!

We spent five weeks on the road while working on this book. We paid for far fewer pizzas than we ate, and we are eternally grateful. Once again, a big thank-you to everyone involved in helping us out!

We take full responsibility for any errors found in this book. We have worked very hard to avoid them, but if we haven't done our homework well enough, it's we who must be blamed.

A heartfelt thanks goes out to The Lisa Ekus Group and to Agate Publishing. Without you there would be no American version of this book. Thanks for believing in the project.

Thanks to Tynlee Roberts for an excellent job of transcribing and editing the English interviews and texts, and the same to Lisbeth Kristoffersen with the "Okie-fied" Norwegian texts.

We also thank Lucas Holm and Mitra Ekström for the digital photo work, and of course our favorite stylist, Ann Kristin Møsth Wang. Say "Cheese!"

Thanks to the suppliers who helped us with premium ingredients for recipe testing and photos.

A special thanks goes out to Elen Marthe S. Carrara: Thanks so much for the trip(s), Marthe. Ciao, bella!

A big thank-you to all the folks at Kagge Publishing in Oslo, and Beniamino Bilali for his work during the photo shoot. Thanks to Magne Christensen and the others from the Culinary Institute in Stavanger, and a big hug to Liv-Anne for all your help with the recipes.

Last, but definitely not least, each of us wants to thank these women in particular. Without you . . . well, you know what we mean:

Kenneth: Merete Rogstad
Tore: Liv-Anne Gjesteland
Mats: Maja Forsslund
Craig: Helle Mellemstrand

ABOUT THE AUTHORS

Craig Whitson is a cookbook author, former restaurateur, and now food product developer. He was born and raised in Oklahoma and in 1980 moved to Norway where he is known as Grillkongen (King of the Grill). **Tore Gjesteland** is owner and managing director of the Jonas B. Gundersen restaurant chain and was co-founder of the Dolly Dimple restaurant chain, both in Norway. **Mats Widén's** photography has been published in more than 10 cookbooks, including *Cognac, Calvados and Armagnac*, which was a winner of a Gourmand World Cookbook Award in 2001. **Kenneth Hansen** operates Blaane Guiding Great Brands AS, where he serves as the Senior Creative Director/Art Director. He has also been involved in several cookbook projects including the award-winning *Cognac, Calvados and Armagnac* as well as *Smak!* and *Himmelsk*.